WHEN OLD TRAILS WERE NEW

WHEN OLD TRAILS WERE NEW
The Story of Taos, New Mexico

Facsimile of 1934 Edition

by
Blanche Chloe Grant

New Foreword
by
Marcia Muth

SOUTHWEST HERITAGE SERIES

SANTA FE

Sunstone books may be purchased for educational, business, or sales promotional use.
For information please write: Special Markets Department, Sunstone Press,
P.O. Box 2321, Santa Fe, New Mexico 87504-2321.

Library of Congress Cataloging-in-Publication Data

Grant, Blanche C. (Blanche Chloe), 1874-1948.
   When old trails were new : the story of Taos, New Mexico / by Blanche Chloe
Grant ; new foreword by Marcia Muth.
       p. cm. -- (Southwest heritage series)
   Originally published: New York : Press of the Pioneers, 1934.
   Includes bibliographical references and index.
   ISBN 978-0-86534-606-2 (softcover : alk. paper)
   1. Taos (N.M.)--History. 2. New Mexico--History. 3. Indians of North
America--New Mexico--History. I. Title.

F804.T2G74 2008
978.9'53--dc22
                         2007028180

WWW.SUNSTONEPRESS.COM
SUNSTONE PRESS / POST OFFICE BOX 2321 / SANTA FE, NM 87504-2321 /USA
(505) 988-4418 / ORDERS ONLY (800) 243-5644 / FAX (505) 988-1025

The Southwest Heritage Series is dedicated to Jody Ellis and Marcia Muth Miller, the founders of Sunstone Press, whose original purpose and vision continues to inspire and motivate our publications.

CONTENTS

I

THE SOUTHWEST HERITAGE SERIES

The history of the United States is written in hundreds of regional histories and literary works. Those letters, essays, memoirs, biographies and even collections of fiction are often first-hand accounts by people who wanted to memorialize an event, a person or simply record for posterity the concerns and issues of the times. Many of these accounts have been lost, destroyed or overlooked. Some are in private or public collections but deemed to be in too fragile condition to permit handling by contemporary readers and researchers.

However, now with the application of twenty-first century technology, nineteenth and twentieth century material can be reprinted and made accessible to the general public. These early writings are the DNA of our history and culture and are essential to understanding the present in terms of the past.

The Southwest Heritage Series is a form of literary preservation. Heritage by definition implies legacy and these early works are our legacy from those who have gone before us. To properly present and preserve that legacy, no changes in style or contents have been made. The material reprinted stands on its own as it first appeared. The point of view is that of the author and the era in which he or she lived. We would not expect photographs of people from the past to be re-imaged with modern clothes, hair styles and backgrounds. We should not, therefore, expect their ideas and personal philosophies to reflect our modern concepts.

Remember, reading their words and sharing their thoughts is a passport back into understanding how the past was shaped and how it influenced today's world.

Our hope is that new access to these older books will provide readers with a challenging and exciting experience.

II

FOREWORD TO THIS EDITION
by
Marcia Muth

Blanche Chloe Grant was born in 1874 in Leavenworth, Kansas. Like many other women of her time, she was from the first an independent spirit. She was interested in the arts and literature and saw a role for women that did not include the usually prescribed domestic life. A graduate of Vassar College, she also studied at the Boston Museum School of Fine Arts, The Pennsylvania Academy and the Art League in New York City. She soon became known for both her landscape paintings and her career as a magazine illustrator.

In 1918, she was asked to go to France as head of an art project under the auspices of the Y.M.C.A.

A move to Taos, New Mexico in 1920 brought about dramatic changes in Grant's life. She developed an intense interest in the rich and varied history of the area. She took on the job of editor of the *Taos Valley News* and began her years of research into the history of Taos and the Southwest. This led then to a series of books, many of which were about Taos and the people who lived there.

Her art also changed and she painted Native American and Western subjects. Although an active participant in the Taos art scene, she continued to show paintings in New York. Gradually her main interests turned to her writing. Her books included *Doña Lona, When Old Trails Were New, Taos Indians* and she edited a biography of Kit Carson based on his notes, all available again from Sunstone Press.

When Grant moved to Taos it was a small village but she soon found that its history was "large." Through extensive research, she put together the facts of the past. These were augmented and confirmed by residents who had knowledge of first-hand accounts.

She discovered that the history of Taos stretched back several centuries to the sixteenth century. It was a settlement that some people claim has a Chinese name or perhaps a Mayan one. It is a village that has been under three flags, Spanish, Mexican and finally American. Early on it became a trading center where trappers and explorers stopped as they moved up and down the western trails. By the time of Grant's arrival in Taos it had become a Mecca for artists and writers.

Taos survived through periods of drought, violence from unfriendly Indians, and religious controversy. It was the home of a brief rebellion against the government of the United States in 1847.

Two of its most famous early residents were Kit Carson and Padre Martinez. Today, in the twenty-first century, books are still being written about those two men as well as the many artists and writers who later settled in Taos.

Grant's book is a wonderful introduction to this ancient village and its inhabitants. There is a vibrancy in her writing that brings the past to life.

III

FACSIMILE OF 1934 EDITION

When Old Trails Were New

The Story of Taos

———

In Indian country lies the village of Taos

When Old Trails Were New
The Story of Taos

by

BLANCHE C. GRANT, A.B.

Author of "Taos Indians" and editor of
"Kit Carson's Own Story of His Life"

ILLUSTRATED

THE PRESS OF THE PIONEERS, Inc.

NEW YORK

1934

TYPOGRAPHY AND PRESSWORK BY
THE PLIMPTON PRESS · NORWOOD, MASSACHUSETTS, U · S · A ·

TO THE MEMORY

OF

TWO CITIZENS OF TAOS

KIT CARSON

THE GREATEST AMERICAN SCOUT

AND

TERESINA BENT SCHEURICH

DAUGHTER OF GOVERNOR CHARLES
BENT TO WHOM EVERY HISTORIAN OF
TAOS MUST BE FOREVER INDEBTED

AND ALSO

LEWIS H. GARRARD

THE BOY TRAVELER OF THE FORTIES
WHO WROTE THE BEST BOOK ABOUT
THE OLD TAOS TRAIL

TABLE OF CONTENTS

LIST OF ILLUSTRATIONS

FOREWORD

Taos history is a part of the larger story of the building of our nation, especially in the West. Taos may boast of a record more varied than that of any village in our whole land, yet even this will always remain incomplete, due to loss of papers, carelessness of chroniclers and limits necessarily imposed on any writer of one volume.

Now that my book is finished, a word of appreciation is due the many good folk of Taos who have helped me build these chapters. It is impossible to give a complete list but, among those to whom I am especially indebted, are Dr. T. Paul Martin, Francis T. Cheetham, Gerson Gusdorf, Bert G. Phillips, L. Pascual Martinez, Mrs. Nancy Witt, Mrs. Albert Gusdorf, and the late William L. McClure, Alexander Anderson, Columbus Ferguson, Benjamin G. Randall, and Albert A. Cummings.

In Santa Fe, I was given generous assistance by Dr. Edgar L. Hewitt, Dr. Lansing Bloom, Mrs. Mary R. Van Stone and the late Colonel Ralph E. Twitchell. To these names must be added others well-known elsewhere, Dr. Herbert E. Bolton, Dr. Frederick W. Hodge, Dr. John P. Harrington, Dr. Charles L. Camp and two great collectors of fine old books, whose work is now finished, Henry E. Huntington and Dr. Joseph A. Munk.

BLANCHE C. GRANT

Taos, New Mexico

When Old Trails Were New

The Story of Taos

I · EARLY RECORDS

ONE DAY, DURING JULY OF 1598, A GROUP OF SPANIARDS came slowly over " six leagues of bad road " from Picuris, a pueblo in the mountains of the great Southwest of America. Finally, below them, they saw a wide plain stretching away to fort-like, mud-block houses standing at the base of gray green slopes, veiled in blue. Perhaps the rocky peaks caught, that night, as they have so many times since, the strange crimson red which won their name when the devout travelers exclaimed, " Sangre de Cristo! "

When cool darkness came over the valley, glowing fires probably brought into silhouette, peaked tents, single-poled marquees, spreading circular as guy ropes pulled them taut. Within one of these, a candle's yellow light guided the quill of a young man, Juan Belarde, secretary to Don Juan de Oñate, the bold, imperious leader of the expedition. " This day," he wrote, " after mass, we went on to the province of the Táos which they also called Tay-beron and others." So came the name of Taos [1] into the ken of white men.

Little did the young soldier realize that he was creating, for the first time in writing, a name that was to live on for centuries. He had heard the Picuris Indians, pointing to the northeast, say that their relatives the *Tao* lived yonder and he pluralized the name as he scratched away in his

---

[1] Taos, pronounced *Touse*, like house.

journal, after relieving himself of his high metal helmet, unloosening his doublet beneath which his fine coat of mail glinted in the candle-light. Listening to his chief, he recorded a new name, " San Miguel," which was to fade as had " Braba " and " Valladolid." The latter title had been chosen by the first white men to see the Indian homes because they fancied a resemblance existed between the pueblo and the drowsy town of Valladolid, far away in Old Spain. These men had come into the valley, in 1540, and were members of Coronado's wandering explorers led by Hernando de Alvarado.

The name, *Taos,* had come to stay. There were other spellings such as " Taosi " and " Teaos." The latter came into existence during the long, cold winter evenings in 1628, when another candle flickered and sputtered while fact and fancy strove for mastery over the quill of the Franciscan, Alonso de Benavides. Drawing his brown cowl about him, he shuddered and bent over the parchment on which he was writing a report of his work as " custos of conversions " throughout the land vaguely known as " New Mexico." Of Taos, he said that there were, in that pueblo, two thousand five hundred souls baptized and all " very well doctrinated." A monastery and church stood there. Of the valley, the scribe wrote most humanly, " It is a land very cold, and most abundant in provisions and flocks."   .

Benavides said nothing of the origin of the name of the pueblo; neither did any other early chronicler. It was strange and new, yet very old. Perhaps the Indians of that day may have known but they made no records. Son had listened to father for generations and it may be the word had been given that the name had originally come from the north. Did they not say, the great chiefs, that their ancestors had come out of a great water to the north? May there have been a land beyond — ancient China? There the word " Tao " still lives, signifying " The Way " or " The right Way." Is it possible that the Taos Indian ancestors were Chinese? Far-fetched that may be, yet wise old men of the pueblo of to-day, speaking in a language resembling Chinese, say that " Taos " means " The gateway to Heaven " or " The place of the sacred mountain." Most of the Indians frankly declare that they do not know the origin of their name in which there seems to lurk a persistent call from the north. Yet, although the word *Tao* was in the country before the Spaniards came, there is such a word to be found in the southland, meaning a peon. Could it be possible that it was brought to the north by that marvelous people, the Mayas? Are the red men descendants of wandering Mayas? No one knows.

Solemn scholars of our day have wandered over sandy roads in the Southwest from pueblo, hogan and teepee, studying words as they went. They have announced that " Taos " is but an adaptation of a Tewa word, " Towih," meaning " Red Willows." True it is that our pueblo has been so called for centuries but that was never the name given by the owners of the mud houses towering square against the mountain sky-line. Appropriate it was and still is, for their busy little river is lined with willow bushes which glow red and orange in the winter. Here and there they give way in favor of ochre gray cottonwoods which stand, like huge, hoary giants, guarding the descendants of an ancient people. They scatter in the fall a glorious shower of golden leaves as if to keep alive the tales of wealth told by the Indians and believed by the treasure-hunting Spanish *conquistadores* and the friars whose lives of daring sacrifice were such that Oñate's comrade Villagrá, in the first epic poem of this country, said that " to ope these heathen lands with valor they assayed."

Probably the sanest explanation of the meaning of the word *Taos* comes from the famous priest scholar Julius J. Hartmann of Albuquerque. As the result of years of study of the Tiwa language, he believes that the Indians told the Spaniards that the pueblo of *Ta* or *Ta-u* lay over the mountains. The strangers were in the habit of adding an *o,* as well as pluralizing with *s,* and so came Ta-o and Taos. The augmentative letter *o* gave added glory to the fundamental word *Ta,* which means vast, great, impressive, and hence was appropriate as a name for their largest pueblo.

So circling through tradition and fact we do not arrive definitely at the meaning of the name of the pueblo which became that of our town in Northeastern New Mexico. What we do know is that Taos is a bit of Old Spain left on a sage-brush desert of a new world to sun itself throughout the centuries; a living monument to ages past; the end of many a long trail, old for the Indian when they were strange to the Spaniard or the American of a much later day; the home of cowboys, trappers, prospectors and scourging Penitentes; the abode of an internationally known group of artists.

Now for the background of the strangest little village in the United States.

Yellowing records of Spaniards, coming north, ever north, tell first of Alvar Nuñez Cabeza de Vaca and three companions, sole survivors of Narvaéz's gallant Spaniards of 1527. Shipwrecked on the Florida coast, the four men, who spent years as slaves to Indians, finally escaped and made their way toward the setting sun. News of their ap-

proach always was ahead of them and with it went the
word that the men could heal the sick. True it is that they
had been very successful in their treatment of those who
were ill and to this was due their Indian name, " Children
of the sun with power to heal and destroy." Finally, after
eight years, the four men found themselves in Old Mexico after one of the most remarkable treks ever made by
man. Cabeza, the leader, clung to an Indian gift, " a
copper hawks-bell, thick and large, and figured with a
face." Strangely enough the tinkle of the copper seems to
have hinted of gold to the Spaniards of the southland.
Cabeza, himself, said little of gold but he did say that the
Indians had told him of permanent habitations. In fact,
he had seen some of them. They had also told of great
wealth in the " land of the hunchbacked cows " as he
called the wide range of the buffalo, lying north of the
land he had explored, land which was probably what we
know as northern Old Mexico, although some eminent
scholars of history insist that Cabeza entered what was to
be New Mexico.

Cabeza touched off the torch which was to lead others
northward, notably Fray Marcos de Niza, a Frenchman of
the Duchy of Savoy. The gray-gowned friar had with him
the Barbary negro of Azamor, Estevan, who had been
with Cabeza, on this journey of his in search of the Seven
Cities, now firmly established in Spanish minds as centers
of great wealth. It was in 1539 that the travelers struggled
over deserts, on and on. Finally Estevan was sent ahead,
instructed to leave behind him crosses to mark his trail.
He sent back to Fray Marcos a " crosse as high as a man,"
which meant it was a great country, so the priest traveled
on. Before he could overtake the scout, Estevan reached
Cibola, a group of seven cities, our Zuni of to-day, but he

found no great wealth. Although he was warned not to enter the first of the towns, stolid and silent on the hot sands, borrowing its only gold from the sunshine, Estevan went on, guarded by two huge dogs. He paraded in all the finery at his command and demanded much. Arrogance proved his death and wise men of the pueblo reported that they had given him "a mighty kick which sped him through the air to the south, from whence he came."

News of the death of Estevan reached Marcos, who went on until he could view at a distance the Indian villages, but he dared not go farther and turned back, as he said, "with far more fright than food." He eventually arrived in the City of Mexico where he told great tales and aroused the desire of others to venture north.

The next year, in 1540, the first great expedition, under the leadership of Francisco Vasquez Coronado, who was accompanied by Fray Marcos, marched northeast from Compostella, whither a group of notable officers of the land had gone to watch them start with spirits high and colors flying. Both spirits and colors were soon fairly dragging in the dust for, search as they would, no gold was found. Finally, Fray Marcos seems to have been forced to leave for the south, branded a liar. Whether he was deliberately such, history has never made quite clear.

Now came upon the scene one, called El Turco, to whom Coronado lent a willing ear, for the Indian told of a land called Quivera where ran a great river upon which the lords of the realm were wont to go in big canoes with golden eagles on the prows. The master of the land took his afternoon naps under a tree on which were hung little gold bells and even ordinary people had dishes of gold! So reported the only historian of the expedition, Casteñada, who wrote that El Turco advised them " that they ought not to load the horses with too much provisions, which would tire them so that they could not afterward carry the gold and silver! " Such obvious treachery made no dent on the Spanish minds intent on believing that much gold could be found. On they would go to Quivera!

Only a few months went by and then the weary and well-nigh bankrupt Coronado and his men returned from a land called Quivera, to be sure, and now believed to have been part of Northeastern Kansas, but very far from being a land of gold. El Turco was not with him for he had proved himself false and had been forever silenced by those he had hoped to lead out to their death on a desert where one, Diego Lopez, had reported, after a scouting trip, that he had seen nothing for twenty leagues but " buffalo and sky."

This tale lends itself to Taos because Coronado made his headquarters at Tiguex, a group of Tigua villages in the Rio Grande Valley, and from there on August 29th, 1540, one of his officers, Captain Hernando de Alvarado, with a small party, set out to explore and came into Taos country. They were the first white men, as we know, to see the pueblo and describe its pyramidal buildings on either side of a river which was bridged " by very long, large squared pines." So to-day stand such buildings but they are not the ones the Spaniards saw in that year of 1540, but were built probably about 1700.

Other expeditions followed that of Coronado, unmoved by his failure, but more than fifty years were to roll by before another large group of venturesome souls were to travel northward. It was in 1598 that Don Juan de Oñate, with eighty-three wagons, seven thousand cattle and about one hundred and thirty soldier colonists

and their families, led the way for many long weeks. Not
all went well for the demon mutiny rose and threatened
disaster. It was then that a woman, known as Doña
Euphemia, " a dame of courage singular," mounted some
slight eminence and, in determined voice, berated the
men who wished to turn back. Listening they heard her
say,

> *What reckoning will you give, being men,*
> *Of what you took under your charge*
> *If you leave all to these coifed dames,*
> *Whom, seeing such baseness, such insult,*
> *I know to be, all sorely affronted,*
> *Full of dishonor and of shame*
> *To see in Spaniards such intent.*
> *When all is lost and we lack all,*
> *Do we lack widely stretching land,*
> *A peaceful river of much water,*
> *Where we may build a noble city,*
> *An imitation and example of many more*
> *Who thus made everlasting name and fame?*
> *Where can we go to better purpose?*
> *Hold your steps, nor think to stain yourselves*
> *With stain so infamous as surely will*
> *Descend upon your children, every one.*

So did the poet-historian Villagrá record this stinging
rebuke. It was evidently effective for the expedition moved
forward until, on a summer day in 1598, Don Juan de
Oñate declared a halt, forty miles southwest of the Taos
pueblo, and said that here he would build the first capital of New Mexico which he had proudly taken, some
time before, " for God, the King *and himself.*" This set-

tlement Oñate named San Francisco, but it was more often called San Gabriel. Here, in spite of one serious attempt to desert the place made by some of the colonists, the first village in New Mexico remained until 1610, when the settlers moved and established Santa Fe.

The greatest credit for the success of this earliest attempt to colonize in the dangerous land belongs to the women of the expedition. Living in constant fear, though the near-by San Juan Indians were usually friendly, hardships did not daunt them. Undoubtedly, Doña Euphemia, she of "spirit great, extremely beautiful, and, too, unusual for splendid, quick and clear mentality," was the mainstay of the women of the colony and kept their courage high.

Oñate would not stay at home. He would go exploring and on one of his trips he visited Taos. Not unmindful of his duty to establish missions, he ordered Fray Francisco de Zamora to the Taos pueblo, where he may have remained until his departure for Old Mexico in 1601. The actual work of building a mission has always been attributed, not to him but to Fray Pedro de Miranda, with the probable date of 1617.

Accused of grave crimes, tried and disgraced, Don Juan de Oñate spent the better part of his later years in Old Mexico trying often to regain and in the end possibly winning some degree of kingly favor, but his settlement lived on and grew strong in the new country.

After the founding of Santa Fe, Indian tradition insists that Spaniards settled in Taos Valley. If so, the earliest settlers were men who had been with Oñate and the evidence of many names, living on to-day in the community, which appear on the list of soldiers coming north in 1598, turns tradition almost, if not quite, into historic

fact. Surely, by 1615, there were settlers in Taos Valley
and near the pueblo. This was not to the liking of the
Indians, who soon begged them to move a league away to
the south and so the present town of Taos had its beginning. No date for this has ever come from the archives.
What we know definitely is that there was a town in 1680
for the alcalde of Taos was the one who sent a messenger
south on that day of fiendish war cries in August of 1680.

There had been angry mutterings against the Spaniards for many decades. As early as 1631, two soldiers,
on guard at the Taos pueblo mission of San Geronimo,
came to warm themselves in a rude hut where the padre
was at his devotions. Indians stole upon them, killed the
soldiers and dragged the priest out to his death. Twenty
years swung by and, according to Taos tradition, a friar
tried to force some of the Taos Indians to lift great stones
and timbers to build a new church. They objected vigorously and, finding their entreaties were of no avail, actually bundled up their belongings and left for the east,
from which few ever returned. They established themselves at a place they called Quartalejo.

It was in this year of 1650, probably, that deer-skin
messages were sent out by swift runners, calling on all
Indians to revolt. All seemed to be going well until the
Moquis refused to be a party to the plans; so the scheme
came to nought. From that time on, however, discontent
grew. The longing for their old-time freedom and religion dominated their souls. The cruelties of the white
man continued as did their counterpart in what the Indians did in revenge.

The red men especially resented being sent down ladder after ladder into the dark depths of mines to dig out
gold and silver which they knew would be all claimed
in the light of upper day by their Spanish masters. Finally

the time came, as tradition has it, when overhanging earth gave way in one mine and fell, burying alive a number of Indians. This may have been true and a real reason for the revolt. Recently, however, through the study of tree rings by the famous scientist, Professor A. E. Douglass, it has been definitely learned that there had been ten years of terrible drought in the land. This may have had more than anything else to do with the decision of the natives to drive out the hated conquerors of the country whom they, very probably, believed to be the cause of the continued disaster which had come upon them.

Meantime, a San Juan Indian by the name of Popé had come to the Taos pueblo. Shrewd and clever, this Indian soon won favor as a leader. He wandered throughout the Southwest and finally had a following of about twenty thousand. The weighty word with him was none other than revolt. He preached this until he believed the time was right. He set the date — August, the thirteenth, 1680. Runners sped away. Secrecy was enjoined on all. No woman was to know the plans but, overburdened by the awful secret, some of the men told the news. Learning of this, Popé changed the day and, on the morning of the tenth, the fury swirled to its height and war-whoops resounded throughout Taos Valley. Arrows hissed. Spaniards fell. On the Indians went killing. Three hundred and eighty lay dead when the red enemy reached Santa Fe.

The messenger from the Taos alcalde was ahead of the murderous host of Indians growing in numbers as they neared the capital. Governor Otermin did his best with his small army of about one hundred and fifty, but despair and fear burned up courage when the white men saw the water lessen in their ditches. Five days afterward, all citizens, carrying whatever they could, were allowed by the Indians to begin the long, weary journey to El Paso del

Norte. At Isleta, they were joined by others, notably two Taos men who had escaped with their lives, possibly because they may have been hunting on the awful tenth of August. They were Sebastian de Herrera and Captain Don Fernando de Chaves.

Now, at last, the Indians were free to dance and to destroy all evidences of the white man!

When Governor Otermin called for volunteers, both of the Taos men, Herrera and Chaves, came north again but apparently never returned to Taos Valley. In fact, they turned south with the governor when reconquest seemed impossible.

Several attempts to regain the " lost kingdom " were made shortly after 1680 but to no avail. The Spaniards had had enough of fighting and the Indians remained hostile, though they were being grossly mistreated by their leader, Popé. Twelve years passed and then, in August of 1692, Don Diego de Vargas was appointed leader of an expedition which was to conquer once more, convert souls but, perhaps above all, find the mine of silver and that of quicksilver, not far away, which a certain, perhaps over-imaginative Captain Toribio de la Huerta, in Old Mexico, claimed he had discovered between the Zuni and Moqui pueblos.

De Vargas conquered the land, again established the capital at Santa Fe but never found the mines. Many of the Indians again came easily under the Spanish flag, but it was not until 1696 that the Taos bent their rebellious heads, made their last stand in their cañon and then surrendered. By 1700, they were willing for the Navajo chief to come to their pueblo and there bow in submission to the white men. Time was even thus soon cutting off the sharp edge of bitterness and Indians were becoming friendly.

II · VILLAGES

The sketchy historical background is finished. now comes the moving picture of Taos itself, which begins to the south in the settlement made by Don Juan de Oñate or his successors in 1598. Since there are no definite records, our imagination must be given play.

About 1615 or earlier, a party of Spanish soldiers, with armor flashing and lances and arquebuses firmly held, started northward. Their horses were heavily laden and so were their pack-burros. Perhaps low wooden-wheeled carts creaked and groaned under their burden of things needed in the building of homes for the men were bringing their families. The goal was Taos Valley where they were determined to establish farms.

Slowly the party moved up the Rio del Norte, camping again and again among great boulders near the river. Finally they filled their waterskins and climbed away from the river and, crushing down sagebrush, dipped into one shallow cañon after another until they found themselves on the rolling land which swings toward the mountains.

" This is the land we saw when we came up with Don Juan," said one of the older men, pulling down his helmet to see the better and pointing with a wide sweep of his hand. " We called it good then. Yonder is the break in the ridge where flows a goodly river. Ever-running it must be for snow lies long on these mountains."

· " Aye, so it does," seconded another soldier. " This is the land. It gives more promise than any I have seen. The Indians live on the flat beneath that rocky peak by a fine

little river. I opine they will be friendly. They were in
1598."

"Right you are, Señor Barela," joined in another.
"We will have no trouble. As for the soil, it is rich,
aye passing rich. We shall build our haciendas near
the Indians, but forts they must be for one can never
tell what may happen. The natives have not forgotten
Coronado."

"We have presents, you know," reminded a woman.
"The Indians like the red cloth my Marguerita weaves.
Then there are the trinkets too."

Such must have been the type of conversation as the
men and women plodded on, up and down, now losing
sight of the mountains and then gaining it again from
a hilltop. Perhaps to their right they saw a group of small
mud houses without windows and near by fields with
ditches. Passing a little river, clear and cool, they pushed
on for now they could see the tall mud houses of the
Taos Indians.

Men sent ahead to hold a parley with the red men
found them friendly. Breathing more easily, the Spaniards began happily to choose their land and build their
homes after the age-old fashion, using adobe bricks for
walls which they topped with great beams on which mud
was tramped down. Undoubtedly, a friar began a rude
hut to serve as a church.

Hard work and many disappointments took their toll
but when life began to be a bit more easy, boys and girls
grew out of their youth and married some of their Indian
neighbors. This bothered the old men of the tribe and
they held meetings underground in kivas and decided
Indians must remain Indian. It was then that they told
the Spaniards that they would give them land a league

away if they would go and build there. This was probably
the beginning of the town of Taos.

Whether there was a definite plaza, no one knows. Certain it is that there was a group of haciendas scattered here
and there over the valley and the land was known as Taos
Country. When the village became Don Fernando de
Taos is unknown but it was so called during the eighteenth century, after 1760.

It is fitting here to study this name, which has been a
matter of much discussion during our day.

Captain Don Fernando de Chaves, who has already
been mentioned as one of the leading men with Governor
Otermin, was given a grant of land by the King. This lay
near the mouth of Taos Cañon, where flowed the small
stream, even in our day called the *Rio de Don Fernando.*
Other Spaniards joined him and the group was early
spoken of as the "settlers at the foot of the ridge." Probably there began what we call Cañon de Taos, a sort of
suburb about a mile and a half from the present plaza of
Taos.

At the time of the massacre of 1680, we know that Captain Don Fernando escaped. He never returned apparently and, in 1710, Cristobal de la Serna, a soldier,
petitioned for this land and eventually owned it.

It is notable in De la Serna's second petition for this
land that he referred to the former owner simply as Don
Fernando. We may therefore imply that Captain Don
Fernando de Chaves was well remembered in the valley
and was so much respected that, later, when the settlers
wished to discard what seems to have been the first name
of the village, San Geronimo de Taos, they decided to
call it Don Fernando — possibly they used the full name
but de Chaves soon gave way to de Taos. The members

of the de Chaves family who now live in New Mexico declare there was a Fernando de Chaves living in the middle of the eighteenth century and believe the town was actually named for him as it was the custom to entitle towns for a prominent citizen. However that may have been, the name went back to the earliest days and undoubtedly that fact played its part when the title definitely became *Don Fernando de Taos,* legal to this day. We know that there was no Spanish king by that name, nor had there been for many a decade. There was a Fernando who was governor in the very late years of the eighteenth century but there is reason to believe the citizens had long since been calling their village Don Fernando de Taos.

Early in the nineteenth century, a Señor Francisco Fernandez lived in Taos in a fine two-story house on the south edge of the town near the big spring. He was sufficiently important and popular to account for the change then made to *Fernandez de Taos.* Then came *San Fernandez de Taos,* but legally there always stood the earlier name. Eventually, many years later, in 1884, to be exact, a young American postmaster, William L. McClure, finding so many addresses on the letters he put away in pigeon holes, decided that the town should be called just Taos and so wrote the authorities in Washington. The oldest and most persistent of all names thus came forever into its own.

Of the life in the village, very little is known. After the massacre of 1760, of which we shall learn later, the people saw the necessity of obeying the royal demand, made on other communities, of becoming walled towns. No separate wall ever stood but the solid rear walls of homes joined those of neighbors and thus formed the town wall.

General view of Taos

For many years, there were communicating doors between all houses. Two gateways led into the central plaza with its common well and through these sheep and cattle were driven for safety during the long night hours. A portal extended all around the plaza in front of heavy wooden doors and walls broken by small windows of mica. As for the people, life was happy enough what with fandangos, gambling, and trading when heavily loaded pack-animals and wagons came in from far away Chihuahua. Gardens and wide fields of wheat, barley and the like kept many men and probably the women busy in the season, while homely duties were always plentiful; yet there was ever time for leisure.

By 1796, the town had grown so well, that there was need of more room. On May first of that year, sixty-three poor families appeared before the alcalde, Antonio José Ortiz. How many families there were all told in the place we do not know but we do know that the poorer ones had petitioned for land outside the old town limits. The alcalde explained to them that the land was to be guarded and that they must equip themselves with fire-arms and arrows and, if they did not so provide for safety they were " to be ejected from said settlement."

The alcalde's own report on this affair in the spring of 1796, which undoubtedly brought about the suburbs, shall we call them, of La Loma and possibly La Placita, is sufficiently interesting to quote.

" Wherefor," wrote Ortiz, " I took them by the hand and proclaimed in clear and intelligible words that in the name of His Majesty — God preserve him! — and without prejudice to his royal interests or those of any third party I led them over said land and they plucked up grass, cast stones and shouted aloud, ' Huzza for the King,' en-

tering upon possession quietly and peaceably and without any opposition whatever, designating to them the
boundaries, which are on the west, the land of Antonio
José Lovato, below in the bottom and above the middle
road; on the east, the Cañon of the Rio de Don Fernando;
on the south, the brow of the hill standing on the opposite side of the river and on the north, the boundary of
the Indians of Taos, notifying them the pastures and
watering places are common." Absurd boundary lines
were these and soon to be lost.

It was three years before the Governor Fernando Cha-
con wrote his approval of this act of the alcalde and added
that the people, being poor, were entitled " to have included on two sheets of stamped paper, the particular
possession executed to each colonist for that correspond-
ing to them as property."

Meanwhile, four miles away from Don Fernando de
Taos, the village of Las Trampas or Ranchos de Taos was
growing and probably boasting of being the oldest settlement in the valley, barring the pueblo of the Indians
near the mountains.

Tradition persistently calls the Taos Indians the first
settlers of Las Trampas. Years after, the family of Romero
seems to have owned practically the whole place. A series
of wills go back to a Diego Romero of 1724.

This Don Diego and his sons probably helped build
the first mission about 1733. Forty years later its walls
fell into decay and the present edifice slowly rose on the
old foundations. Its windowless apse, save for one opening under the roof and out of sight, its heavy mud abut-
ments and quaint interior belong to the long ago. Catholic it is in name but actually Penitente in ownership.

By 1787, another Romero, Joseph, did not know where

the boundaries of his land were and so he applied for an establishment of lines because the archive reads: " The papers of said ranch of said Joseph Romero inherited from his father were destroyed or taken away by the Comanches, a savage tribe at that time in continuous war with the people of New Mexico."

Sometime later, on October 20, 1795, a Catarina Romero sold a plot of land of eighty *varas* to Ventura Romero for $170 and declared, " The lands are bounded on the north by the settlers of Don Fernando river *at the foot of the ridge* (Cañon) etc." Again she sold to the same Ventura, " a Tower, with three rooms for three articles one for each room, and said articles are a gun and an iron pan and a copper kettle weighing twelve pounds with which said Catarina acknowledged herself paid and satisfied."

With property boundaries so indefinite it is small wonder that many disputes arose. Most unique of all was the trouble over the dividing line between San Fernando de Taos, as the old archive calls our Taos, and San Francisco del Rancho or Ranchos de Taos. This controversy grew so hot that finally men traveled, in 1840, as far as the City of Mexico to have a decision rendered. One of these men, José Miguel Archuleta, was asked forty-one years later concerning the matter and said that a decision was given by President Anastacio Bustamante and this was that a string reaching from the church door of either place was to be doubled and the point was to be on the dividing line!

It would be rather interesting to know if Señor Archuleta ever had the contract to furnish the four mile string for this accurate method of finding the dividing line between the two quarrelsome towns. Incidentally one cannot but wish for the record of this whole affair which was undoubtedly destroyed during the revolution of 1847.

Before we leave the discussion in regard to the establishments of villages, it will be well here to consider two others not actually allied to Taos but so closely identified in interests that they are near neighbors — the towns of Arroyo Seco and Arroyo Hondo. Very probably there were settlers in both of these places as early as 1795 but they were not made definite centers for ranch people until the year 1813 when vacant lands were opened by proclamation. A man, by the name of Nerio Sisneros, petitioned on March 27, 1815, as follows: " I and various associates being in need of lands with which to support our families, pray you that the Rio Ondo place be granted to us for our support, considering that said tract does not injure any one, as it is distant from the league of the Indians and is suitable for the formation of a town as the administration is near and pasture, water, firewood and timber abundant." This request was apparently granted and in 1823 the people around Arroyo Seco sought the same recognition, although the date of the founding of the town is about 1818. Other smaller groups of people gathered, here and there, in the valley of Taos and always around a little church with a steeple.

Ranchos de Taos Church

III · THE MASSACRE OF 1760

Now for the story of the sad year of 1760, never to be forgotten in Taos Valley.

An old man of that year could have told a stranger how Taos had grown in importance since he was a boy for he would have remembered more than one expedition which had tarried in the old town for a few days for supplies before venturing on into unknown country. Juan de Uribarri had come in 1706, when the man was but a boy, and had gone on hoping to make a pact with the Apaches but when he had reached them he found the Indians had guns — that meant Frenchmen were in the mountains. Fourteen years later, Villazur had come also, bent on finding out more about the Frenchmen who were trading and trapping on Spanish territory. Yes, the old man would have gone on, there were eleven of that party who had come back to Taos to tell of a vicious attack made by Indians in tall grass. All the other men were killed. None of the survivors could have told of the Frenchmen who came upon the scene soon after the fight and picked up leaves of Villazur's diary which were to be rediscovered over two centuries later among old archives in Paris far across the great ocean.

The Mexican would have shaken his head and sighed, as he puffed away at his pipe, over the futile efforts of the governor who had tried to remedy matters by issuing a decree against trading with Frenchmen, for it had done no good. He would have added that the real menace to the valley was not the French but the fierce Comanches who came into the country about 1704 and had caused trouble ever since. That junta down in Santa Fe in 1748, where men had discussed means of keeping them away from the Taos fairs, had not accomplished anything. Men might talk and decree but the devilish Indians came into the valley just the same. Yes, it was true that, for some time, the Comanches had not been so hostile, but then again the old man would have shaken his head. One could never be sure about them. The Utes and Apaches were bad but the Comanches —

How much such an old man could have told about his century if he had been able to write! That task was left to Bishop Tamáron, who came on a tour of inspection of all the missions, in the spring of 1760. He rode in a high coach which swung under festive arches erected in his honor at the entrance of each pueblo. Once he was tipped over in this royal carriage of his but escaped unhurt. The pompous manner of the Bishop evidently amused an Indian down in the Pecos country for he imitated and mocked the super-dignified man and then what happened? The tale came soon enough. A bear came down from the mountains and gnawed his head off — yes, sir! gnawed his head off!

Meantime the Bishop was wandering on, making notes. Approaching Taos over pine-covered mountains he found a village of Apaches living under the protection of Spaniards — probably our Ranchos de Taos of to-day. Here he was entertained by a rich Indian and then journeyed on, crossing ditches of snow water which he called rivers. Finally he reached the Taos pueblo and was greeted by a Franciscan friar.

A sizable place was this to the Bishop when he learned that there were one hundred and fifty-nine families numbering over five hundred persons living in the buildings, three in number then, one of which was across the river, that stream where, in winter, women broke through the ice to bathe their children, thinking thus to make them hardy.

The pueblo church, with its image of the patron saint of the community, San Geronimo, was large and here the Bishop sought to have the Indians confess and make the act of contrition but not all could do so in Castilian! This did not please the Catholic dignitary who chided the poor friar beset with troubles of which the visitor could not even dream. But the near-by thirty-nine Spanish families of one hundred and sixty members undoubtedly were a source of joy to the Bishop who, in turn, prayed that they might be spared any further misfortune at the hands of the Comanches.

The Bishop did not tarry long enough to see the seventeen tents of this dreaded tribe spring up suddenly on the plains, nor the seventy more which appeared by the end of June. Some of these, perhaps all, were friendly and they were honest when they said that there were others of their tribe who were not to be trusted. Some they said were now up on the Las Animas River, hunting buffalo. Early in July came about three thousand. Of what happened then, the Bishop wrote from reports he had heard, but seventy years later a little girl was to tell what she saw and knew, to the famous trader-writer, Josiah Gregg. She was Madame Sale dit Lajoie then and lived, as she had for most of her life, in St. Louis.

This one-time Señorita Villapando of the year of 1760 lived in a large house with four towers and within the patio was room for many neighbors who came hither because there was much ammunition stored there. The master of the house was not at home. Had he been, the tale might have been far different.

Years before, when his little daughter was but a wee child, Comanches had come to the house. The chief wanted the girl but the father shook his head and then said that if the chief would keep his tribe at peace in the valley he would give him his daughter when she should be grown. He consented and went away and kept his promise fairly well but the day came when he rode in to claim his prize. The girl flatly refused to go with the Indian. Her father was not there to pacify the chief so, angry, he mounted his horse and told his followers to raise the war cry.

Brandishing their lances and bows, the Indians besieged the house of Villapando. There were not enough people within to hold out against so many Indians, who, with savage yells, began to batter down the great door. Seeing this give way, Madame Villapando — the Bishop called her an Indian — "taking up a lance, went to defend it, and they killed her fighting." The heroine of Taos Valley was not able to protect her young daughter nor halt the terrible Comanches in their fury for they swept over the valley, killing and carrying away fifty Spanish women and children. They traveled north singing as they went.

Precious time was lost before the Governor with a thousand men set out on the trail of the murderers. They spent forty days following the Comanches but accomplished nothing. The Spanish women were never recovered. The Comanche chief found he had an unwilling bride in the Villapando girl and soon sold her to another group of Indians who, in turn, bartered for her with a Frenchman who married her and took her to St. Louis.

The following year, Comanches returned to the valley on the same day that Manuel Partillo Urrisola and his soldiers arrived, in response to a letter which the alcalde of Taos had dispatched to him. Urrisola found the Comanches defiant and announcing that they had brought back some captives for ransom. This was refused by the Spaniards and the result was war. " Comanches were killed until the fields were covered with them, not one being willing to yield himself alive," according to Urrisola. More than four hundred lay dead but in the mountains to the north were many more brave warriors of the tribe. Would they come again?

This proved, however, to be the last massacre to take place in Taos Valley, partly owing to the fact, that the citizens of Taos had learned the necessity for the stout home wall about their town and henceforward were more than ready to meet Indian enemies.

IV · TAOS FAIRS

During these troublesome times Taos continued to boast of its fairs which, for about seventy-five years, at least, were annually held. It may be that they were part of the life of the community from almost the very beginning of Spanish life in the valley, though we have no record of them until during the eighteenth century. Such occasions were an elixir of life to the small community. Their flutter and flurry made hearts beat faster and stirred to activity an otherwise anemic condition which has often accounted for fallen walls and lost boundaries.

A sentence or two from the Bishop's record of his visit to Taos concerning the fairs will be informative. He wrote: "The governor comes with a great part of his presidio and people from all over the kingdom to those fairs, which they call ransoms. They bring captives to sell, buckskins, many buffalo hides, and booty that they have taken in other parts — horses, guns, muskets, ammunition, knives, meat, and various other things. No money circulates in these fairs but articles are traded for each other and in this way those people provide themselves."

One other glimpse of the fairs was written in a cell in the convent of San Matias de Istacalco on July 23, 1754. "This mission [Taos]," wrote Fray Manuel de San Nepomuceno y Trigo, " is the last of this Holy Custodia, twelve leagues north from Picuris and is the first one to which most of the tribes come together for their fairs which are governed by the moon and which the Governor of the Kingdom and the lieutenant-governor attend with many *vecinos* and soldiers."

No description of the fairs has ever been found. We know that they were first held at the pueblo and later in the plaza in the town and were exciting events, as were their counterparts in Chihuahua five months later in January. Beyond such bare facts, imagination must have license. We will roll back the years to a day in early August of 1755 and write our experiences as they might have been.

Along the tumbling little river or by the still smaller irrigation ditches, under the shade of bushes, willow or cottonwood trees, peaked teepees are rising. Brown-skinned Indian men with buckskin about their waists and eagle feathers bobbing in their black hair stand watching the squaws lifting the poles in place and tying on buffalo robes to make a shelter. The women wear one piece of cloth or skin caught on the right shoulder only and bound at the waist with many-colored belts, the ends swinging as they walk to unroll their bundles of beaded skins, shining silver jewelry or bring out some pottery to be polished again.

Yonder comes slowly a burro dragging two poles on the ground supporting bundles of skins, women and children. The sun beats down pitilessly but the travelers move on across the open space and near the river, they tumble off and before we know it their teepee is cutting its angle out of the near-by blue-green mountains. There goes another and another. Now the women are squatting down and arranging their wares about them.

A yell breaks the silence. Across the sagebrush desert toward the west comes a band of horses. The riders are lifting bows in the air. Each one is whooping now as he rides with great skill. Dust rises in a mighty cloud behind them, hiding distant blue mountains and making the on-

coming comrades seem but phantoms until they too ride
in and halt sharply, dismount and tie their animals in the
shade of rude corral shelters. They laugh and joke as they
pass along by the teepees and hail some newcomers who
have just arrived. These prove to be Spaniards from Chihuahua and San Juan in wooden-wheeled carts loaded
down with cloth, wine and even gold. The drivers push
back their wide straw sombreros, draw in their yellow,
green or red sashes under their boleros of black embroid-
ered stuffs and stretch out their short legs in black trousers, slashed to the knee to admit a triangle of red. They
look tired after their long trek of perhaps a thousand
miles but they are not too tired to jabber as they undo
their bundles, roll off casks or pick up smaller packages
of finer stuffs from Old Spain. Singing now, the traders
display mantillas and shawls, brilliant and finely stitched,
and slippers of dainty colors, or rebozos of coarser material for daily wear about the Spanish women's shoulders
for these things are not for Indians. The people of the
valley will be coming soon.

In fact, before the traders have their goods ready, horses
come galloping in with men and women from yonder
ranch where Señor Pando lives or that one to the west or
south where the Godey or Lucero family live. Here they
come, with rebozos half hiding the faces of the women
who clutch at their skirts a-flying. Pulling down their
sombreros, the men lean far forward to scan the crowd
near the river.

Other Spaniards are coming now from the great door
of the Mission with its two mud towers looming almost as
high as the pueblo buildings which terrace their way up
to two small rooms on top where several blanketed Indians stand on guard. The leader of the Spaniards stops

suddenly and points to the mountains. All eyes follow his lead. Yonder come slowly down a trail, burro after burro heavily loaded with pelts.

" The Frenchmen," calls out some one. " They are past due."

An hour later, the crawling train of burros disappears into the cañon and then comes slowly into the eastern gate. Their drivers, speaking excitedly in French, deftly throw off the packs and turn the burros loose to forage for themselves. With the Frenchmen are one or two who look like white men from the far eastern colonies on the Atlantic. They are always straying from their homes, those Englishmen.

Now the whole crowd are moving here and there, beginning again their bargaining for mink, otter, deer, beaver or buffalo skins. Yonder they are bartering for beads, knives or swinging rare blankets in the air. On the far corner, they are handling gold or silver, testing turquoise, jingling jewelry, necklaces, rings and balls.

By the wall a group of Comanches are threatening a trader. Lances are in the air, far too high. Knives gleam. Red headbands are loosening and fluttering. Indian eyes are snapping with a fire that is wolfish. Grunts and growls. A distant war drum sounds. It is the wrong time for such. More growls. Knives flash. The trader falls. The chief leans over, grabs the bright blanket he wants. High he throws it and away they go, off over the desert in a cloud of dust. No one dares follow.

A few men gather around the unfortunate fellow on the ground, pick him up and carry him up a near-by ladder to the first roof of the pueblo. Some Indian women are caring for him now. The men are coming down. They join the crowd below who, on the whole, have paid little heed. Too many such things happen at the Taos fairs. If the Comanches would only stay away!

There is another quarrel over near the corral. A few gather around to listen.

" Si," cries an excited Spaniard, " but the price of a horse is now but 12 to 15 skins. The governor has said so! I'll give no more."

" No care for *jefe*. Me want more," growled an Apache.

" I'll not give more. The price is set and you know it. Enough. Here is a knife for that skin. That will be our only bargain. That is the exchange."

" It is fair," calls out another Spaniard coming up to join the crowd. " I have to stand by the new prices. Why, I have just had to trade ten arrobas of good green cloth for two horses. I wanted at least three. Have I not traveled far over death-bringing deserts to get here? Aye, but I had to take two. The governor has so decreed. I could get no more."

" Ugh! " grumbles an Indian. " Have we not had such ransoms for many, many moons? My grandfather has told me about them. Why does a Spaniard dare tell us about prices? "

" Aye, why," echoes the trader as he turns to leave the crowd. He knows well how the Indian is cheated. The white man buys with what he calls cheap pesos, imaginary though they are, and sells for those of higher value. The Indian does not know the difference now.

" If the Governor does not keep his hands off, the redskins will catch us at this trading business. They'll make demons of themselves and then there'll be the devil to pay," the fellow mutters to himself and walks leisurely over to where some old Indians are squatting on the ground near a teepee.

Over the hum of the bargaining crowd comes another yell, this time from across the river near the south pueblo. A hand to hand fight is on. The trader ducks under an arm. A knife flashes but does not hit. See! The man is on the ladder, up and over the wall. No Indian follows, nor white man either, for is not that the home of the fiercest of the Taos?

" Comanches again," whispers a wrinkled old Indian as he shades his eyes with a hand, tough and strong, like leather. " Comanches — bad. Utes and Apaches bad too but Comanches — ugh! Trouble some day, big trouble. You see. Taos Valley red. Blood."

" Perhaps," answered the Spaniard squaring his shoulders proudly. " There are many of us now, Ventura. We will fight. We can protect our own."

" No good. Many Comanches come. Many horses, lances and fierce looks, Señor."

The trader rises and, as he crosses the big logs thrown over the river, the Indian nods his head.

" Spaniard think he too strong. Some day, he know. Si, and some day after many, many moons, come pale faces from the east. Then we will be free of the men from the southland. They come! "

The Indian falls into silence and looks far toward the east. How does he know?

When the sun falls low, the whole crowd forms in two long lines on the hard beaten ground on the north side of the river. Old Indian men with eagle feathers wave the people back farther for it is the time for the *gallo* or a chicken pull.

Swinging a rooster by the legs, a young buck comes into the open space, digs a hole and puts the bird into the ground, allowing only the head to stick out. The eyes of the frightened rooster roll wildly. Struggle is impossible.

From the western and eastern gates come horsemen, young Indians with brown bodies marked with white earth and loins covered with flapping cloth of gay colors. With wild cries they rush toward one another, making for the rooster. One Indian swings skilfully from his saddle, swoops down but misses the bird. Another dashes up but his horse is going too fast. Yet another, holding in his horse, dips and pulls the rooster from the ground and swings it in the air. It falls lifeless to his wrist. He swings it again and hits a passing rider. His horse staggers ever so slightly but it is enough. The hand on the dead rooster's neck loosens, an Indian grabs it and begins striking out at the others who are trying to wrest it from him. Feathers fly as one after another catches the bird. The old Indians wave the eagle feathers at their favorites as they speed past. The Spaniards and Anglos shout as an Indian finally makes his complete get-away with the tattered prize. The game of *gallo* is over.

Night cuts in quickly. The Indians disappear into adobe walls or teepees. Fires sputter into flame. The Spaniards mount and hurry away into the darkness. The mountains, forgotten during the day, loom up now, high and dark, like huge sentinels, guarding the valley. A day at a Taos fair is over.

No records of the Taos fairs after the beginning of the nineteenth century have been found. Probably the establishment of stores brought about their decline. Trading in covered wagons between Taos and Chihuahua continued until in the 'sixties but real fairs, no.

Possibly due to debts contracted at the fairs as well as other causes in the process of living, there grew up a sys-

The Signal

Painting by J. H. Sharp

tem of peonage which was allowed to exist until 1867. Apparently no man dared to oppose the custom which forced son after son, as well as other members of the family, to remain eternally in debt usually to some landowner. Twenty years had gone by under the flag of the United States but nothing had been done. Finally a brave Mexican girl, Mariana Jaramillo, dared to refuse to let her own father sell her into bondage as part payment for his debt. She won and there came an end to this slavery from which there had never been a hope of freedom.

During the years of the passing of the Taos fairs something happened far to the east which was to bring a very different type of life and trade to the old Spanish town.

News was scarce and old when it reached the village and created little if any interest, but, in 1803, there came through a bit of news that must have made some stir among the gossips who have ever sat in the sunshine of Taos plaza. This was that President Jefferson of that far eastern country, now called the United States, had signed a paper. He himself said that, in doing so, he had stretched the constitution of the government until it cracked. That crack was heard in Taos. Louisiana was not far away. From now on all the land skirting the Mississippi to the unknown northwest belonged to the republic of the States. Just what was to follow?

Rumors came filtering in sub rosa that there was to be established a government in this newly-acquired land by a certain Aaron Burr but the idea that New Mexico, so long under Spanish colors, would ever belong to the United States was not even the subject of a wild dream.

Here we pause. Could it have been possible that Captain Zebulon M. Pike, the American, had dreamed? He came through this Southwest in 1807–9, making a daring,

lonely trip with a few men and almost no supplies. Into
the Rockies, across the Sangre de Cristo range, he traveled, passing through Ojo Caliente somewhat to the west
of Taos. On the way, he made both Indian and Mexican
know what the flag of the States looked like and even
raised it on the Spanish side of the line!

Before he had left St. Louis, dark, ominous war clouds
brooded over the nation. Spain was looking distrustfully
toward the United States. It seems evident now that certain authorities at the Capital had sent Pike. The man,
the Spaniards called, " Mungo Meri Paike," could have
been on none other than a spying expedition. He learned
much of this adjoining land and, at Santa Fe, fell under
suspicion and was forced to give up his papers. Pike
turned the trick, however, and won the right to proceed
down to Chihuahua.

Along with this story runs another which affected Taos
more and was in keeping with the Pike story in spirit. In
1804, a Canadian Frenchman, Bautiste La Lande, was
sent by William Morrison, a merchant of Kaskaskia, Illinois, down into the Southwest to investigate the chances
for trade. He has been called the first American trader
to enter New Mexico but he does not deserve that honor.
There were others, now unknown, because the Spanish
government issued a decree, as early as 1723, restraining
commerce with all traders from the east.

Equal to the new game, La Lande came on cautiously
with his burros loaded with goods. Pike said that La
Lande sent in a messenger and the Spaniards came out
with horses and carried him and his goods into the province. Selling his merchandise, or rather that of Morrison,
at a splendid profit was an easy matter. Then La Lande
decided to use the money, thus acquired, for himself and

proceeded to become rich. So runs the tale but there were extenuating circumstances. La Lande was forbidden by the authorities to leave the country and so made the best of the matter. No one knows whether Robinson of Pike's party of a few years later ever had the chance to present the bill against La Lande which he had brought with him from Kaskaskia.

Becoming a guide, La Lande was mentioned by that other famous traveler of the name of Pike — Albert Pike of 1831 and 1832. The French Canadian married and, after having several homes, came to live in Ranchos de Taos. Family tradition insists that he died and was buried there. Certain it is, that his daughter Josepha lived in Ranchos for many years and her home was pointed out as that of " La Francesa," the French woman.

During all the early years of the century, Taos was well known as an important trading post. Little did it dream that within its walls there was constant play and counterplay and the stake was the control of the borderlands between two great powers.

V · ONE HUNDRED YEARS AGO

TRADER FOLLOWED TRADER WITH PACK MULES OR BURROS, stopping, now and then, to *cache* their goods when there was danger. This digging a hole, hiding pelts, bales of merchandise and what not and then skilfully covering all with earth and sod was often resorted to and the man found guilty of stealing from such was doomed to have his arms broken and then be turned loose in the forest to live or die as Fate decreed.

Trade became a matching of wits. Bribing of officials was common. Duties were very high and articles such as shoes, silk, coffee and tobacco were contraband. Small wonder that men who risked their lives on the dangerous trails from the east defied Spanish law. So much so was this the case that we find in the index of 1814 of the famous frontier paper, *The Niles Register,* " Trade — see Smuggling! "

Inviting were the profits to be made in the trail trade whether or not the traders evaded the customs. A carelessly written note found on a manuscript in the Bancroft Library in Berkeley, California, runs, " Average profit before the Mexican war was 200% on first cost. Overlanding freight was $12 per 100 lbs. from Ind. (Independence) Mo. to S. Fe and as much more to Zacatecas. Net freight from N. Y. to Z. via S. Fe was 20%." We know also that as high as six hundred percent was made by some of the earliest traders. One of the first wagons to come was bought for $150 and sold for $700 when the owner Becknell reached Santa Fe in 1822. A wagon from the East! The day of the burro was doomed, that of the covered wagon was at hand.

The years from 1824 to 1830 were red letter years in the history of Taos. The great overland trade was on in real earnest. In 1824 came the first covered wagon train with thirty-five wagons, $30,000 worth of merchandise and eighty men. Part of this caravan under the leadership of August Storrs followed the mountain road to Taos. Spanish decrees against trade with the easterners were things of the past; the two republics held out welcoming hands to each other.

What a year that of 1824 must have been in the old town. Citizens bestirred themselves to acquire the title of " Villa " in the new Mexican republic. That meant much more to them than the political acrobatics in which Lower Mexico was allowing herself to indulge. In fact, this " Villa " was alive with all sorts of local activities. As a center of the fur trade for the Southwest, it far outdistanced Santa Fe. Trappers with or without licenses could bring in their peltries. Mountain men often came preferably to Taos where they swapped horses and yarns and outfitted for their next journey into lands of ice and snow.

Probably as early as this, Old Bill Williams was in town. Once, doubtless under the influence of the potent home-brew, *aguardiente* or Taos whisky, Williams supplied the loafers on the square with some fun and set needles flying indoors. He bought a whole bolt of calico, threw it out by the yard length and then told the women to go to it with their scissors. Laughter was followed by regret when the men again set out for the mountains or for the Gila River. Then the village lapsed into its easygoing life.

Many history-making men called Taos, home, during those years. Big stalwart Ewing Young of Knox County,

Tennessee, was one. He led many an expedition into the trapping country. But fur grew scarce and he left for the west in September, 1831, to become a settler in Oregon.

John Rowland and William Workman were well established and remained until 1841 when they had good reason to leave for California because their names were connected with what seemed to the authorities to be conspiracy against the government and had shown sympathy with the unpopular Texans. They must have known that elusive man Kincaide, possibly a friend or relative of the Carson family back in Missouri, who lived in Taos and took the runaway Kit Carson into his home in 1826.

William Wolfskill was also a citizen. He fitted out a trapping party, in February, 1824, bound for the headwaters of the Colorado. Ewing Young was of the group and they were out until June. In 1828, Wolfskill returned to Missouri and came back with a caravan of one hundred wagons. He sold his goods to Young, who became his partner. Both were restless men. Young soon went on an expedition to the Gila while Wolfskill traveled to Paseo del Norte after " wines, brandy, pinoca etc. which he brought up to Taos in the spring of 1829." During the last days of September, 1830, Wolfskill left Taos for California. Striking off to the northwest, his party opened up a new pathway which ever after was known as the " Wolfskill Trail." It followed the Colorado River, crossing just above the Grand Cañon, through the Great American Basin to Sevier, thence southward to the Rio Virgin, down the Colorado to the Mohave, then through Cañon Pass to San Bernardino and Los Angeles. Here Wolfskill spent the rest of his life and became noted as the owner of the most wonderful vineyards on the coast.

The sure decline of the fur trade, which all foresaw, led

many a man westward. Then, too, moving on was the fashion. "At that time," wrote the pioneer John Bidwell in his journal, "when a man moved west, as soon as he was fairly settled he wanted to move again." Another old-timer frankly admitted that he came west "because the darn thing wasn't fenced in and nobody dared keep him off."

Living in this section were the Robidoux brothers. Luis made his home in Taos and later became the founder of Riverside, California. Bidwell said he remembered hearing a Robidoux, probably Antoine Robidoux, noted as one of the first boosters for California, remark, "There was but one man in California that ever had a chill there and that was a matter of so much wonderment to the people of Monterey that they went eighteen miles into the country to see him shake!"

Certain it is that Taos mothered more than one settlement on the Pacific Coast. Huge droves of sheep were driven from New Mexico to the west which helped build up the wealth of the now rich state of California.

To return to the year 1824. There seems to have been but one account of the town written by a man who was actually here that year. This is found in *Pattie's Narrative*. The Patties, father and son, were splendid wanderers and kept a record of all the places through which they passed. According to them, Taos had nine thousand inhabitants but they were probably mistaken because a census report made by Fray José Pedro Rubin de Celis under date of December 31, 1821, gives — "San Geronimo De Taos; Indians 753, Spanish and others 1260, Total 2013."

"On the evening of the 26th (1824)," wrote the younger Pattie, "we arrived at a small town called St. Fernando situated at the foot of the mountain on the

west side. The alcalde asked us for the invoice of our
goods which we showed him and paid the customary
duties on them — I had expected to find no difference
between these people and our own but their language.
I never was so mistaken. The men and women were not
clothed in our fashion, the former having short pantaloons
fastened below the waist with a red belt and buckskin
leggins put on three or four times double. A Spanish knife
is stuck in by the side of the leg and a small sword worn
by the side. A long jacket is thrown over and worn upon
the shoulder. They have few arms generally, using upon
occasions which require them, a bow and spear and never
wear a hat except when they ride. When on horseback
they face toward the right side of the animal. The saddle
which they use looks like ours would with something
like an armchair fastened upon it.

" The women wear upon the upper part of the person
a garment resembling a shirt and a short petticoat fastened around the waist with a red or blue belt and something of a scarf kind wound around their shoulders. Although appearing as poorly as I have described, they are
not destitute of hospitality, for they brought us food and
invited us into their houses to eat as we walked through
the streets.

" The first time my father and myself walked through
the town together we were accosted by a woman standing in her own doorway. She made signs for us to come
in. When we had entered, she conducted us up a flight
of stair steps into a room neatly whitewashed and
adorned with images of saints and a crucifix of brass
nailed to a wooden cross. She gave us wine and set before us a dish composed of red peppers ground and
mixed with corn meal stewed in fat and water. We could

not eat it. She then brought forward some tortillas and milk. Tortillas are thin cakes made of corn and wheat ground between two flat stones by the women. This cake is called in Spanish, *metate*. We remained with her until late in the evening when the bells began to ring. She and her children knelt down to pray. We left her and returned. On our way we met a bier with a man upon it who had been stabbed to death as he was drinking whiskey."

Albert Pike, the famous Mason, was another writing wanderer. On one occasion he spoke thus of approaching Taos: " Directly in front of me, with the dull color of its mud buildings, contrasting with the dazzling whiteness of the snow, lay the little village, resembling an oriental town, with its low square, mud-roofed houses and its square church towers, also of mud. On the path to the village were a few Mexicans wrapped in their striped blankets and driving their jackasses heavily laden with wood towards the village. Such was the aspect of the place at a distance. On entering it, you found only a few dirty, irregular lanes and a quantity of mud houses.

" On the evening of my arrival, I went to a fandango. I saw the men and women dancing waltzes and drinking whiskey together; and in another room, I saw a monté bank open. It is a strange sight — a Spanish fandango. Well-dressed women (they call them ladies), harlots, priests, thieves, half breed Indians, — all spinning around together in the waltz. Here a filthy, ragged fellow with half a shirt, a pair of leather breeches and long dirty woolen stockings and Apache moccasins was hanging round with the pretty wife of Pedro Vigil; and there the priest was dancing with La Altragracia, who paid her husband a regular sum to keep out of the way and so lived with an American. I was disgusted —."

Later another said the town was but " a collection of mud houses built around a miserable square or plaza." In 1822, Thomas James saw the town as peopled with those who had " not sufficient enterprise to seize the offer," referring probably to the obvious possibilities of the valley.

The quaintest record of the early twenties is that of Major Jacob Fowler, a lover of adventure for its own sake and also the crack speller of his time. Doubtless he never had the slightest idea that his notes written in 1821–1822 would ever see the light of day for he gave easy play to his pencil as he jotted down the happenings on his way, accompanied by his negro slave, Paul. Here are some of the entries made in his journal:

Wensday 1st may 1822

We Went down to St. flanders (San Fernandez de Taos) in the nibor Hood of touse (pueblo de Taos) and find Conl. glenn Is gon to Sta fee, We Remained Here two days vanbebers Party Head came In and the french party is Heare AllSo.

We Were Informed that Spanish army Had Returned that they Hag taken one old Indean and Some two or three old Horses that Ware So poor the Nabaho Cold not drive them up the mountains, for it appers The Went up the Steep mountain and Role down Rocks on their pursurs So that the Ware Compled to discontinu the pursute."

A bit of news came into Taos evidently, for under the heading of " wensday 8th may 1822," the Major wrote, " We heare That Congrass Has Convened at maxeco." About this time, he and his party went exploring in the "nibor Hood of touse" and so he wrote of the Rio Grande: "As Soon as you come to the top of these Clifts and look down you are so struck With Horror that you Will Retret In an Instant." Of the journey back, he said, "So We loade and moved on Crossing a Crick Which Ren west threw the villege Steered a little South of East about twelve miles over a High Butifull plain to the villege of St. Flander (San Fernando)."

Three years later, in 1825, a Dr. Willard, probably Dr. Rowland Willard, of St. Charles, Missouri, made a few hurried notes while he tarried in town for several months. It was he who made a flag with an American eagle on it and, floating it to the breeze, put on a Fourth of July celebration in the plaza and paraded around receiving from the Mexicans shouts of "Viva la Republica."

In 1831, a trapper by the name of George Nidever wandered in with a party from the north. Many years later he dictated his experiences, calling Taos Valley "a great wheat country." In Taos, which he called "San Fernando," he found Rowland with a flour mill and Workman with a store, where traps were expensive. Four dollars to fourteen are prices mentioned by men of that day.

Nidever could not stay in the settlements. He left on a trapping trip and, returning on July 4th of '31, went with one hundred and twenty skins once more into Taos. Of the trading, he said: "These we sold in San Fernando at $4 per pound, or an average of $10 per skin. In those days although there was a heavy duty on all beaver skins brought into New Mexico, no one ever thought of paying it and, as in our case, they would be smuggled into town in the night."

So went the days and nights in Taos, one hundred years ago.

VI · TRAILS

Wʜᴀᴛ ᴡᴇʀᴇ ᴛʜᴇ ᴛʀᴀɪʟs ᴡʜɪᴄʜ ʟᴇᴅ ɪɴᴛᴏ ᴛʜᴇ ʙᴜsʏ ᴛʀᴀᴅ-
ing post a century ago? Trails ever play at hide and seek.
Some slip away forever in rock and brush; others grow
eternally new.

Indian trails were many, spoke-like paths they were,
which took their well-nigh hidden way over mountains,
by streams and across prairies, radiating from the Taos
pueblo, long before the white man came from east of the
north star or from " the land of everlasting summer " as
the red man called Old Mexico.

At the base of the Rockies, ran the old Kiowa Trail,
where mounted Indians still gallop. Across the Rio
Grande Cañon twisted the Navajo Trail, now unknown
to both white and red traveler. To the southwest, the
Taos may yet go his way to his Picuris friends while over
the eastern mountains no Indian ever gets lost.

In making his thin paths, the Indian shrewdly followed
the buffalo, that " new kind of ox, wild and fierce," of
Coronado's day and recognized later as " the best civil
engineer in the world," for he unerringly found the low-
est course over the mountains. After him came the smaller
game, then the stealthy red hunter and finally the white
man profiting by all.

With the advent of the covered wagon, trails became
definite established routes to Taos.

The first caravan route in importance was that which
curved from the east, south to San Miguel, after making
an ever-widening line over great plains annd deserts, and
became known as " The Santa Fe Trail." Few of the

wagon masters would follow the first official survey of the trade route, which came down what we know as the Black Lakes road to Taos Cañon and on into town. This was a shorter line to Santa Fe but it was through mountains and so not as easy as that to the south, which was really far more dangerous, for hostile Indians could lurk along that trail, notably at the Point of Rocks. In spite of murders and burning of wagons, and piles of bleaching bones, the daring traders usually followed this southerly route, though there were always some who preferred the mountain trail which led to Taos, "the first settlement in the Spanish country."

Winding down from the north was probably the oldest trail of them all which was specifically known as "The Old Taos Trail." It started at Bent's Fort as did the more important one just mentioned, but left the Arkansas at a point between the present Las Animas and La Junta in Colorado and curved down through Robidoux or La Veta Pass, west of the beautiful Spanish Peaks, through the Rio Colorado basin and then on through the Questa country, entering Taos probably along our Pueblo Road, though Indians say the first thoroughfare was a half mile or so to the east and came up Couse Hill.

The third trail struck off southwest from the present Dodge City, Kansas, to Rock Creek, then slightly northwest to Vermijo River to the site of Springer and then southwest to the Rio de Don Fernando in its cañon and out on to the flat plain of Taos Valley. The greater part of its way was through the so-called Cimarron country to the east and for that reason it was often called, "the Cimarron Route." Old-timers remember this as the one most used by the wagon trains which came into town and separated to follow three well-traveled roadways leading to smaller communities in the vicinity of the trading post.

An old citizen of Cañon, Señor José Helario Lucero, once pointed out to the writer the small rounding, yet rather flat-topped hill easily distinguished across our plain to the east and said it was the site of an old lookout. There, either an Indian or a Mexican always kept guard as it commanded the trail for many miles. A sentinel daily carried a cross down to the road and carefully looked for signs of hostile Indians. Then back up the mountain path he would climb carrying the cross he had left below the day before. Such was the time watch of the day.

If signs of enemies were discovered, down the western mountain slope would come the sentinel to build a fire. Its thin spiral of smoke could not be seen by the Indians hiding along the wagon trail but would be seen by the townfolk and warn them of danger so that they could send out relief parties. When, at last, weary weeks of travel were over and the tired oxen pulled the heavy wagons out of the cañon, another sentinel would proclaim the news from a round tower which used to stand near where is now the studio of E. Irving Couse on the slight rise into town and to the left as the caravans entered Taos.

Long before the wagons could move into the plaza, the cry " Los Americanos! Los Americanos! " rang through the town. At once preparations were made for a dance while the smell of delicious food filled the air. Shouts of welcome came from those who hurried to the wagons ready to buy. All sorts of goods there were to interest them, iron, leather, cotton cloth and even pianos and dainty slippers from Paris!

Newspapers from the East continually cited our Taos man, Charles Bent, who many years after was to hold the proud title of Governor of New Mexico, as a captain of wagon trains. In 1831, he made the first venture with wagons drawn by oxen and succeeded in coming along the trail in safety.

Finally the day of military escorts came, soldiers guarding the wagons to the line where Spaniards met them. Thomas Forsythe wrote, in 1831, of this sort of meeting, to Lewis Cass, then Secretary of War, as follows: " It was a remarkable scene — this gathering of the military forces of two nations in protection of an international commerce. It was moreover one of the most heterogeneous gatherings conceivable, for the Santa Fe caravans embraced every class and condition of men to be found in the frontier settlements of either country. Never, since the days when Coronado penetrated to the Kansas plains, had the barren and treeless prairies witnessed a more interesting spectacle."

Of the growing trade, a newspaper reporter wrote: " The inland trade between the United States and Mexico is increasing rapidly. This is perhaps the most curious species of foreign intercourse which the ingenuity and enterprise of American traders ever originated. The extent of the country which the caravans travel, the long journey they have to make, the rivers and morasses to cross, the prairies, the forests and all but African deserts to penetrate, require the most steel-formed constitutions and the most energetic minds."

Not all of the energetic minds in the wagon trains belonged to Anglo-Saxons, let it be said right here. Rufus Sage, a traveling writer of the forties, after telling of a prairie fire which his party had to fight and during which a load of powder had exploded, scribbled: " None of us were quite so brave or present-minded as several Mexicans, in the employ of Messrs. Bent and St. Vrain, on an occasion somewhat similar. While journeying across the grand prairies, the powder wagon accidentally caught fire. This was noticed immediately by the Mexican attendants who hurriedly clasped it upon all sides, to prevent the vehicle from being blown to pieces, while one of them proceeded deliberately to extinguish the flames."

So we have a picture of heavy light and shade. Some traders fared well; others badly. The lure of the trails never faded. Taos became distinguished as a port of entry in 1837 and was closed in 1843. The ban was lifted, however, before much damage had been done and the trade grew apace especially between the years 1840 to 1880 when the first railroad train came chugging into the Southwest but not to Taos.

VII · BENT'S FORT

At the other end of the long, long trails, standing alone on a wide prairie, near a river, stood a large mud house, built around a spacious patio. Since stories have ever called forth their mates, so it is true that no tale of Taos is complete without that other, running contemporary with it for several decades, the story of old Bent's Fort.

For years, this famous trading post and fort was the center of the life of the plains which skirted the Arkansas River, not far from the present town of Las Animas, Colorado. Here William Bent and his Indian wife lived and worked peacefully while, two hundred miles away, Charles Bent, a brother, was the most important merchant in Taos.

Almost all traders and trappers of the early nineteenth century knew both of these men as well as both places, Taos, "the paradise of the mountaineer," and Bent's Fort, the towers of which "rose over the uncultivated wastes of nature like an old baronial castle that had withstood the wars and desolations of centuries."

The history of Bent's Fort, also called "William's Fort," goes back to the sharp crack of an ax, one dark night, in old New England, when, according to family tradition, grandfather Bent clambered on board a certain unwelcome ship that swung with the tide in Boston Harbor, weighed down with chests of tea. The spirit guiding the strong arm, as it wielded the ax, that night, came down through the years to his son Silas Bent who dared to take his chances in an overland trip to St. Louis to become judge of the Superior Court in 1804, just after the city had come under the stars and stripes. Four of his sturdy sons carried on this spirit when they, in turn, journeyed fearlessly into new, dangerous land on the Upper Arkansas where again sounded the crack of an ax.

Pioneer blood told especially in the veins of two of the sons, Charles and William, who wandered into the mountains trapping, when they were mere boys. Finally, one day, Cheyenne Indians crossed their path and they quickly made friends with them. Chief Yellow Wolf evidently had a long pow-wow with the young fellows who had, by that time, already built their first stockade. The Indian told them it was too near the mountains and consequently too far from the haunts of the buffalo. If they would build down near the mouth of the Purgatoire where it joins the Arkansas he promised to bring his band there to barter. It was probably this suggestion which induced the young men to build their fort where they did. They soon found that they had done well to follow Yellow Wolf's advice, for their post became the real center of the fur trade of the Rockies.

From 1829 to 1832, the walls of the fort rose, four feet thick, walls of sun-dried brick. Huge logs, dragged from a distance, spanned these to make the roof. Smaller poles and brush were then laid across and on top was thrown and tramped down a heavy covering of adobe or mud.

The windowless outer walls of the rooms made the wall for the fort while the inner side faced a large *placita*. In this enclosure, Indian women went silently about their work, for Owl Woman, daughter of White Thunder, keeper of the medicine arrows of the Cheyennes, was mistress of the post as wife of William Bent. It was she, no doubt, who planted the cactus which softened the straight top line of the walls with gray green. The deadly thorns also proved an ever-present guard against thieving Indians who would not dare their sting.

On the northeastern and southwestern corners rose small towers about thirty feet high and ten in diameter inside. Here were loop-holes for gun or cannon. More loop-holes pierced the upper part of the walls which were built breast-high and so made the roof a safe promenade.

In a watch tower over the wide front gate, some one always sat, ready to use the long spyglass which swung easily on a pivot. There was never a swirl of dust out on the desert but the glass was brought into play. Just above, in a belfry where two white eagles lived, hung a bell which clanged out summons to meals, "meals which were mostly of dried buffalo meat and bread from the unbolted meal from Taos, repasts which lacked sweets and condiments" as one sugar-hungry guest of the day wrote.

In the morning, when the gates were opened, Indians cautiously slipped from their tents about the fort into the *placita* and watched with shifting eyes while traders and clerks hurried about their work. On the roof promenade marched the patrols with rifles loaded while guards stood ready with flaming torches beside the cannon. When the day was done, the gates again swung to and the locks clicked. Without, the Indians examined their newly bought store of beads or blankets, horses or mules, or lounged around under the influence of the whisky which they had secured from traders. Their camp fires glowed and died away and throughout the night the Indians knew a sentinel paced back and forth on the roof of the fort.

Such was the picture of the trading post as the young

lawyer Thomas J. Farnham saw it in 1839. Almost ten years after came a young writer, an English soldier sportsman, George Frederick Ruxton. He found life much the same. The cactus still grew around the upper walls and below busy people moved about in the small living rooms, store, magazine and council chambers.

Meals were now more palatable for the wagons brought more sugar and salt. " Over the culinary department," said Ruxton, " presided of late years a fair lady of color, Charlotte, by name, who was, as she loved to say, ' de onlee lady in de dam Injun country ' and who, moreover, was celebrated from Long's Peak to the Cumbres Españolas for slap jacks and pumpkin pies."

Far more to the point than any words of our day, is his description of the fort: " In the corrals, groups of leather-clad mountaineers, with decks of euchre and seven up, gamble away their hard-earned peltries. The employees, mostly Frenchmen and Canadian voyageurs, are pressing packs of buffalo skins, beating robes, or engaged in other duties of a trading fort. Indian squaws, the wives of the mountaineers, strut about in all the pride of beads and ' fofarrow ' jingling with bells and bugles and happy as paint can make them. Hunters drop in with animals packed with deer or buffalo meat to supply the fort. At any hour of the day or night, one may safely wager to see a dozen cayeutes or prairie wolves loping around, or seated on their haunches and looking gravely on waiting for some offal to be cast outside. Against the walls, groups of Indians too proud to enter without invitation lean wrapped in their buffalo robes, sulky and evidently ill at ease to be so near the whites without a chance of fingering their scalp-locks; their white lodges shining in the sun, at a little distance from the river banks; their horses feeding in the plain beyond.

" The appearance of the fort is very striking, standing as it does hundreds of miles from any settlement, on a vast and lifeless prairie, surrounded by hordes of hostile Indians; and far out of reach of intercourse with civilized man; its mud-built walls inclosing a little garrison of a dozen hardy men, sufficient to hold in check the numerous tribes of savages ever thirsting for their blood. Yet the solitary stranger passing this lone fort feels proudly secure when he comes within sight of the Stars and Stripes which float above its walls."

Such was the place where the Bent brothers began to trade with Indians and trappers. Ceran St. Vrain, a young Frenchman from St. Louis, soon joined them and the firm name for years was Bent and St. Vrain. As early as 1832, Charles Bent was established on the plaza in Taos attending to business at this Spanish end of the line. St. Vrain joined him here. The two married Mexican women and their homes were noted for hospitality. Both of them liked to lead their own trains across the trail and both were popular as leaders. In St. Vrain's caravan of 1846, there was a young man, Lewis Garrard, who evidently admired his leader for he wrote of him: " Mr. St. Vrain was a gentleman in the true sense of the term, his French descent imparting an exquisite indefinable degree of politeness and combined with the frankness of an ingenious mountain man made him an amiable fellow traveller."

Of St. Vrain's life in detail little is known. His real name was Ceran de Hault de Lassus de St. Vrain — a name that reflects French-Flanders ancestry. The last Spanish governor of Upper Louisiana was a relative, Don Carlos de Hault de Lassus. His mother's name was Debreuil. Her lessons in thrift, piety and courtesy found definite lodgment in the heart and mind of her wanderer son of whom no one wrote without bespeaking him a courteous, kindly gentleman.

Ceran St. Vrain married Louisa Branch of a well-known Taos family and, again and again, bade his dark-eyed wife good-by to become leader of an outgoing wagon train for St. Louis. His life paralleled that of the Bents and, like them, he was a fearless, daring man who never paled before danger. He lived to a ripe old age and died October 29, 1870, at the home of his daughter in Mora where he had for many years been a merchant, after the days of trading posts were over.

His will of April 2, 1866, shows that he knew the old trails were still far from safe. He began the document: " As man's life is uncertain and as I am about taking a trip of some risk across the plains, should I be so unfortunate as to be killed or die on my transit, etc." and named his three children, Vicente, Felix and Felicitas St. Vrain as among his heirs.

William Bent died on May 19, 1869, in his later stockade home on the Arkansas. He left four children by his first wife who died at the birth of Julia, the youngest. Her sister, Yellow Woman, became Bent's second wife and their son Charles, though educated to the best of his father's ability, reverted to type and became a desperado much dreaded for years by his father's people.

Charles Bent, the brother, with his bride, Maria Ignacia Jaramillo, a Mexican woman of good family, established their home near the road leading to the Taos Pueblo. To his store on the south side of the plaza came all sorts of traders, outfitting for the trail or mountains. He became a stanch friend to Indian, Mexican and American. Of commanding personality and keen mind, he lived up to the ideals of his early training and his conduct was

Ceran St. Vrain

Governor Charles Bent

such that he had a right to believe that his life was safe among those he called friends. The fact that this did not prove true must have broken his heart when he fell at the hands of assassins on that cold morning of January 19th, 1847.

So much for the men who built Bent's Fort. What of the fort itself?

The halfway mark of the century was not quite passed when William Bent deserted the old fort for a better stockade home some thirty-eight miles down the river, but not, however, until he had tried to sell the older building to the government as an army post. When he failed in that, he decided that it should stand no longer and resorted to the use of powder. An explosion lowered part of its walls in 1849, instead of 1852 as the date is often given.

Matters were in a bad way. The fur trade was on the decline. In a letter under date of October 5th, 1849, written at the Indian Agency at Santa Fe, Agent James S. Calhoun wrote: " One of the owners of Bent's Fort has removed all property from it, and caused the fort to be burnt. Mr. St. Vrain, long a citizen here, in every way reliable and intelligent, says a worse state of things has not existed in this country since he has been an inhabitant of it. This fact is sustained by Mr. Folger and others, etc."

The old fort was, however, not entirely burned, for it was actually used as an express station later, but, as a trading post, it passed into history as the most unique building of its time and region.

VIII · TRAPPERS

Bent's GREAT TRADING POST COULD NOT HAVE THRIVED without the mountain men, — rough, hardy, blunt of speech, embittered mayhap in their deepest souls, through some misfortune of earlier years — adventurers or criminals who had fled from the frontier settlements. " These aliens from society," as one who knew them said, " these strangers to the refinements of civilized life who would tear off a bloody scalp with even grim smiles of satisfaction were fine fellows, full of fun and often kind and obliging." Such, in brief, were the types of men who made a success of the fur trade.

The earliest trappers were in the Southwest during the years between 1815 and 1821, and probably before, but it was at that time that the fur trade began in earnest. It has been estimated that one hundred men were at work in the basin of the Rio del Norte, called later Rio Grande, during 1821 to 1823. Then came the red-letter years from 1824 to 1826, when the Colorado Basin was fairly flooded with mountain men who relentlessly sought the beaver, leaving, with about $100,000 worth of beaver skins, a country forever ruined as a hunting ground. Laws were of no avail; guards too few.

During the next ten years, trappers shifted their activities to the west along trails named for Pattie, Jackson, Young, Armijo, Wolfskill and Smith. Instead of hundreds, there were now thousands of men at work and so thoroughly did they sweep the land of fur-bearing animals that, by 1837, the trade in pelts went into a rapid decline. The covered wagon and the burro had been rivals — the

one meant trail trade, the other fur trade with the burro
in the lead — but now the whole interest became centered
in the wagon. True, trappers were many but they continued their work far to the northwest.

Among the men who outfitted in Taos, we already
know the names of Wolfskill, St. Vrain, Young, Bill Williams and Kit Carson. Then there were Milton Sublette
and probably his three brothers, Peg-leg Smith, Jim
Baker and many others.

Most worthy of all was Jedediah Strong Smith, who
rounded out eight years of mountain life and no doubt
knew Taos well. He was a rare spirit, " an intelligent,
Christian gentleman who repressed my youthful ardor,"
said J. J. Warner who sought him out for advice, " and
fancied pleasure for the life of a trapper and mountaineer
by informing me that if I went into the Rocky Mountains the chances were much greater in favor of my meeting death than of finding restoration of health and that,
if I escaped the former and secured the latter, the proba-
bilities were that I would be ruined for anything else in
life than such things as would be agreeable to the passions
of the semi-savage." Smith finally left the mountains and
entered heart and soul into the wagon trade, but met an
untimely end when, famished for water, he stooped to
scoop out a little from a sandy depression in the desert.
The whizz of an arrow and the great Smith fell.

Kit Carson, "a credit to the diggin's that gave him
birth," was born in 1809 in Kentucky. When but a boy
in his teens and an apprentice to a saddler, Carson heard
tales of the West which led him to run away and join a
caravan bound for Santa Fe. In 1826 he came into Taos
to make his home. Devoted to Ewing Young, he learned
his mountain trade from him, though many have claimed

a hand in that, notably Jim Bridger of the north country. As Carson developed into manhood, he became one of the hardiest of all the mountain men, little bow-legged man that he was, with keen blue eyes and voice almost as soft as that of a woman. His experience in trapping led him far afield and gave him a knowledge of the West which eventually brought him into the company of Colonel John C. Fremont, the explorer, and won for him the title of America's greatest scout.

Older than Carson was Bill Williams, born William Sherley Williams, about 1788 in Kentucky. His father's name suggests New England while that of his grandmother on his mother's side was Lewis, of the same stock as Meriwether Lewis of the Clark expedition of 1804. Receiving an education unusual in frontier settlements, William Sherley became a preacher. Then something happened and the mountains claimed him for life. Only once in later years did he try to live in a settlement. No one knows just where this experiment was tried. He set up a store but, becoming disgusted, threw his goods out into the street and, seizing his gun, left for the mountains.

Earlier than most men in the West, Williams was wont to travel alone when trapping. Shrewd and diplomatic, he became the enigma of the mountains. He was dual in character to a marked degree, helpful and kind here, and thieving and desperate there, and became known as a " hard case," half savage and always equal to outwitting the red skins until, of course, his last encounter. A natural leader was Williams when on rare occasions he would consent to travel with a group.

Among those who actually knew him was Albert Pike, of the early thirties, who said: " As a specimen of the genuine trapper Bill Williams certainly stands foremost.

He is a man about six feet one inch in height, gaunt and red-headed, with a hard weather-beaten face, marked deeply with the small-pox. He is all muscle and sinew and the most indefatigable hunter and trapper in the world. He has no glory excepting in the woods and his ambition is to kill more deer and catch more beaver than any other man about him. Nothing tires him, not even running all day with six traps on his back. His horse fell once, as he was galloping along the edge of a steep hill and rolled down the hill with him, while his feet were entangled in the stirrups and his traps dashing against him at every turn. He was picked up half dead, by his companion and set upon his horse and, after all, he out-witted him and obtained the best set for his traps. Neither is he a fool. He is a shrewd, acute, original man and far from illiterate. He was once a preacher and afterwards an interpreter in the Osage Nation."

Another man who knew Williams well was Richens Wootton, a one-time Taos sheriff, who drove the first sheep to California in 1852, and was favorably known around Taos, though given to skylarking on a white horse which he liked to ride into a saloon and shoot out the lights. When he was an old man, he dictated the following about Williams: " He was a queer character. I never knew where he came from, or how long he had been in the country, although I have sat by the same camp fire with him a hundred times. All I ever knew was that he had been a circuit preacher in early life in Missouri and had been in the mountains longer than any of the other trappers. He had been so much among the Indians that he used to look and talk like an Indian and had imbibed a great many of their superstitions and peculiar notions. Poor old fellow, he was a warm-hearted, brave and generous man, and in whatever state he continues his existence, I hope he is happy."

This hint of belief in after life probably refers to the fact that Old Bill or " Lone Elk," as the Indians called him, used to warn his companions that they should not shoot a certain kind of buck elk after he had taken the long trail for his spirit would come back and live thus. We wonder if Williams had his wish after that spring day in 1849 when he and his companion Dr. Benjamin Kern, who were searching for valuables cached away by the Fremont expedition of that year, were killed by Utes.

So much of interest lurks around his name that one longs for the manuscript story of his life, which he is said to have written, only to go up in smoke in the seventies when the Crow Agency in the north burned to the ground.

Of lesser caliber were other men who drifted into Taos. Such was Peg-leg Smith, a daring fighter but not a great character any more than was Jim Beckwourth who loved to spin his yarns out a little too far. " Peg-leg was really a trafficker in horses among the Indians," said Horace Bell, a major in the United States Army. " It was on one of these Rocky Mountain forays that he lost his leg, which was amputated below the knee by an Indian surgeon under the direction of Peg-leg himself, the only surgical instruments used being a hunting knife and a small Indian or key-hole saw." So much for the grit of horse-loving, jolly Peg-leg who liked to show he could dance a jig, wooden leg or no.

El Cojo, or the lame man, was in Taos with the Gwinn Heap party, at one time, and won this from the leader: " From the time of our arrival in Taos, Peg-leg had been surrounded by his friends and boon companions, relating to them his late exploits on Grand River, and his frequent libations to Bacchus in wretched Taos brandy had rendered him incapable of keeping his seat on horseback. I left him practising the Apache war whoop in the square of Taos and did not see him again until the wagons and men had arrived at the Cubebra and I was prepared to depart. He then made his appearance, looking very sick, unhappy and repentant."

Of bear fighting fame was Jim Baker, as well as a man who had positive convictions about the Indians, as " the most onsartinest varmints." When Baker was an old man, he settled down to quiet life. Among his treasures was an organ stored in his barn loft. A traveling tuner repaired it and " Old Jim was happy then. Often his cramped old fingers moved over the keys and low melodies, quivering with love and pain, filled the shadows of the cabin."

Among the mountain men, women were held in high esteem. Most of them married Indians and were usually kind to them and proud of their dusky offspring. Sometimes they employed cave-man tactics, according to Ruxton, who said the trappers " would often undertake an expedition to the settlements of New Mexico where not unfrequently they adopted a young Lochinvar system in procuring the required rib and have been known to carry off *vi et armis,* from the midst of a fandango in Fernandez or El Rancho de Taos some dark-skinned beauty — with or without her own consent is a matter of unconcern — and bear the ravished fair one across the mountains where she soon became inured to the free and roving life fate had assigned to her." This could not have happened often for the trappers, as a rule, felt that a girl brought up in a town was unfitted to live in the mountains.

When the time came for the mountaineers to gather at Green River or some other point for the great rendezvous of the north, the men traded briskly for a while and then when dull times set in they mended moccasins, dried meat, cleaned their guns and tried their strength in wrestling and other sports.

Sometimes these men wandered far afield and then, undoubtedly, they met with the same hospitality of which Captain R. B. Marcy wrote, after greeting a good wife from whose face and form, though young, hard work had stolen all beauty.

" Mighty few humans comes this-a-way," she said as she led the way indoors.

" What's yer name? "

" Marcy," replied the Captain.

" Massy. I knowd a heap o' Massys down in ole Mississippi. Me and him allers 'lowed that them Massys was considdible on bar and other varmints. Wal, now, stranger, my ole man he ar out on a bar track but I sort o' reckon maybe you mought git to stay. There's narry show of vittles in the house barrin' some sweet taters and a small chance of corn."

When once their trapping season was over many of the men went down the Missouri to St. Louis to sell their pelts and with pockets full of money would make their way to the banks, sometimes getting lost, for, as one fellow put it, " the confounded cañons here are all so much alike I couldn't tell one from another." At one of the banks, there was, once, by chance, a James B. Finley who saw a trapper come wandering in and of him he scribbled: " His dress and appearance were those of a backwoods trapper and the bank room being filled with the gentry they looked upon his greasy buckskin hunting shirt and leggins as though they feared he would touch them and spoil or soil their delicate clothing, and after looking around the room, he threw down his first check — then his second, third. Then the cashier said, ' Where are you from, Sir? '

" The trapper replied, ' Just from the moon, Sir! '

" ' How did you get down, Sir? '

" ' Why, I just greased my hunting shirt, Sir, and slid down the rainbow! ' "

After depositing his rich haul from the pot at the end of the rainbow, the mountaineer would wend his way to the Rocky Mountain House which used to stand on a back street in that old fur-trading center. Here he would fall a victim to some card shark who would call out as he squatted on his buffalo robe and slammed down his money, " Ho, boys! Hyar's a deck and hyar's the beaver (rattling the coin) . Who dar set his hoss? Wagh! "

Away slipped the hard-earned dollars either in the games or at the dance where the French coquettes gathered. There the men delighted in performing queer antics, since they were too clumsy for real dancing and were more at home when allowed to give Indian dances with the accompanying songs and cries.

Outfitted for another long stay in the mountains, away would go the men to earn more dollars in the land of snow and ice. Here they would camp and puff at their pipes before rolling themselves in their blankets. Then some old-timer would begin to tell of his experiences and, if a tenderfoot were near to listen, might give him a thrill by telling of the carcague, an awful creature, part wolf and part bear. Many a man actually believed such an animal existed for had they not heard their companions say they had seen it bound right into camp, seize their meat and be off in a flash? Or perhaps, the old man would tell of a trip he once made far to the southwest where he had seen the " Munchies," white Indians, yes, sir, white! If he were in the mood he might say he had been made a king among those Indians who had no guns and no word for *enemy* in their language. There was no end to what such a liar might venture unless some one broke in to tell a true story.

There was one they sometimes told in low, quiet tones. It was that of Hugh Glass, a hunter in the north who stopped by a stream to drink and, as he rose, was struck by a bear and unmercifully wounded. When he reached for his gun and finally downed his adversary he fell unconscious and was later found and taken to camp, where he lay showing little or no improvement as the days went by. Since the whole camp could not tarry longer, two were chosen to remain behind to care for the invalid, a man by the name of Fitzgerald and a boy who, tradition insists, was none other than Jim Bridger of much fame later. Glass did not seem to get any better. Believing that he was doomed to die, the two watchers decided they would move on. They took everything, even his knife, and, while the sick man dozed, they slipped away, thereby committing one of the worst crimes possible in the mountains.

Soon Glass opened his eyes and looked about. He knew the signs. He had been deserted! This thought gave him courage to live if but for revenge. He staggered to his feet and, munching berries, when he could find them, he slowly made his way to a fort where he startled everybody by his sudden appearance, this man all believed dead.

Strangely enough it was here that he found the boy and forgave. He was after the man, but Fitzgerald was gone, gone to hide in the army. He needed killing, the narrator would assure his audience with a shake of the head. Glass? Well, he finally forgave the man too and instead of taking care of his marred old body he went into the mountains and was finally killed by Indians.

A deep silence would have fallen over any such party of men in the wilds by this time. Each would have sat wondering if he ever could forgive a man who could desert him and leave him to die, aye and even take the knife! There would have been discussion and many shakes of the head but the end would always have been the same. Hugh Glass *had* forgiven!

Perhaps to break the gloom some man would have risen and announced that, after he had had his sleep he was going to take the Taos Trail instead of making for St. Louis, this time, and there would " trap a squaw." There too he would indulge in the whisky of local brew announcing, " Then thar's Touse arwardenty; it's d——d poor stuff — kin taste the corn in it — makes me think I'm a hos, a feedin' away fur plowin' time; an' I allers squeals, an raises my hind foot to kick when any palou comes about my heels."

If a whole party came down the western slopes and to Taos, there was always a welcome. The dance was an inevitable part of such a welcome, though it often, if not usually, ended in a fight with the mountaineers grouping themselves together in the center of the room to raise chair, gun or club and finally drive everybody out of the hall. Again tales of happenings in the mountains, next day, would be related as the men loafed against the poles which supported the portals around the plaza.

Some of these men evidently knew a young minister, W. G. Kephart, in Santa Fe well enough to chat away many an hour. What he said in a letter he wrote on October 25, 1852, sums up the whole story of the mountain men and so is well worth quoting: " I have sat by the fireside and conversed with men not older than myself, who were, nevertheless, *old* mountaineers; men who had thrown themselves into these mountain wilds and savage fastnesses in their green boyhood, spent their lives with the wild savages and beasts of prey for their companions. I have listened with deep and sometimes painful interest to their stories of imminent perils and hair-breadth escapes, told, not with the blustering swagger of the bravado, but with a real touch of *melancholy regret* at the prospect of encroaching civilization. These men are drawn to this mode of life first by motives of gain; they become inured to its hardships, familiar with its dangers and eventually deeply attached to it. The far-famed Kit Carson and others in this territory who have as much fame at home as Kit himself are all comparatively young men."

Among these young men were many from Taos who knew the Rocky Mountains well, especially Carson's " celebrated forty five " yet we have not even their names. There were Taos Indians who went as friendlies and were as bold and daring as any who roamed the wilds. Only the Rockies could tell their stories and they lift up their heads as of yore — silent.

IX · A TAOS BECOMES GOVERNOR

DURING THE HEYDAY OF LIFE FOR MOUNTAINEERS AND
for Bent's Fort, where there was little to worry over and
where no Indian battle ever took place, there were troublesome times in Taos and Santa Fe.

Tales of Indian atrocities saddened both towns. Many
a relief party had to gallop away to the rescue of men
fighting for their lives on some lonely stretch of the long
trail to the East. Indians plundered, pillaged, burned
wagons and homes and scalped their victims. White men
often acted like savages and were most unfair to the red.
Losing faith, Indians became exasperated beyond control because of the white man's injustice. Again and again,
unoffending Indians were shot for no greater crime than
that of running after the wagons, when they were desper-
ately hungry.

Josiah Gregg, the most famous of the traders of the
forties, was bitter in his denunciation of his people for he
believed that the Indian would act well if so treated. At
one time, he fell in with a band of Comanches and had
the opportunity to tell them about the United States and
the President in Washington who wished them to make
peace with the white man.

In reply, the Comanche chief said: " We are rejoiced,
our hearts are glad that you are arrived among us; it makes
our eyes laugh to see Americans walk in our land. We
will notify our old and young men — our boys and our
maidens, our women and children, that they may come
to trade with you. We hope that you will speak well of
us to your people, that more of them may hunt the way

to our country for we like to trade with the white man."
When he left the next morning the chief said: " Tell the
Capitan Grande that when he pleases to call us we are all
ready to go to him."

Gregg's comment on this experience runs: " I have no
doubt that the chiefs of the Comanches and other prairie
tribes if rightly managed might be induced to visit our
veritable ' Capitan ' and our large cities which would
doubtless have a far better effect than all the treaties of
peace that could be concluded with them for an age to
come." Such an experiment, however, was never tried
and troubles increased.

Meanwhile, though Indian mischief was still a matter
for consideration in Taos, there were affairs of a political
nature happening to the south which boded ill. In fact,
such had been the case since about 1821.

In 1828, the hatred of the Spaniard, held by all Mexicans, showed itself in an expulsion law which swept the
country of all real Spaniards except where money purchased the right to stay. Then avarice, greed and misrule
could not but produce an explosion.

Governor Albino Perez was sent by General Santa
Ana to take his chair in 1835. Since he was not of the
country, he was distrusted. His greatest handicap was the
profound ignorance he encountered on every side. There
had been only the most feeble efforts on the part of
government or church along the line of education. He
announced a plan for schools which, had it been carried out, would have meant much to the people of New
Mexico.

Only a few priests had cared about schools but Padre
Martinez of Taos was one. Shortly after coming to his
parish in 1826, this gifted priest had established a school

for both boys and girls. This was an unusual step for any Spaniard to take, not to say priest. Several of his boys later went to Congress and of the girls, who were allowed to come, practically every one became more or less of a power in the community. For his pupils, the padre brought in the first printing press which ever came to Taos and published his own school books and for four weeks, in 1835, he published a paper called *El Crepúsculo* or "The Dawn," a name truly suggestive of the thinker that he was.

The early government officials had not desired schools. Even priests were denied the right to certain scholarly pursuits. Years before, at San Juan, in 1807, Zebulon Pike told of meeting a priest who was at heart " a great naturalist." Pike showed him the few astronomical instruments which he had and the priest listened carefully to his explanation of the sextant. Since the padre seemed to be versed in the ancient languages and several sciences, Pike was at a loss to understand why he had never studied mathematics. The priest explained that the government took great care that no one should study " anything which would have a tendency to extend the views of the subjects of the provinces of the geography of their country or any other subject which might bring to view a comparison of their local advantages and situations with those of other countries."

Governor Perez brought a new thought into the land, as far as schools were concerned, but he also announced what was known as the " departmental plan " in the Mexican Republic. Direct taxation was to go into effect. The people were not used to such a system and when they heard a rumor that this was to include a tax on poultry and even on husbands for living with their wives — false,

no doubt — excitement and indignation ran high, as well
it might.

Meantime, knowing of and perhaps creating much of
the discontent among the people, the former governor,
ambitious Manuel Armijo, a man of subtle, snake-like
character, was fairly writhing with joy. In all probability,
he was the real promoter of the trouble which took shape
in 1837.

Again it took but a match to start a great conflagration
and again at Taos came the first sputtering fire. Under
what was believed to be an order from Governor Perez,
Don Ramon Abreu had the alcalde of Taos arrested and
imprisoned on a trifling charge. Mob fury took charge
of affairs. The people released the alcalde and both Mexicans and Indians took arms and marched south. The first
revolution since 1680 was under way. It gathered force
until a meeting took place at Santa Cruz de la Cañada,
where a proclamation was made against the departmental
plan, the tax and the disorder which the revolutionists
claimed others were attempting to create. As was to be
expected the rebels declared they would defend their
country " until we spill every drop of blood to obtain the
victory we have in view."

Although then only six years of age, my late neighbor,
Señor Sostenos Trujillo, said he remembered the men
marching at La Cañada. He and his brother were left to
guard their home, while the women and little ones took
to the hills to hide behind cedars and piñons. He recalled
distinctly seeing Padre Martinez making his way toward
Santa Fe where he took sides with the government.

Finally, the insurgents camped around Santa Fe. The
inhabitants of the city were in great fear but nothing of
an untoward nature took place at that time. Before long

the insurgents had their wish and a new governor was elected — José Gonzales, not of Taos but of the Taos pueblo! An ignorant man was he, of whom the best that could be said was that he was a good buffalo hunter!

Then murder began and the former Governor Perez, Don Abreu and many prominent men lost their lives, their property being confiscated.

Governor Gonzales took the reins of government and on the 27th and 28th of August called a general assembly where a committee was appointed who reported on the grievances of the people. Assenting to all this was that arch fiend, General Manuel Armijo, who now proceeded to work his will after having " pouted and plotted " at his Albuquerque home. He sent messengers south to report in his favor to the officials in Mexico City for whom he now declared. Meanwhile, the Gonzales government had repudiated that southern government and was proceeding to make plans to appeal to Texas.

Gathering a few soldiers together, General Armijo marched on Santa Fe. Gonzales fled and Armijo took possession of the office he coveted and began an iron rule which was to last eight years, having for his office a room in the old palace where hung human scalp-locks as a wall decoration! He put to death former friends and supporters. No one held anything but contempt for Manuel Armijo.

The fate of the Indian Gonzales was sad enough. As reported by a governor of a much later day, L. Bradford Prince, it was as follows: " The story is that Gonzales, on being captured at Cañada, was brought before Armijo, who was then in the outskirts of the town. On seeing the General, Gonzales came forward with hand extended, saying, ' How do you do, Compañero? ' as was proper be-

tween two of equal rank, as governors. Armijo replied,
'How do you do, Compañero? Confess yourself, Compañero.' Then turning to his soldiers he added, 'Now
shoot my Compañero.'" Standing by was Padre Martinez of Taos who had to receive Gonzales' confession and
watch the monster Armijo have his way.

X · THE TEXAS–SANTA FE EXPEDITION

DURING THE YEARS FOLLOWING 1837, WHEN ARMIJO WAS ruling and proving himself a coward and tyrant of the first magnitude, some misguided men came marching from Texas. They thought the time was ripe to lead New Mexico out from under the heavy yoke of the Mexican Republic. All land east of the Rio Grande they claimed for the Lone Star Republic.

John Rowland and William Workman of Taos were apparently of a similar mind. A friend of theirs was a man who later became the second mayor of Los Angeles, California, Benjamin Davis Wilson. Many years later Wilson was induced to tell the story of those days to a representative of the Bancroft Library, and it runs as follows:

" Messrs. John Rowland and William Workman, who were old residents of that country (at Taos) and had been in correspondence with prominent parties in Texas, learned that an expedition was being fitted out to come and take New Mexico as part of Texas. They were convinced that the plan might succeed, but, in the meantime, prominent foreigners in New Mexico would probably be sacrificed to the fury of the Mexicans.

" As it was, Armijo had information that the Texans were coming. This was in the summer of 1841. It was even whispered that we were in correspondence with the Texans. One day (when) that Armijo was haranguing his rabble to rise to a man to meet the foreigners who were coming to destroy their customs, religion etc., a French Creole from near St. Louis, who was a bold gambler and

named Tiboux, made some insulting remark in a sten-
torian voice. This came very near being the destruction
of all of us, for the whole wave of the rabble moved toward
us, but fortunately Armijo called them back, promising
to punish the offenders. However he (Tiboux) was not
found out and came to California with us in the fall.

" Under the circumstances, Rowland, Workman and
myself together with about 20 other Americans including William Gordon and William Knight, concluded
that it was not safe for us to remain longer in New Mexico. We formed a party and were joined by a large number
of New Mexicans. In the first week of September, 1841,
we started from our rendezvous in the most western part
of New Mexico, a place called Abiqui, for California."

Such is the story of the Americans of Taos who were
interested in the ill-timed effort of Texans to rescue New
Mexico, as they believed. The hasty departure for the
west undoubtedly saved the men and enabled them to
establish themselves and even become prominent on the
far western coast.

One other fact linked our town with the Texas-Santa
Fe expedition. A Mexican from Taos, known only by the
name of Carlos, marched with the men from the East. It
was he who stepped forward from the ranks, when the
wilderness around Red River had proved too much, as-
suring the men that he had trapped through that country
and felt sure he could guide them to safety. Since he was
known to have established a reputation as an honest fellow when he was mail carrier between Austin and San
Antonio some time before, he was immediately appointed
a member of the Spy Company.

A short time later, Carlos and others went out apparently on a reconnoitering trip. They separated and, one

by one, the men came back to camp but Carlos did not return. Had he found that he did not know where they were and dreaded to say so or did he fear the authorities at Santa Fe and so did not dare continue as a guide? Many kept their faith in the Mexican but he did not return. Was Carlos lost? No one knew. There was nothing left for the Texans to do but march on with only their wits to guide them.

No account of their great suffering on the trail and in the vicinity of the capital need be given here save for one instance. Armijo ordered the Texans to march for ten leagues to meet him. When they arrived he immediately commanded them to march back, saying that he would talk with them the next morning.

The Mexican Don Jesus, who was their leader and a tool of Armijo, dared to remonstrate, declaring that the men were not able to walk ten leagues more. To this the Governor replied: " They are able to walk ten leagues more. The Texans are an active and untiring people — I know them. If one of them pretends to be sick or tired on the road, *shoot him down and bring me his ears!* Go! "

When the tired men turned to leave the place, they spied in the crowd the runaway Carlos, seated on a mule, with arms and breast bandaged. It was said that he had been stabbed by a nephew of Armijo because he had been suspected of being connected with the Texas expedition. His own story was never learned.

Through treachery, the Texans failed. The cruelty and suffering were great and the tale of the awful march down into Mexico was soon reported in the Lone Star Republic so it was not long before a band of men came marching, as avengers, declaring themselves eager to right the wrongs done to the Texans. The *Houston Telegraph* made this announcement as they were leaving, " Col. Snively with the troops under his command left Coffe's Station on the 25th of April and took up the line of march for Santa Fe — Just as the cavalcade started, the banner of the Single Star was unfurled and, spreading its glorious folds to the breeze, seemed to shine forth as the harbinger of brighter days. The troops hailed it with joyous acclamations."

Hearing of the coming of the men under Snively, Governor Armijo sent out to meet the invader, a company of one hundred men, practically all of whom were from Taos and the Taos pueblo. Captain Ventura Lovato of Ranchos de Taos was in command. The men marched for many miles and found no enemy.

Meantime, according to Rufus Sage, who was not actually with the advancing army but was not far away, the soldiers under Colonel Warfield had joined those of Snively, and, sighting the Mexicans, waited for them under cover of a sand-bank, while the Taos men pressed on, ignorant of the proximity of the enemy, until they were suddenly halted. Then a parley took place which ended with this declaration from the Texans: " We have come to fight and shall unless you surrender. But, that you may know with whom you have to deal, we give you thirty minutes to decide whether to fight or surrender. If you choose the former, a signal from your sword will announce the answer."

The Taos men held a hurried discussion. The Mexicans wanted to surrender, but the Indians, fifty in number, scorned to do so, saying they had come to *fight* and not to surrender, like women, at the first appearance of an inferior army. It was an Indian who advanced with drawn sword.

The battle was on and the Taos line was broken immediately by the Texan fire. Cries for mercy filled the air. Within five minutes the conflict was over and twenty-two of the Taos company lay dead; thirty were wounded and all the others but one were taken prisoner. Not a Texan was hurt.

Had Armijo with his seven hundred soldiers been near, the outcome would probably have been different, but Armijo was fifty miles away at the Cimarron and, on hearing the fate of his advance company, ordered an immediate retreat for he did not care to meet with Snively's men, no, not he!

There seems to be but one account by any man present and he was apparently with the Texans. He evidently wrote a letter which fell into the hands of the editor of the *St. Louis Era* and this much was printed:

" MISSOURI RIVER
On Board Steamer Tobacco Plant;
July 28 (1843)
" We were joined by Col. Warfield about the 4th of June. On the 19th of June we came in contact with the advance guard of Governor Armijo's army, (about 100 Mexicans) under Cheveler's. About 100 Texans engaged in the attack on them. After firing three rounds, we broke their ranks, killed five, wounded twenty-three, took all the rest prisoners, without having a Texian hurt. The Mexicans were fortified in a ravine near the trace or orad, about 16 miles from the Arkansas River.

" Armijo, however, like an old fox tired of the chase retreated back beyond the Semerone and as the caravan did not arrive at the expected time, we supposed that the company had returned to Missouri. We therefore sent the prisoners homeward."

In the end, Captain Cook of the United States Dragoons forced the Texans in their "uniform of rags" to surrender to him, claiming they had invaded the territory of the United States and were desperadoes. Released in July, they returned to Texas, having accomplished nothing.

In Taos, indignation ran high when the news came in. Lovato's men had not wanted to go and rumor had it that Armijo had even given the command that, if necessary to force the men to go, they should be tied to their horses until they were far out on the plains. Taos men had been slaughtered and to no avail. Something should be done. It was. Without giving them a chance to carry anything with them, all citizens who had ever sided with the Texans were driven out of town. Taos would have none of Texans or their sympathizers.

XI · WHITMAN'S RIDE

LEAVING POLITICAL TROUBLES IN THE SOUTHWEST, WE turn to another event of much greater import, the ride of Dr. Marcus Whitman to Washington.

There have been many famous rides through the West. In the very early days, so goes the tale, possibly true, a woman, failing to secure justice when she plead with a Spanish governor for the honor of her daughter, buckled gold in her belt and rode alone through Indian country, over plains and mountains to the City of Mexico. There she found a listener and the result was that the man who thought " 'tis only a woman " fell from his proud seat. Messengers, in relays, rode to carry the news of the annexation of Texas to the United States. Our own Carson galloped away to the East four times with Washington as his objective. He always had companions enough on long journeys. Never has a man with only one other and an occasional guide started out at the beginning of winter to ride four thousand miles or more against wind and storm, over deserts and well-nigh impassable mountains, to rush on in the face of warnings and discouragements with the great unselfish purpose of saving for his country a rich land which was slowly drifting under the protection of another flag.

Marcus Whitman knew there was " an empire to be lost or won." He asked young Lovejoy who had recently come from the East to go back with him. It was already October. Time was precious. In spite of the fact that they knew full well that they would reach the Rockies when the snows were deepest, the two men set out from Walla

Walla, far to the northwest. Warned at Fort Hall that either the Indians or the British would try to halt their march, they never wavered, but on they came as the poet Hezekiah Butterworth said:

> " On, on and on, past Idaho,
>   On past the mighty saline sea,
>   His covering at night the snow,
>   His only sentinel a tree.
>   On, past Portneuf's basaltic heights,
>   On where San Juan Mountains lay,
>   Through sunless days and starlight nights,
>   Toward Taos and Santa Fe."

Every honest account of the famous ride by the Protestant missionary doctor, Marcus Whitman, says that he came through Taos. Every account gives his real mission. Where there has been an effort to discredit Whitman, the underlying motive is so apparent that no scholar can for a moment doubt what it was. There never lived a great man that small men did not attack him. So it was with Whitman.

The most authentic record of this wild ride comes from the man who accompanied him, Amos Lawrence Lovejoy. After describing some of the hardships endured on the way, he wrote, " With our new guide, travelling slowly on, we reached Taos in about thirty days. We suffered considerably from cold and scarcity of provisions, and for food were compelled to use the flesh of mules, dogs, and such other animals as came in our reach. We remained at Taos some twelve or fifteen days, when we changed off our animals, made such purchases as our journey required, then left for Bent's Fort, on the headwaters of the Arkansas River, where we arrived about the 3rd day of January, 1843."

From Bent's Fort, Whitman rode on alone save when he could join some caravan bound east. On he went to Washington where he was privileged to say, " Thank God, I am not too late." Oregon was saved to the United States and in a small measure Taos helped to save it.

Back of this remarkable ride lies a story of four Nez Percé Indians who were undoubtedly seen by traders from Taos when they were in St. Louis in the winter of 1832–3.

Over the many miles from their Oregon home these Indians came to St. Louis. At first, they did not tell their mission but finally they broke their silence and told General Clark, Superintendent of Indian Affairs, that they had come to learn of the white man's " Book from Heaven " and ask for teachers for their people. Their fathers had known Lewis and Clark and they had learned much from hunters and trappers. Longing to know more of the truth led the men east to the white man's great city.

General Clark, who was a devout Catholic, realizing his position as Great Father to these truth-hunting Indians told them Bible stories and took them to the cathedral. He also led them about the city to let them see how the white men lived and took them to ride in wagons on wheels which delighted them. Winter wore away and the time came for them to start on their long return journey. Two of them had died. Two were to start on the morrow but only one of them was destined to reach his people and he never lived with them again.

General Clark arranged a dinner for them. Before the evening was over one of the Indians rose and in tones that spoke of sorrow and disappointment addressed his audience in words that cut to the heart, these hundred years after.

" I came to you over a trail of many moons," said the Indian, "from the setting sun. You were the friend of my fathers, who all have gone the long way. I came with one eye partly opened, for more light for my people who sit in darkness. I go back with both eyes closed. How can I go back blind to my blind people? I made my way to you with strong arms, through many enemies and strange lands, that I might carry back much to them. I go back with both arms broken and empty. The two fathers who came with me — the braves of many winters and wars — we leave asleep here by your great water. They were tired in many moons and their moccasins wore out.

" My people sent me to get the white man's Book from Heaven. You took me where you allow your women to dance, as we do not ours, and the Book was not there. You took me where they worship the Great Spirit with candles and the Book was not there. You showed me the images of good spirits and the pictures of the good land beyond, but the Book was not among them. I am going back the long sad trail to my people of the dark land. You make my feet heavy with burdens of gifts, and my moccasins will grow old in carrying them, but the Book is not among them. When I tell my poor blind people, after one more snow, in the big council, that I did not bring the Book, no word will be spoken by our old men or by our young braves. One by one they will rise up and go out in silence. My people will die in darkness, and they will go on the long path to the other hunting grounds. No white man will go with them and no white man's Book, to make the way plain. I have no more words."

This speech drilled its way into many a heart. It found lodgment in the soul of Marcus Whitman and there began his work for Oregon Indians. There too began the tale of the famous rider, who, on his way, weary and well-nigh exhausted, rested in Taos.

XII · KEARNY AND BENT

THREE YEARS AFTER CONGRESS HAD BEEN COMPELLED TO listen to the fur-clad messenger from the Northwest and Oregon was saved, affairs on the southwestern border came to a climax.

Trouble had been brewing for many years, as we know. Americans had suffered many indignities that called loudly for redress, yet Congress was loath to give attention for another war was far from desirable.

Mexico still claimed Texas though it was now a part of the United States after nine years under its own rule. Mexico also insisted that the Americans were the aggressors and called upon their patriots to arise against the intruder.

On the other hand, in a message to Congress, President Polk declared: " We had ample cause for war against Mexico long before the breaking out of hostilities but forebore to take redress into our own hands until Mexico herself became the aggressor by invading our soil in hostile array and shedding the blood of our citizens."

On the thirteenth of May, 1846, war was declared — a war of which Americans have never been proud, for it is quite impossible in the light of facts to believe that war was necessary. Once on, it proceeded to the sorrow of our southern neighbor.

General Stephen Watts Kearny left Fort Leavenworth with his troops and halted for a time at Bent's Fort. Among the marching men were Colonel Doniphan and his thousand Missourians. They were later joined by several of our Taos men, notably Dick Wootton who became a guide and messenger for Colonel Doniphan.

Lieutenant-Colonel W. H. Emory was sent on ahead from Bent's Fort as an advance guard and from his diary comes the most interesting first-hand account of those stirring days.

"Aug. 2, 1846 — I looked in the direction of Bent's Fort and saw a huge United States flag flowing to the breeze and straining every fibre of an ash pole planted over the centre of a gate. The mystery was soon revealed by a column of dust to the east advancing with about the velocity of a fast walking horse. It was the Army of the West. I ordered my horses to be hitched and as the column passed took my place with the staff.

"Aug. 5. Captain Cook of the First Dragoons was sent ahead the day before yesterday to sound out Armijo. Mr. Liffendorfer, a trader married to a Santa Fe lady, was sent in the direction of Taos with two Pueblo Indians to feel the pulse of the pueblos and Mexican people and probably to buy wheat if any could be purchased and to distribute the proclamations of the Colonel commanding.

"Yesterday Wm. Bent and six others forming a spy guard were sent forward to reconnoitre the mountain passes.

"Aug. 11. Matters are now becoming very interesting. Six or eight Mexicans were captured last night and on their persons was found the proclamation of the Prefect of Taos, based upon that of Armijo, calling the citizens to arms, to repel the 'Americans who were coming to invade their soil and destroy their property and liberties,' ordering an enrollment of all citizens over 15 and under 50. It is decidedly less bombastic than any Mexican paper I have yet seen. Colonel Kearny assembled these prisoners altogether, some ten or twelve, made a speech to them and ordered that when the rear guard should have passed they should be released.

"In the course of the week various deputations have come in from Taos, giving in their allegiance and asking protection from the Indians. That portion of the country seems best disposed toward the United States. A Taos man may be distinguished at once by the cordiality of his salutation."

On marched the Americans, learning soon that they were to meet General Armijo near Las Vegas, for he had suggested a parley but at Las Vegas there was no Armijo! Kearny then, with a nerve which amazed Washington, proceeded to tell the people that he was taking the country and that Armijo was no longer governor. He met with applause. In reality, he was acting under the impulse of the moment rather than following official orders. From Las Vegas he marched south to Apache Pass where reports said he would meet armed resistance. Again Armijo was not there! Arrant coward that he was, he had fled with *plenty of money* to Old Mexico from whence only after many years did he dare to return.

When, in the capital, Kearny found the acting governor, Juan Bautista Vigil y Alarid ready to swear allegiance to the United States though he voiced the sentiments of his people well when he said: "No one in the world can successfully resist the power of him who is stronger. Do not find it strange if there has been no manifestation of joy and enthusiasm in seeing the city occupied by your military forces. To us the power of the Mexican Republic is dead. No matter what her condition she was our mother. What child will not shed abundant tears at the tomb of his parents."

After the occupation of Santa Fe, Colonel Philip St. G. Cooke made this entry in his journal: " The Indians have been coming in, and seemed pleased at the new order of things; temporary civil officers have been sworn in. The authorities of Taos have submitted and the prefect taken the oath of allegiance. Some of the civilized Indians or ' Pueblo ' Indians from that quarter have visited us. These are a remarkable element in the New Mexican population."

Indians from the other pueblos as well came soon to give assurance of their allegiance to the newcomers and considering the fact that for years their wise men had prepared them for the event, it is not strange that they came readily.

At Pecos, long years ago, had not the mighty Montezuma planned a fine city and started with his own hands a fire which was to burn forever? Had he not planted a tree upside down and told his children that, if they kept the fire aglow until the tree should fall, a people, pale of face, would come out of the east and free them from the Spanish yoke? Montezuma had gone to live in the sun. Year after year had passed with no one to the rescue. Now, at long last, the pale faces had come and at Pecos had fallen the old tree with a mighty crash! The prophecy was fulfilled. So ran the story for most of the Indians.

Among the Mexicans at Taos and in the north generally there was no such tale to ease their fears and quiet their indignation at this quick taking over of their land. Throughout the territory the populace, led by the clergy, muttered. In Taos, there were meetings on the loma, where windows were darkened while within only a dull lamp lighted faces growing more and more discontented. There were no meetings in the churches as at Santa Fe.

The lawless element continued to find their way to the home of Pablo Montoya but he controlled only a part of the citizens of the town. Some remembered the insurgent rôle Montoya had played in 1837 and would have none of him. Yet even Montoya's voice of protest cannot rightfully be called treason.

Meantime, unmindful of mutterings, Kearny shaped events so that on the 22nd of September he announced the officers for the new territory of the United States. Taos was in the lead. Charles Bent, the merchant of our town, was considered the best man for the position and was appointed Governor. Then on the 25th, Kearny left for the West. His work was done as he saw it. Without shedding blood or firing a single gun, he had won a rich new land for his country.

XIII · THE REVOLUTION OF 1847

ALLEGIANCE MAY BE BUT A WORD. THE OATH OF OFFI-cials may not reflect the true feeling of a people. A conquering general may come and go and yet leave behind him growing discontent. So it was in New Mexico, now floating the flag of the United States.

All was far from well in Taos and Santa Fe. By December first, there were more meetings in dark, unwonted places where men plotted the overthrow of the new government. Many priests were privy to these councils. Our Padre Martinez was accused of being among the number. This may have been true as it probably would have been of you and me, had our country been taken in such a manner as General Kearny had used. Rumors and the talk of servants condemning Padre Martinez were afloat then and have persisted throughout the years, but actual proof has never come to light. That he knew of the discontent or of the plan for revolution is probable, but that he believed affairs would culminate as they did seems hardly possible in the light of his known character and activities. More eager for revolt was Don Tomas Ortiz who had his eye on the governor's chair and associated with him was Don Diego Archuleta who came to Taos for aid. This would surely not have been necessary had the powerful, masterly Martinez been a party to all the plans.

Midnight of December 19th and then Christmas eve were the dates set for the church bell to sound the signal in Santa Fe for the seizing of the artillery and the searching out of Governor Charles Bent, wherever he might be, to do him to his death. Such were the ugly plans of the revolutionists — " each having pledged himself to the others on the cross that he would be faithful and vigilant in consummating their designs as speedily and successfully as possible."

No woman was to know the secret. Any honest record of proceedings must state that the men themselves gave away the plans. It matters little whether they walked up to the commanding Colonel of the United States Army or not. They talked, probably in their cups. A little mulatto girl-wife of one of the conspirators listened, it is said, and became the heroine of the day. True to woman's hatred of underhanded methods and any plan which means death, it is probable that she pulled her black shawl about her and dared to go to the famous gambling woman of the day, Madam Tules, because she knew the Americans well, or she may have gone directly to headquarters to tell what she knew. This checked the first plan for revolt. Later new ones developed. Again the Governor was the target.

Governor Bent, undoubtedly, was aware of the state of affairs. Held in high respect and esteem by most people, was this citizen of Taos of whom tradition states that he had often acted as a physician to his townfolk. Certain it is that he had endeared himself to Mexican and Indian alike and had often befriended both. He was absolutely fearless and, probably thinking he might quell some of the dissatisfaction at home, he came to Taos on a visit, where he was warned, for men could no longer hold the awful secret; but he would accept no guard.

In the early gray of the morning of January 19, 1847, a thrifty merchant's wife was busy sweeping out their store. Her husband Peter Joseph was away in Santa Fe. She heard strange cries and the sound of horses and went quickly to the door. Rushing by went a group of people whom she recognized as Indians and people from Ranchos. She probably saw the Taos, Tomasito and the unprincipled fellow Montoya.

Intuitively she sensed danger and, catching up her shawl, she hurried next door. There she found Señor Valdez already up and carefully cleaning his gun. Knowing that Mrs. Joseph was an American from New Orleans, he urged her to go at once to the priest's home a short way down the road. Soon there were other Americans hurrying along the same street. They, too, went through a door opened by Padre Martinez, still in his night clothes. The door closed but it was not long before it opened again. A fellow came out, mounted a swift horse and started southward from the house, carrying the news that mischief was afoot in Taos.

There is a story that a few men were made prisoners the night before and that the mob which gathered the next morning meant to force the alcalde to release the men. This, however, was a mere pretext, if, indeed, it were true. The day fixed for an uprising may not have been the nineteenth but the plans for the revolution were matured. Whisky did the rest.

The mob roar grew. Men with guns flashing were everywhere. Crowds gathered on the roofs and saw well-known Americans fall in the streets. Then the maddened men swept into the placita of the Bent home. They broke down the door and filed through the rooms. Neighbors held their breath in terror. Soon back came the surging crowd and with them they brought the bleeding scalp of Charles Bent.

Teresina Bent, then only five, always keen of mind and memory, remembered that day all her long life. Doubt-

less she heard her elders tell the story too. Her version of
the affair is far and away the most reliable account. Here
is her story as she told it many years after to that other
beloved Governor, L. Bradford Prince:

" I was only five years old at the time but I well remember every circumstance as if it were but yesterday.
It was early in the morning and we were all in bed. We
were awakened by the noise of many people crowding
into the placita. My father was home from Santa Fe on
a short visit and had refused a military escort. The night
before he was warned of danger and urged to fly, but,
though there were several horses in the corrals, he declined. He had always treated everybody fairly and hon-
estly and he felt that all were his friends, and he would
not believe that they would turn against him. Hearing
the noise he went to the door and tried to pacify the
crowd yelling outside. In the adjoining room, my mother,
Mrs. Carson and Mrs. Boggs who were with us, and we
children were trembling with fear, all except my brother
Alfredo. He was only ten years old, but had been reared
on the frontier. He took down the shotgun and, going to
my father's side, said, ' Papa, let us fight them.'

" While my father was parleying with the mob, Mrs.
Carson and Mrs. Boggs aided by an Indian woman, who
was a slave, dug a hole through the adobe wall which
separated our house from the next. They did it with
only a poker and an iron spoon; I have still the poker
that they used. We children were first pushed through
the hole and then the women crawled through after us.
My mother kept calling to my father to come also, but
for a while he would not. When he did try to escape, he
was already wounded and had been scalped alive. He
crawled through the hole, holding his hand on the top

of his bleeding head. But it was too late. Some of the men came after him through the hole and others came over the roof of the house and down into the yard. They broke down the doors and rushed upon my father. He was shot many times and fell dead at our feet. The pleading and tears of my mother and the sobbing of us children had no power to soften the hearts of the enraged Indians and Mexicans.

" At first they were going to take the rest of us away as prisoners, but finally decided to leave us where we were. They ordered that no one should feed us, and then left us alone with our great sorrow. We were without food and had no covering but our night-clothing, all that day and the next. The body of our father remained on the floor in a pool of blood. We were naturally frightened as we did not know how soon the miscreants might return to do us violence.

" At about three o'clock the next morning some of our Mexican friends stole up to the house and gave us food and clothing. That day, also, they took my father to bury him. A few days later we were allowed to go to their house. Mrs. Carson and Mrs. Boggs were sheltered by a friendly old Mexican, who took them to his home, disguising them as squaws and set them to grinding corn on metates in his kitchen."

Had Carson and Boggs been in Taos in all probability the terrible affair would not have happened because both Mexican and Indian stood in awe of them. Alas, Carson was in California and Boggs was far out on the plains with United States mail.

Meantime all was deep sorrow or wild frenzy. The mob swept across the desert to Arroyo Hondo and approached Turley's mill and distillery. Turley, like the

ill-fated Governor, banked on his friends and did not believe there was any real danger until the mob appeared.
Then he told the angry men that he would never surrender himself or his comrades.

A desperate fight began. Eight fell. Turley escaped to
the mountains on the night of the second day of fighting,
but he met a veritable Judas and was betrayed and killed
without a chance for his life. His mill was completely
sacked and gutted and the crumbling walls still stand in
the Hondo Valley, a silent reminder of the awful struggle.

Ruins of Turley's Mill in the Hondo Cañon
Destroyed in 1847

XIV · THE TRIAL

NEWS OF DISASTER TRAVELS WITH INCREDIBLE SPEED. Soon far to the northeast as well as to the south the sad tale was told. To the east, a lone Indian fired in the air as a sign of surrender and then approached a party of Americans, including Lewis Garrard. In broken sentences he blurted out the story of the battle in Taos and the murder of Governor Bent. Then he hurried along to Fort Bent.

A mountaineer by the name of Louy came into the same camp and eager questions brought forth this version of the affair: " *Well,* you see the Purblos was mity mad fur the 'Mericans to come to thar diggins an' take everything so easy like; an' as Injun blood is bad and sneakin', they swore to count coups when they could. So when Charles was down to Touse to see his woman, the palous charged afore sunrise. The portal was too strong fur 'em an' they broke in with axes an' a Purblo cached behint a pile of dobes, shot him with a Nor'west fusee twice and skulped him."

The men were on their feet at once and ready to start out to make " a heap of wolf meat." At Bent's Fort the Indians were soon offering to march in a body to Taos and scalp every Mexican within reach, but William Bent sadly declined to allow them to take vengeance into their hands, telling them the soldiers would go if it was necessary.

Soldiers did come but from the south. Colonel Sterling Price with his men hurried north to the stricken town. By January 27th, he was marching up the Rio Grande and, on the 28th, he was joined by the doomed Captain Burgwin, one of the best loved soldiers who ever entered Taos Valley. As the men proceeded on their way news came that the mob were now in a cañon which rises to the height of about a thousand feet on both sides and so afforded a splendid opportunity for the enemy to wipe out the entire command, which numbered only 479 men.

Captain Burgwin, Captain St. Vrain and Lieutenant White were sent on into the very heart of this Embudo Cañon and, charging up the rocky slopes, put the mob to rout. Proceeding to Las Trampas in the mountains, they joined the main body of soldiers who were plodding on through two feet of recently fallen snow.

On their arrival in Taos, they learned that the enemy were strongly entrenched at the pueblo. About seven hundred had fortified the place, many of whom were in the old adobe Mission church and on the roof as well. Here centered the first day's fighting which brought no definite results. On the second day, finding they could make no impression on the walls of the church, the Americans dug a hole through the west wall and then used their guns to advantage. Within as well as on the roof, Big Nigger, a Delaware Indian from the Missouri frontier, did his best to keep up the fight. But it was of no avail. Finally, the large front door was pushed in and then, as an old Indian José Inez Romero said, as he pawed the air with his hands: " Indian, he like prairie dog." In their fright, they tried to dig themselves in.

Aghast at the turn of the tide and their loss of 175 men, the Indians and their Mexican allies begged for peace. This was granted.

Meantime up in the mountains, probably on Palo Fle-chado Hill, instead of being as far away as they thought,

The Mission at Taos Pueblo
Destroyed in 1847

Garrard's party caught the sound of what seemed like distant thunder, yet, as it was not the right time of year for such, they concluded they were really hearing guns and that a battle was on far below them.

" The wind rose at dark," wrote Garrard, " driving most of us down by the water's edge where, sheltered . by the high banks, we talked and smoked. The Canadians were above us, chattering in their usual glib style when a sound like distant thunder filled the air. Down they rushed, all talking at once. We knew it could not be thunder at this time of year and the conclusion at which we soon arrived was that a battle was taking place in Taos. — Fitzgerald and Bill Garmon came from Taos with the report of the excitement occasioned by numerous arrests. Fitz was a private of Captain Burgwin's company of dragoons at the battle of the Pueblo de Taos. When the breach was made in the church, whither the enemy had retreated as a last resort the dragoons attacked with bombs, holding the shells in their hands until the fuses were nearly burned and then tossing them in to do their work of devastation. The first two Americans who entered the church fell dead; the third was unhurt; the fourth killed and Fitz was the fifth. He was a man of good feeling but, his brother, having been murdered by Salazar, while a prisoner in the Texan expedition against Santa Fe, he swore vengeance and entered the service with the hope of accomplishing it. In the fight, at the pueblo, three Mexicans fell by his hands and the day following he walked up to the Alcalde and deliberately shot him down. For this cold-blooded act he was confined to await a trial for murder.

" One raw night, complaining of cold to his guard, wood was brought in which he piled up in the middle of the room. Then breaking through the roof he noiselessly crept to the eave. Below a sentinel wrapped in a heavy coat, paced to and fro, to prevent his escape; but, when the guard's back was turned, he swung himself from the wall and with as much ease as possible, walked to a mess fire, where his friends who were in waiting, supplied him with a pistol and clothing. When the day broke, the town of Fernandez lay far beneath him in the valley, and, two days after, he was safe in our camp."

Evidently leaving Fitzgerald and his companion to make their way east, Garrard and his companions came down into the valley, skirting the Rio de Don Fernando and hurrying on to reach Taos.

The time for the trial was at hand when Garrard and his party came into town. Montoya had already paid the price. Tomasito, the Indian, was shot before he had an opportunity to have a trial. The remaining group, accused of having a part in the murder of Americans, were a wretched, ignorant lot, the dupes of Montoya.

The trial was a travesty on justice. Even the judge on the bench had lost his son in the revolution and had no right to act, but the trial proceeded and sixteen were doomed to hang. The jury were blinded with blood in their eyes. One of the twelve was John L. Hatcher, Garrard's companion, who expressed himself emphatically, "This hoss has a feelin' hyar," he broke forth one day, "for poor human natur in most any fix but for these palous he doesn't care a cuss. This coon has made Injuns 'go under,' some wagh! but he's never sculped 'em alive; this child's no niggur an' he says its onhuman, again natur, an' they ought to choke."

The people were apparently of the same opinion, especially the Americans, though a pall hung over the town unused to such a grim proceeding as hanging men.

The sheriff Metcalfe was a son-in-law of Estis, the tavern keeper, where Americans bolstered themselves against the event of the day with much whisky. When he announced that he did not have the necessary rope, he was immediately proffered rawhide lariats and hempen picket cords. Then he went to a near-by store and ran a bill which read " To soft soap for greasing nooses. . . . . $12\frac{1}{2}$." With several Americans to lend him moral support, Metcalfe went to the jail. Of the crowd there, Garrard said: " A more disgusting collection of ragged, lousy, greasy, unwashed *pelados* were, probably, never before congregated within so small a space as the jail of Taos." Outside a brass howitzer stood ready within four feet of the entrance.

Finally the poor fellows were marched out to a field north of town. The howitzer on the jail roof was planted so as to command the whole place and the soldiers and mountain men, including Garrard, stood with guns ready in case an attempt at rescue was made. A government wagon with two mules stood under the gallows. Before the wagon slowly pulled away to leave bodies swaying in the air, an opportunity was given for each to say a few words. Only one said he had committed murder and deserved his fate.

" The one sentenced for treason," said Garrard, " showed a spirit of martyrdom worthy of the cause for which he died — the liberty of his country; and, instead of the cringing, contemptible recantation of the others, his speech was firm asseverations of his own innocence, the unjustness of his trial and the arbitrary conduct of his murderers. With a scowl, as the cap was pulled over

his face, the last words he uttered between his gritting
teeth were, ' Caraho, Los Americanos! ' The atrocity of
the act of hanging that man for treason is most damnable;
with the execution of those for murder no fault should
be found."

The whole affair was well-nigh too much for the men
in the town and probably more whisky was drunk that
afternoon than ever, before or since, has been consumed
in an equal length of time in Taos. Garrard was to hear
one last echo of this day when he was leaving for the
East. As a caravan bound for Santa Fe passed, an uncouth
fellow, a lieutenant in the Missouri volunteers, who had
assisted the sheriff, Metcalfe, called out, " How are ye —
would ye like to hang any more Mexicans? Now wasn't
that a tall time down to Touse! "

XV · LEWIS H. GARRARD'S VISIT

THE NAME GARRARD IS NOW FAMILIAR TO READERS OF this story of Taos and an account of his visit to the Southwest is chronologically in order. Among those who set out with the caravan bound from Missouri to Taos under the leadership of Ceran St. Vrain in the fall of 1846 was this young man of eighteen, Lewis H. Garrard who had but recently left his home in Cincinnati, Ohio, in search of health. He carried with him a note-book and pencil which he used constantly during his trip and the result was, three years later, the publication of his delightfully boyish book, entitled " Wah-to-yah " and " The Taos Trail." This has proved, through the years, to be the most interesting as well as the most reliable account of travel of that heyday of the covered wagons. The trail had become fairly safe, but there was always the possibility of an Indian attack and other adventures which lent spice enough to satisfy any traveler who courted danger.

The talented Garrard will forever be remembered in Taos as the boy traveler for he never has grown up in the minds of the people of the town. Naturally he did mature into manhood, however, and studied medicine but was kept from practice by ill-health. When the Civil War came, he was the one, of four sons in the family, who was forced to remain at home for the same reason. He married and had two daughters and lived until 1887. Unfortunately, he never wrote another book except to edit some of his grandmother's letters, but as Dr. Garrard he retained the same delightful personality of the forties which won for him the love of Taos people.

On the afternoon of the 12th of September, 1846, Garrard joined the caravan of great Pennsylvania wagons which were soon rocking from side to side in the deep ruts of the trail. Mexicans were swinging their heavy whips over sluggish oxen. Leaders were riding up and down the line to see that all was well with the wagons while Garrard was talking and chirruping to his horse, glad to be bound out on such an adventure as a trip across the plains.

His horse Paint was given to "malicious dodging" and, one morning, the boy was unable to catch him, so he threw his saddle on a wagon and walked along listening to the stories and songs of the Canadian teamsters who loved to carol in honor of some Creole beauty or of their La Belle France.

When meal time came there was great rejoicing for often this did not come but once a day. No wonder one of the men said, "Darn this way of living, anyhow; a feller starves a whole day like a mean coyote and when he does eat, he stuffs himself like a snake that's swallowed a frog and is no account for an hour after." Appetites appeased, there was joking and many shouts of laughter when, having narrowed his eyes for possible lurking Indians, some one told of a woman in the settlements who asked a mountaineer just in from the west, "Are the *hostile* Indians as savage as those who serve on foot?"

Garrard wrote at length of the roasting on sharpened sticks of fat and lean buffalo meat, of the fellow who called out, "Hyar's the doin's, and hyar's the coon as *savys* 'poor bull' from fat cow; freeze to it, boys!" At his own mess fire, a whole side of ribs had been roasted and he ate with great satisfaction, declaring: "Talk of an emperor's table — why, they could imagine nothing half so good! The meal ended, the pipe lent its aid to complete our happiness; and, at night, we retired to the comfortable blankets, wanting nothing, caring for nothing. One remarkable peculiarity is there about buffalo meat — one can eat even beyond plentitude, without experiencing any ill effects."

When all had gone to bed, many a night, Garrard would sit by the fire alone. " It was my favorite pastime to take a blanket, and lie on the ground with it wrapped around me, with back to the wind, apart from the noisy camp, to read or scrawl a few words in a blank book, of the events of the day, or think of friends far away; " wrote the boy, " or perchance, nodding, and, in a dreamy state, with the warm sun beaming on me, build castles in the air. . . . On every opportunity, I endeavored to resume the thread of the last reverie, and dream away, sometimes in a conflict with Indians, or rescuing a fair maiden from the hands of ruthless savages; or, again, chasing buffalo, and feasting on the fat of the land. Any one, in the Far West, is romantically inclined."

Finally the wagon train pulled into Indian country and Garrard eyed with interest the redskins and envied them their carefree life, speaking of it as undoubtedly " the acme of happiness." A band of Indians wanted to trade so this was begun with much ceremony. " Shaking hands," he writes, " we sat in a row with several of the principal warriors. The pipe of red marble, four inches in length, was passed around, containing a mixture of tobacco and the bark of the red willow or swamp dogwood. First the chief took the pipe, and after presenting its mouth to the sky, and to the ground, he drew four whiffs — blowing one towards the heavens, one to the earth, one to the east and the other to the west. Each In-

dian did the same. Some must have the pipe presented
to them stem downward; others with the bowl resting on
the ground; and others, again, with the stem upward.
All have their peculiar *medicine* or religion, and they are
as punctilious, in this matter, as ever a Hidalgo in politeness." After the ceremony, the trading began and soon
the Indians rode away.

Garrard finally reached Bent's Fort where he had his
first meal at a table, in fifty days, and was assigned a place
to sleep indoors though it gave him a sensation of op-
pression to be shut within four walls, but as he said: " We
didn't have to guard against Indians." The next morning,
the boy climbed to the roof and had a fine view of the
Spanish Peaks which seemed only a few miles away but
were, in reality, one hundred and twenty.

When his pencil was busy, he described the fort much
as had other travelers except that he mentions a billiard
table, " in a small house on top of the fort, where the
bourgeoise and visitors amused themselves "; and he also
jotted down the fact that " in the center of the court is
the ' robe press '; and lying on the ground was a small
brass cannon, burst in saluting General Kearney." Little
did he dream then, what following after Kearny was to
mean to him for the General had but recently gone on to
take New Mexico.

Apparently Garrard allowed the wagon train to go
without him. Instead he traveled with a party of mountain men, having many experiences, and learning on the
way of the tragic happenings at Taos. His most important
companion was John L. Hatcher, the mountaineer, whose
opinion of the settlements was along this order: " Darn
the white diggin's, while thar's buffler in the mountains."
Nevertheless, one morning he shouted, " Whoopee!

Lewis H. Garrard

From a daguerreotype of about 1846. Courtesy of his son-in-law, T. B. Wilson

Are you for Touse? This hos is thar in one sun, wagh! Louy, the cavyard's out picking grass — half froze to travel."

Agreeable to the idea of reaching Taos, Garrard rode along with the party on a mule and finally emerging from the Cañon saw the town for the first time, " its walls, as well as those of the minor towns, mica lime — washed to a dazzling whiteness." When in the plaza, Hatcher and he were greeted by Fisher, another mountain man, with, " How are ye? I swar you look tired; come in and take a ' horn ' — a little of the arwerdenty — come — good for your stomach."

Later the genial St. Vrain invited the boy to be his guest and he was glad of that. Of his first night there he wrote, " At supper, I sat at table and ate potatoes, for the first time in several months. A fandango was to be held that night but, declining an invitation to attend, a mattress was unrolled from the wall, where, in daytime, it served for a seat and I turned in between sheets. Yes! sheets! For months I had enveloped myself with blankets, in the open air, pulling off no clothing but the blue blanket top-coat, which, with my saddle served as pillow — but now a change came over the spirit of my dream. A house, table, vegetables and sheets — to say nothing of the charming smiles of woman and the Taos aguardiente."

Lingering for some time in the old town, Garrard strolled about, noting this and that pretty señorita as well a youth of eighteen might. He laughed at the burros lazily wandering up and down the streets hunting for food and then walked out to the Indian village which he described thus: " Two irregular, immense piles of adobe — towers and loopholes everywhere visible — and a broken, blackened ruin, composed the celebrated

Pueblo de Taos — the stronghold of bravery, and the terror of the Vale of Taos."

Of the homes in the town itself, he said: " Many houses have windows or mere holes in the wall; and, in lieu of glass, large plates of mica are used, which serve the purpose well. The court, in front of each house, brings everything within a small compass, besides excluding thieves, except in case of a regularly burglarious attempt. From the outside nothing but bare, high walls are visible, thus allowing no scope for architectural display, and giving an antiquated, foreign air to the town, in the eyes of all from the States."

Garrard, as we know, was present at the famous trial in that spring of 1847 and his is the only account written by one who was actually in the court-room. For many years, the townsfolk remembered his visit with pleasure and we, of to-day, note with pride that when the young man finally turned his mule's head toward the eastern mountains that he did so " with some reluctance."

XVI · PADRE MARTINEZ

THE HORROR OF THAT YEAR OF 1847 DID NOT AT ONCE hide its ugly face. It seemed to peer about at unwonted times and hold in check efforts at stabilizing peace and so several years passed before matters were arranged for a general assembly or legislature in Santa Fe. There, in 1851, the highest honor fell again to Taos. Reverend Antonio José Martinez was elected the first president of the council which, at its second session, announced the formation or division of the new territory into counties one of them being called Taos.

This remarkable man, Padre Martinez, deserves special comment. He was for many years the most powerful man in the community, but no complete story of his life has yet been written. The Mexican churchman has never been willing to tell the whole truth, and no Anglo-Saxon has been quite fair.

Born in Abiqui of the well-to-do Martinez family whose name runs back several generations to a General Martinez of Spain, the young boy lived, as is usual in such an isolated community, doing his share at herding sheep. Though he had little opportunity for education he, nevertheless, learned to love books. At nineteen he married the sweetheart of his boyhood days. She lived but a year and left behind her a little daughter who, in turn, followed her mother, when she was but twelve. Broken-hearted the young man turned to the priesthood. He left for Durango in Old Mexico where he completed his studies with credit. Then he returned to New Mexico and, in 1826, became the priest in Taos.

His forceful personality brought him to the notice of
the authorities in Old Mexico. Having been made a member of the Chamber of Deputies, he rode, at least once
and possibly twice, on horseback over the many weary
miles to the City of Mexico. He managed to study law
and came to have a wider view than most men of affairs
of his day. He even dared denounce his own church for
its abuse of power and published articles to support his
opinions.

The profound ignorance in his community, he fought
by establishing a school, printing books and editing a
newspaper which appeared for four weeks only and was
printed on foolscap.

The fact that Martinez published the first newspaper
in New Mexico is too well established in Taos to permit
any statement to the contrary. For several years, *The Taos
Valley News* carried " El Crepúsculo " as a sub-title,
when there were many living who could have corrected
this, had it not been fairly used.

Loyal to the government in power, even sitting in
council with José Gonzales, in 1837, Padre Martinez decided in 1847 to side with the United States, believing a
better day had come for his people. Realizing that he
must explain to his pupils about the change which had
come he said, one day, in part: " Boys, you came to this
college with the purpose of studying to be ordained
priests; and in this connection I have labored as much
as possible so that you may attain your goal. But, having
changed governments, it is also necessary to change ideas.
The character of the American government goes in complete harmony with the tolerance of freedom of worship
and an entire separation of church and state. Hence, you

can logically infer that the clergy has lost its predominance."

A pupil asked him what kind of a government they were under.

"Republican," replied the priest. "You may compare the American government to a donkey [docile] and on this donkey ride the lawyers and not the clergy." This reference to a donkey has been considered a term of reproach to the government of the United States. Had this been so intended it is hardly probable that his relative biographer, Don Pedro Sanchez, would have recorded it.

From those years even until our day, the Padre has been the subject of much discussion. His motives were impugned. On the one hand, he was vigorously supported and, on the other, as severely condemned. There seems never to have been a middle ground. The particular question eternally in the air was the attitude of the priest toward the revolution. Was he the power behind the revolution as it showed itself in Taos or not?

During the days of the trial in 1847, rumors were set afloat by American men, no doubt, that Padre Martinez himself had been saved from hearing the dread sentence of death, only by paying a large sum of money. A heavy chest was seen carried out of the home of the priest. There was and still is no other proof. If such had been the case, the Americans seem never to have thought that they were accusing their own military court officials of taking a bribe.

As little as possible seems to have been made of the messenger also seen to mount his horse at the padre's door on that cold January morning and speed southward to give news of the uprising. That Americans found

refuge at that same door must be admitted and there is
no gainsaying the fact that it was straight to the padre's
home that Colonel Price went to hold the first court-
martial, which condemned to death Montoya, the leader
of the revolution in Taos.

The family of the German trader Guttman have pre-
served a tradition, given without proof, however, that
Padre Martinez bought balls and powder for the Mexicans to fight the Americans. Opposed to such a statement
is that of an old man, José de la Cruz Santistevan, whose
word was above reproach. He told his family that he,
with Padre Martinez and others, escaped in the night and
hid in a cellar at Ranchito to get away from the revolutionists " because they were not of the party." Others in
the community have repeatedly said that the Padre tried
to keep the people from revolt.

On the other hand again, Señorita Rafaelita Valdez
often affirmed that the servants in Taos families said that
it was their people with whom Padre Martinez worked to
bring about the revolution. Perhaps the most puzzling
of her stories is the one she related about a group of people being in the large main room of Padre Martinez's well-
kept home when Pablo Montoya, then facing death, was
present. The priest took the occasion to berate Montoya
in the most scathing terms for having had any part in the
revolution while Montoya stood with his foot upon a
chair, holding a handkerchief over his mouth all the
time, as he listened to the priest. He gave no word in
reply. Was this chance or was Montoya unable to listen
without smiling? At least, we know that Montoya held his
peace and did not accuse the priest of having any connection with the revolution.

Forty years after the death of Martinez, George Anderson came to Taos and built up several paragraphs condemning the priest, using such phrases as "generally regarded," "probable complicity" and "circumstantial evidence." Investigation into the sources or probable sources of the information upon which Anderson based his opinion leads one to believe that, in every case, he sought out those known to be thoroughly prejudiced. True, W. H. H. Davis, in his "El Gringo" of the fifties, mentioned the priest as of the party favoring the revolt but he, like Anderson, gives *no proof*. Mere rumors do not make facts.

It is probable that deep in his heart, Padre Martinez hated the headstrong Americans and was, in turn, cordially hated for his power, because he was the real leader of the town. If he had not resented the high-handed action of the Americans in taking over the land he would hardly have been man. Once convinced that the Americans had come to stay he as much as said, "You win. Now, let's go!" To call him a "turn coat" was hardly fair or just.

It is again probable that Martinez was cognizant of the fact that discontent and ideas of revolt were in the air, but it does not seem credible that he believed the result would be murder. That he deliberately advised the killing or driving out of the Americans is hardly possible when one considers the nature of the life he had lived previous to that time or afterwards. He was always a wise friend of the people of Taos. His acts of kindness were many. His one great weakness was his inability to keep his vow of celibacy, which he declared was imposed by man, not God.

The character of thought in the late forties may show itself in the fact that, as far as my own research has carried

me, there is only one printed statement to the effect that
Dr. David Waldo, the first physician to come to Taos,
became a Mexican citizen, duly sworn. During the war
of 1845, he joined the American troops, thereby de-
serving the name of " traitor " to his adopted country.
The light side-stepping of this fact and the severe condemning of Padre Martinez by the Americans give a hint
of how the wind blew. Charles Bent had little use for the
priest and often referred to him in his letters as " The
Calf," and Martinez retaliated by threatening to expose
the smuggling fostered by the firm of Bent and St. Vrain.
Regulation halos would not have fitted either head.

In 1854, came a stunning blow. Padre Martinez, os-
tensibly for immorality, was solemnly unfrocked! The
story of this links the name of Martinez with that of
Bishop Lamy of Santa Fe. The latter was a man of fine
parts undoubtedly but he does not deserve the enlarged
halo given him through a recent book in which he is referred to as " Bishop Latour." Lamy was a man of power
with the one great fault of love of money as is shown in
his " squeezing money out of the poor people " as a relative of his told the writer.

Bishop Lamy *would* build his cathedral. He must and
would have money. At one time, he demanded of Padre
Martinez that he collect tithes beyond a reasonable
amount from the Taos parish. Martinez refused to
knuckle to the Bishop, and dared to answer in the press
of the day. This was, of course, galling to the superior
officer who proceeded to make an investigation into the
private life of the priest. He found, for a truth, that Padre
Martinez had broken his vow. He had taken a common
law wife, and, the father of several children, was man
enough to acknowledge them.

Back of the whole matter lies another fact. Martinez
and Lamy had been friends when the latter first came
into the country without funds. Martinez had loaned his
friend a thousand dollars. When Lamy did not pay the
note, Martinez took the amount due him out of the
church funds which he had to send to Santa Fe. This
broke the friendship and created ill-feeling.

In a letter written at Don Fernando de Taos, under
date of July 9, 1860, to the Illustrious Sir Bishop Don
Juan Lamy, which is probably typical of earlier letters,
Martinez openly accused the Bishop of disregarding the
laws of 1833 in forcing the people of Las Trampas especially by insinuations etc. to pay " a high arbitrary tax
without written arrangements." He declared that the
preaching of the Bishop had " scandalized " the people
and made bold to add, " It seems worldly goods is the object of said preaching."

Martinez referred to the rather famous circular letter
of Bishop Lamy, written on January 14, 1854, in which
he suspended forever the two Taos priests, for there was
another Padre Lucero, " so they will not administer the
Holy Sacrament nor give Holy burial to those who do not
pay in full the tithes." The law no longer allowed priests
to force payment of tithes!

Before as well as after 1854, priest and bishop, many
times crossed swords with Martinez usually holding the
upper hand. Finally Bishop Lamy could no longer brook
the spirit of this man. He delegated another to carry out
his order. Then, in solemn open meeting, Martinez was
unfrocked. So much beloved was this priest and greater
man, that, still unconquered by Lamy, he built his own
church and a great part of the communicants of his
former parish came to him. According to his son, the late

Vicinte Romero, a Protestant, his father wanted to establish an Episcopal church.

We can not leave the discussion of the life and activities of Padre Martinez without considering a rumor which persists to this day that the priest obtained a grant of land from the Indians and never paid for it. The facts are that a land deal had been brewing for two years before the revolution. The Indians said they needed money. Martinez told them that they were wards of the Mexican government and unless they secured permission to sell they could not do so. A group of Indians even went into Mexico to get the necessary papers and were allowed to sell. The American government was not yet well established and the deal was made. This chanced to come up the same spring as the trial but the date shows it was not a matter of record until April 26, 1847, according to Book A, page 54, in the Surveyor General's office in Santa Fe. The sum of $532.05 was the consideration. The document was signed by five Indians, their cross mark being witnessed by Santiago Martin and F. P. Blair.

The finding of this record should put an end to the ugly talk about Padre Martinez having obtained land from the Indians in a fraudulent manner. The five Indians may have used the money themselves and the pueblo, as a whole, never have known about the transaction.

The perspective of years since the passing of Padre Martinez in 1867 still leaves the question of the real character of the priest an open one. Do the scales tip in favor of the padre? Who can tell for a certainty? To the mind open for truth and humanly tolerant, there comes a vision of a great soul, not entirely white, and a powerful personality. Positive it is that his name will outlive

Photograph by C. E. Lord

The grave of Rev. Antonio José Martinez
Kit Carson Cemetery, Taos

those of his detractors, at least in our valley, and long after the words in marble have been blurred by the elements. On the headstone in the little cemetery in Taos was cut in Spanish — " The legislature of the territory at the time of his death called him the ' honor of his country.' "

If love of bombast be back of these words of a group of men, practically all Catholic, for an unfrocked priest, is it possible that conviction lay behind the words of the historian Ralph E. Twitchell, who in a second volume of his writings gives adverse criticism of the priest without citing his authorities and in a fourth volume says, " Among her (Taos) citizens were to be found some who led the territory in almost all lines of thought and action, notably the Presbyter Antonio José Martinez, who, beyond all doubt, was the ablest and most learned man claiming New Mexico as his birthplace, taking part in or directing the affairs under Spanish, Mexican or American rule up to the time of his death."

XVII · RICHARD H. KERN'S DIARY

MOST INTERESTING OF ALL THE STORIES OF THE FORTIES
is that of the rescue of the first artists who ever came to
Taos. There had been United States Army lieutenants
who had made sketches before, notably Douglass Brewer-
ton who was here in the summer of 1848, but, as far as
now known, the first real artists to come were Edward
and Richard Kern of Philadelphia, Pennsylvania.

Artists were necessary members of every great exploring expedition which ventured into the unknown West.
Maps and sketches had to be drawn, birds and flowers
collected and sometimes commanders of forts commis-
sioned overnight. So it happened that these two young
men were with Colonel John C. Fremont on his ill-starred,
fourth expedition of 1848–9.

Usually Kit Carson was with Fremont, but during
that terrible winter when his company became " skeleton
men leading skeleton horses " his guide was Old Bill Williams. Dick Wootton had been of the party but, on reaching the mountains, he gave the Sangre de Cristo range
one long look and turned his horse back toward Hard
Scrabble, saying: " There is too much snow ahead for
me." He probably knew full well that Fremont's over-
confidence in his own judgment would cause him to
press forward when caution urged retreat.

On went the other men, however, ready to follow their
leader. Straight and soldier-like rode Colonel Fremont.
Ahead of him was Old Bill, a man then past his prime.
McGhee followed the mountaineer and later described
him as " leaning forward upon the pommel, with his rifle

before him, his stirrups ridiculously short and his breeches rubbed up to his knees, leaving the legs bare even in freezing weather. He wore a loose monkey-jacket or buckskin hunting shirt and for his head covering a blanket cap, the two corners drawn up into two wolfish, satyr-like ears, giving him somewhat the appearance of the representations we generally meet with of his Satanic Majesty, at the same time rendering his *tout ensemble* exceedingly ludicrous."

Laugh at your leader and crack goes confidence. Fremont may have smiled as he looked at his strange guide. He, like others in the army, thought little of the mountain men, many of whom were ignorant, coarse fellows. Williams was different, a man of brains and not appreciated by Fremont. So when Old Bill pointed out the safest route, Fremont decided that he would show his guide that he could go anywhere he wished and deliberately gave orders to follow another trail.

" The outlook was gloomy, indeed, but there was no grumbling among the men," said Breckinridge, another member of the party, long afterward.

" In camp there was a disagreement between Colonel Fremont and Williams. Williams was a man who said little but he was a long time with Fremont that night and when he turned in (we bunked together) he said that they disagreed in regard to the route we should follow. He said the snow was deeper and the weather more severe than he had ever known it to be before. He said he had advised a route out of our difficulties, to go south round the San Juan Mountains and then west along what is now the line between Colorado and New Mexico."

Disaster followed and Fremont paid dearly for his stubbornness. After the party had stumbled on for some time, leaving several to die, three " strong men," including Williams, were sent ahead to secure aid at Taos. Meantime Fremont blamed Williams for his own mistake; but no mountain man ever supported his charge.

The men arrived. Their news spread rapidly over the town, and soon many of Carson's " celebrated forty-five " were on the way to Arroyo Hondo and probably beyond to rescue the starving men.

Later in the spring, Benjamin J. Kern, the doctor brother of the artists, and Old Bill returned to the mountains to find valuable papers which the members of the expedition had been forced to leave behind. These included some Fort Sutter documents which Edward Kern had with him for he had been commander at that well-known California fort and probably the papers he carried were of great importance. There was also a collection of birds cached away but they were never found. In fact, Kern and Williams never returned, as has already been said. They were killed and their bodies were not recovered.

The real story of this Fremont expedition is best told in a diary kept by Richard Kern in a little yellow leather covered book which was in his pocket when he, too weak to walk, was put on a horse and brought to Taos across the sagebrush desert from Arroyo Hondo. Written in pencil, growing faint with the years, the diary was not easy to follow but has been copied as accurately as possible and probably tells most by what lies between the lines. Permission to use it for the first time here was generously granted by the owner, the late Henry E. Huntington of San Marino, California.

THE DIARY OF RICHARD H. KERN

ARTIST WITH THE FREMONT EXPEDITION OF
1848–1849

Raised camp No. 1 on Boone Creek near Westport Friday afternoon Oct. 20 1848 about 3 Oclk, and went as far as Mission Creek 6 miles where we made Camp No 2 The afternoon was clear and pleasant; and everything went off well with the exception of some packs on wild mules and they went off too.

Sat. Oct 21. Raised camp No. 2 about 11 oclk A.M. and had a great day of trouble on account of our road at the commencement, passing through a wood with thick underbrush We travelled over prairie and through timber, some of the latter being very pretty and made camp No. 3 on Mill Creek 14 miles from the last early in the afternoon. Dr was swiming, when one of our best men, Moran received a severe kick in the face from a wild mule [1] and Medic had to dress his face as well as himself.

Sunday Oct 22. We raised camp about 10 A.M. and in about an hours time the rain commenced pouring in torrents and so continued for the rest of the day. We reached camping ground early in the afternoon having made 22 miles. We were on the edge of a fine creek well timbered with old trees. Made sketch of camp next morning.

Friday Oct 27, our route lay through a very singular country consisting principally of hills, high and steep. Near the apex of each was a ledge or shelf of soft friable calcareous stone laying horizontally (some 3 or 4 feet long;) and presenting at a distance the appearance of

---

1 " A bad beginning " — note in E. M. Kern's diary

old dilapidated and extensive fortalices, built by a Titon but mouldering away like their builders. The stone is of a light color.

— Sketch —

Abrasion has worn away large pieces which are deposited-on the faces of the hills, rendering the descent very uncomfortable.

We made 2[20?] miles and camped in a grove of mossy cup oaks on — . Had Wild Turkeys.

Sat Oct 28 The Country lost that castellated hilly appearance and became more rolling, flattening out into broad plains We saw for the first time one of the Smoky Hills (from which this branch derives its name) its blue head looming-up blue and far off, the only elevated land for miles.

Near our camp — Buttes in the direction of Council
— Sketch —
Grove Smoky Hill (Butte?) lies far to the right and near the Camp. — The Hill is not represented above We camped on the edge of a prairie near timber and made to-day 27 miles

Sunday Oct 29. Started early cool and cloudy — Smoky Hill about 10 miles off — The country still hilly and much of the character of yesterday I passed near the Butte it appears to be about 400 feet high and covered with grass.

Saw Buffalo for the first time, every one in camp much elated. Crossed the Smoky Hill fork; it is about 60 feet wide & where we forded it 3 feet deep. The whole character of country changed. An immense plain extending for miles & miles level as a board, and covered with grass. Smoky Hill Buttes rose up far off and solitary, the only ones of their kind. Towards evening the country became

Pages of Richard H. Kern's Diary

About one third actual size

more hilly and rugged, very little timber to be seen and that small and scarce.

Capt Cathcart went with Scott & Martin to run Buffalo; which escaped him — leaped down a perpendicular bank 20 feet high into the river and ran away on the plain. The Capt — in attempting to follow them nearly drowned his mule; he lost his revolver and powder flask and broke his ram rod, and came into camp in his stocking feet. He cut a very sorry figure.[2] We made about 30 miles and camped in a thicket in a hollow well protected from the cold wind.

Monday Oct 30th Raised camp early this morning. Soon left the plains and entered a singularly hilly country. It is rugged and the rocks are lying about in masses and separate ones, as though thrown so by some convulsion of Nature. It was generally a series of valleys from 3 to five miles (— illegible?) by these hills. The rocks very singular in shape sometimes appearing like cottages with doors —

— Sketch — Rock Shapes —

then like forts — and men in broad brimmed hats sitting in large chairs

Buffalo Bulls still abundant but no cows yet. After passing these hills we came upon a fine Table land, and encamped on a small creek quarter before 1 having made 20 miles Quite a number of bulls were killed and 2 cows. Ned went with Godey to run buffalo. Cold clear & windy. picked up an astragulus veinunatu [?] the last of the season.

*Tuesday Oct 31 — 1848 — *Jim Secundi and the rest of the Delawares left us this morning. The country is at starting broken into small hills & gullies — Smoky Hill

2 looking like Don Quixote in extreme trouble.

Fork winding far in the distance. We soon came to it and rode in the meadows that formed its bottom.

— Sketch —

Whilst the Indians were our guides we travelled in a bee line, but to day's course was a perfect zigzag, losing several miles by striking the river too soon.

Plenty of Buffalo in Sight in large bands and the country gradually more hilly. Timber abundant along the river which is very narrow, but no where else. Our general course was the same as the river, and we camped at 3 oclk near a high bluff, having made 28 miles. Cold & windy today, with occasional clouds.

It is late, and Godey has just come in with some parts of a fat cow he has killed, and all are stuffing as much as possible.

Saw prickly pear for the first time.

Wednesday Nov 1st — Hills same character as yesterday. Buffalo still plenty saw the largest number to day. The river wound to the left, to course easily distinguished by high bluffs, presenting near their summits in many places bald faces of white clay, while below they were broken into smaller hills. The hills our route passed over were broken into gullies at their bases, — (where) occasional water courses

— Sketch —

The river banks were alternately blue — in bottom Encamped in a grove of small cotton woods near a high clay bluff having made 28 miles. Godey killed an (lean?) cow today, Cool cloudy at starting but clear and warm afterwards.

[3]*Thursday Nov 2nd* 1848 — Our route still on right

[3] Nov. 2 — Went to kill beef Scott wounded an old bull, who stood till Ned drew it — when he and Cathcart shot him in the head. — Diary of B. J. Kern

bank, and over high uneven hills broken into gullies. We crossed the river about 8 miles from camp near a very bald high & perpendicular bluff. Near this place the Pawnees made their Buffalo meat during the summer. There are a great many shanties, built of bent branches and covered with leaves. We found some hoes, & hatchets &c —.

Godey Scott Capt Cathcart Ned Ben Creutzfeldt & self went over to see a wounded bull. We were within 10 feet of him but as he had one of his forelegs broken he could not charge us. Ned made a fine sketch of him before Capt C had killed him. Am with — (?) on the left bank lay over the same kind of hills, as on the right. There are a great many perpendicular clay bluffs shut in at a great distance. No trees visible most of the day until about 1 oclk as we rose over the brow of a hill we saw some about 6 miles off, and we were sure of camp which we made about 3 oclk having travelled 30 miles. The day cold and cloudy prognosticating a Storm.

The night very windy and cold.

Friday Nov 3 — Cold and uncomfortable, and before starting snow commenced falling attend (ed) with severe gusts of wind. We only made 10 miles and camped in a little area nearly surrounded by trees. Carver saw two Indians being the first that have been seen. Toward evening clear and cool, very little wind, and the moon shining beautifully. hilly country again but not so bad as yesterday.

Sat Nov 4. Clear but extremely cold, the thermometer being 16° at sunrise. Got off about 8 1/2 oclk — the wind sharp and strong over the plains. The country gently hilly — very few Buffalo, plenty of prairie wolves, but all at a respectful distance.

As my mule had just been shod, the snow and dirt

balled on her feet rendering my position very unpleasant, as sometimes one leg would be 3 or 4 inches, lower than the others. Her movements were all kind that can be imagined. I had the pleasure of being thrown over her head, and landed in safety on the ground. The thermometer rose to 40°. Missed the trail and with 3 others came into camp late. Camp in a deep hollow near a rapid stream probably a tributary of the Pawnee Fork travelled 25 miles — Stream unknown.

Sunday Nov 5 — followed the general course of the creek we struck yesterday, it being on our right, — country Hilly and table land. Fossils very abundant. Camped in a hollow on the same creek having made 25 miles —

Monday 6 — Snowed whilst raising camp. Our course lie (s) toward the Arkansas — Country destitute of timber, Hilly & table land as yesterday. Camped in a small grove of timber, elm and cotton woods made 25 miles.

Tuesday Nov. 7. Intention to day to strike the Arkansas if possible. The country mostly vast table lands gradually ascending and when you reached the summit of one, the same prospect presented itself. Not a stick of timber in sight, occasional ponds of clear water were found on the tops of these plains. Our prospect for camp was indeed desolate; water there was plenty of and for fuel, we should have had to depend on Buffalo manure. At last some Buttes appeared in sight, as we rose up the brow of a hill and a few miles further brought us in sight of the Arkansas. We camped among some old and scattered cottonwoods having made 40 miles.

Wednesday Nov 8 Our object today was to reach Choteaux Island supposed to be about 25 miles off and camp there to rest the animals as some of them were giving out — We travelled on expecting to see the Island, and as it (was) not a good camping ground presented itself we continued on until 8 in the evening, and then had to ford the river, amid rushing ice and camp among some Cotton Wood trees having been out 11 house and travelled 52 miles — It was a hard day on the animals and two were left behind. Thermometer at starting 19° and cloudy and windy. The banks of the Arkansas are low and sandy and hardly any timber to be seen on this side though we passed occasional groves on the other.

'*Thursday Nov* 9 — Made a late start, morning cold cloudy and windy — The clouds gradually passed off; the day became warmer, and we had a sight of the Rocky Mountains, hardly to be distinguished from the clouds, so far off were they and so indistinct — (Crossed out — evidently were clouds) Came across a large village of Kiawas, with some Camanches. Camped near them and were exceedingly annoyed during the rest of the day and evening. They were a set of wild looking rascals, mostly clothed in Buffalo robes and carrying bows and arrows. The dark sooty color of the robe gave them the appearance of ⁵ sweeps wrapped in their blankets.

Made 18 to 20 miles.

Friday Nov 10 — (The Kiowas and our party raised camp together, Having traded meat &c) & moved on pell mell together. It was a queer compound civilization and barbarism — travelling in company. We made a short camp and stopped near each other —

— Sketch (of tepee) —

They were encamped around us, and Ned and I were as busy as we could be sketching them. There were some

---

⁴ "Nov. 9. Passed St. Vrain & Fitzpatrick's camp of last night " — Edward M. Kern. His diary was blank after this date. Most of his notes were about seeing buffalo and hunting — not as interesting as the other two diaries.

⁵ chimney sweeps

very fine looking men among them and some regular
Scarecrows. At a distance with their robes on they looked
like so many Master Journeymen & apprentice sweeps,

The night was a queer one — Indians singing our men
shouting and singing dogs barking horses neighing and
mules to. The old chief [6] haranguing and telling them to
be honest (necessary advice), and above all the clear
moonlight and camp fires. It could not be imagined. One
of the boys was playing most dolefully on the flute,
" Home." I have *been* a great medicine man; looking
somewhat like Syntax drawing the beasts There were
several Spanish boys and girls among them they had
stolen them from Monterey (?) 3 years ago — day clear &
pleasant.

Thermometer 50

Saturday 11 — Thermometer at breakfast 16′ —
Raised camp before the red devils; overtook Aubrey's
wagons on the road his mules nearly given out. Saw large
groups of heavy timber forded the river and camped
on the opposite side, in a place destitute of timber, and
had to supply ourselves from an adjoining island. Henry
Wise missed camp and slept out near us — made 18
miles —

Sunday 12 Thermometer 22. raised camp at 8 oclk,
and continued along the southern bank of the river —
Soil sandy, and bad travelling for the animals, the (day)
increased in warmth until it became disagreeable. Struck
a road at last and got along better. Animals began to give
out, and we camped after a hard march of about 28
miles — Henry Wise not in camp, camped among large
and small cottonwood rushes and rattlesnakes — Met
several war parties of Arapahoes going out to steal horses

---

[6] Nov. 10 — Chief " Little Mound " — B. J. Kern

from the Pawnees. The Kiowas & Arapahoes were camped near us —

We went on this side of the river, because the sand was deep and travelling bad and there was a good wagon road on the opposite side.

[7]*Monday Nov 13* — Eat breakfast by moonlight. By the time camp was raised cold cloudy and windy — moved 5 or 6 miles and camped by the Arapahoes Hard to trade with — Dr & mules

Been after the Utahs.

Tuesday 14 remained encamped among the Arapahoes until 3 oclk when we raised and moved 5 miles and camped in a fine grove of trees in a bottom affording good grass. Dr traded medicine for 3 mules —

Wednesday 15 — Made 23 miles and camped in a hollow, almost destitute of timber and within 2 miles of Bents Fort. Country sandy and hilly, with plenty of timber; day cloudy cold and windy. —

Thursday 16 — Snowed during last night and part of this morning. All of us used warm water & Soap — quite an epoch — did not move camp — At work on sketches.

Friday 17. Camped in same place — Cold early, but warm and pleasant after a while — At work on sketches and letters. Saw the Mountains, made sketch of same.

Saturday Nov 18 — raised camp about 11 — moved towards Bents Fort, and were detained this side of it until near 1 oclk camped about 4 with plenty of timber having made 15 miles — Morning thermometer 12° — warm and thawing during the day.

7 Nov. 13 — Rappahoes — Syphilitic Ophthalmia very prevalent to day an old fellow came to me for med. & I traded for a mule he returned. trade after an hour — so I mix cow (?) Lab & Hydr Pot — at the fire to the astonishment of the injines one of whom hug'd me to the great danger of my becoming lousy — Major Fitzpatrick is with them making presents &c — B. J. Kern

Sunday Nov 19 — Therm. 11′ at sunrise — moved at 8 oclk followed Indian trail, still on the south side, Cold & cloudy — Mountains in full view Thermom. at sunset 39° —

Made about 20 miles and camped in a fine grove — small cotton wood with plenty of grass —

Monday 20 — Followed trail, which went over bottom and tableland winding up steep sand hills &c Mountains still in full view — Day pleasant — camped in a bottom with plenty of grass and timber — made about 20 miles.

— Sketch — Sand hills —

Tuesday 21 — Started at 8 Oclk — Still follow trail — Country same as yesterday Made about 15 miles and camped near Mormon town, or Peublo [8] on the other side — Plenty of large cotton wood — There is a fort built of Adobes — a miserable looking place — The inside resembling a managerie — a compound of Spaniards horses mules dogs chickens and bad stench.

Wednesday Nov 22 — Left Pablo this morning — Crossed the Arkansas to the right side. — Country broken into Castellated Hills, stones [?] Sand bluffs at the top, with numerous sand hills at the base — Saw cedar

— Sketch —

for the first time — being small growth — but old looking — sand stone yellowish — Hills at the base gray — Camped in fine bottom — made 12 miles — day warm and delicious — like an October day east — rained during the night.

Thursday 23 — recrossed and the road left the river, over sand hills — Country not bluff like yesterday — Fine effects in the mountains — those to the left the snow was falling whilst Pikes Peak, and the Red Hills shone

---

[8] Pueblo de San Carlos qui Bouit on the Fontaine.

out in the beauty of an April day — Occasional clouds
hid the mountains from sight, Camped at Hard Scrabble,
White Oak Creek — a miserable place containing about
a dozen houses corn cribs and corrals. It is the summer
resort of the hunters — the houses are built of Adobes,
and are very comfortable — they seemed like palaces to
us, as we enjoyed the luxuries of table & stools.

Friday 24th — Still at Hard Scrabble — finished sketch
Walk — No trail.

Saturday 25 — Left about 1 1/2 oclk moved about
3 1/2 miles to camp among scrub oak — The evening effect on the mountains the prettiest we have seen copper
color with lake in the lights, and black blue and Ind red
in the shadows —

Sunday 26 [9] — Walk no trails — Entered the mts along
White Oak Creek — road hilly — Snow — Camped in
pine grove — passed fine rocks — copper color green
blues (?) and brownish black — very fine rocks near
camp

— Sketch —

Monday 27. Passed through the canon of the White
Oak Creek — Sandstone — white & salmon color. probably 1200 to 1500 feet Rocks high rugged & bald, plenty
of snow — Camped in a little valley without water —
Walk.

Tuesday 28 — gradually descending — less snow —
passed immense pile of rocks — white & wet. Mts in view

[9] One of the men McGehee wrote of this date —
"On the 26th of November (1848) we entered the Rocky Mountains,
which had been for days looming up before us, presenting to view one continuous sheet of snow. The snow already covered the mountains and was rapidly deepening. I have frequently since called to mind the expression of one of
the men as we rode along before entering Hard Scrabble. As we looked upon
the stormy mountains so portentous of the future, he said, 'Friends, I don't
want my bones to bleach upon those mountains.' Poor fellow, little did he
dream of what the future would be." — *Century*, March 1891

— summits (?) broken into valleys — farther on more. Camp whole range in view — color Blackish brown and white — Camped among cottonwood near a smaller bluff, no water — made [— illegible?] Snow 2 to 3 feet deep, road winding — Walk.

Wednesday 29th Mts still in view — Gap do — road winding and over hills, plenty of Pines — Views back like Bastion. Fell far behind and came about 3 miles behind camp used up. Camp near Canon of Rock Creek — Ned sketched same

Thursday 30. Snow in morning and had to wait for Haylor & Sorel to bring up mules. Riding again. Snowed before starting

Dec. 1st — Small [?] Spanish Peaks in view — Camped Huerfeneau (?) and near Gap, in a valley among Pines — very windy & uncomfortable —

Saturday Dec 2nd 48 — Road through the Canon of Wafeneau — Day windiest we have yet met — Road over immense hills — Snowing in spurts —

— Sketch —

Camped in the snow among willows — Commenced snowing and by morning about 5 inches snow.

Sunday Dec 3d — Snowing when started Road — Robidos (?) — 2nd hill dividing ridge, and saw water of Rio Grande Road steep in many places and bad on account of fallen trees — Saw valley of Rio Grande — very little snow. Road through pines cotton wood & quaking asp — Camped in cedar grove on —— Creek —

Snowed

Monday Dec 4 Snowed all day moved about 4 miles to grove of Cotton wood —

Tuesday Dec 5 — Raised camp moved about a

mile and returned on account of severe wind & snow storm —

Wednesday Dec 6 — Cold & clear — Godey led camp over immense sand hills with from one to 6 feet snow — we all looked like old Time or Winter — icicles an inch long were pendant from our mustache & beard, — camped near a creek in a little valley among cotton wood — Col Pruess, King, Creutzfeldt & Old Bill went to examine the mountains Saw fine gap — During the day at 12 Thermom. below zero — clear moonlight —

— Sketch —

Thursday — Dec 7 — Started to cross the valley — strike the Rio Grande nothing but sand, snow, sage bushes & greasewood — cold, cloudy & snowing — The valley is completely surrounded by immense ranges of rugged Mts — Made 22 miles & camped in the plain, with sage for fuel — & snow for water —

Friday Dec 8 — Still over the same plain — snowed all day — camped on the Rio Grande timber thick — & plenty of snow —

Saturday Dec 9 — Moved in valley of the River on the east bank snow very deep — everything cold & ghostly — and as we moved along we seemed entirely out of place — Struck in the canon of the Nun[?] — Singular formation, Clay with immense stone & rock in it — had to turn back & take over the hills — Day very foggy & indistinct. Crossed the river & camped in the Cotton wood — day very cold — plenty of Elk signs

Sunday Dec 10 Stay until 12 M. & moved about 3 miles further up — Mts rugged and piney — in many places perpendicular walls of rocks — Godey and 5 others went out after Elk — brought 2 in — day rather warmer — had fine camp —

Monday Dec 11*th* Started for long camp struck creek
cold & hilly ride — dry clear — hills very steep, & rugged,
trail winding among small pinions affording shelter from
the wind — Mountains very steep and rough — fine valley — camped among cotton wood

Made about 12 miles —

Tuesday Dec 12 Started through little valley to our
right and soon entered a series of Cañons — It was a
very hard day on men and animals as the road wound
the sides of the Canons in many places almost perpendicular, We camped on the hill side at an immense height.
Had two very fine views down and up the canon.

— Sketch — Moonlight —

Made from 5 to 7 miles.

Dec 13 *Wednesday* Had very difficult time passing the
animals over the hills — after that the road became easier
— pass through large pine forests, the snow being several
feet deep on the trees. Struck two beautiful valleys one
running out of the other and camped on the one to the
left —

about 7 miles

Thursday Dec 14 Trail wound up the side of pine hills
and through snow valleys — passed over an immense
bald hill supposed to be the dividing ridge. Had from
the summit of this hill one of the finest mountain views
in the world. Made sketch — Camped in deep pine forest
on the edge of a little valley —

5 miles.

Friday Dec 15. Very bad hill at start. Afterward road
passed over summits of hills — had the weather been
clear it would have been beautiful Godey's mule Dick
gave out. Camped on the side of a hill — Snowed all day.

3 miles

Saturday Dec 16th [10] Made start to pass what was supposed to be the dividing ridge, passed dead mules and pack and riding saddles lying on the trail — It looked very desolate and cheerless After hard work we reached the summit of the hill but the wind and snow were so dreadful we had to return.

Had the animals gone over the hill or had we remained there half an hour longer the whole party might have been lost — returned to our old camp fires amidst a furious snow & wind storm which continued all day and night.

[11]*Sunday Dec. 17th* A party of the men went ahead to beat a trail, and after hard labor we reached the summit of the same hill and saw the trail winding up the oppositie hill where a little grass was visible, affording some chance of life for the animals. The snow on the hill we were descending was very deep — from 3 to 15 feet; several animals died — We unpacked on a small point and

[10] Saturday Dec. 16 Sun rose with strata of rosy fleecy cumuli which soon increased & hid him Commenced snowing and blowing Men sent ahead to break the road — Started about 10 Oclock & soon reached the ascent clear of all timber compelled to wait in a bitterly cold wind for the van to reach the top packs falling off — passed packs & pack saddles devoid of ñads which had been eaten by the mules last night — when we reached the top it was so cold & windy that none could see ahead & the drifting and falling snow obscured everything in danger of all being frozen we took the back trail & we lucky enough to reach our last camp one mule froze on the way & we passed one near one of the fires in the last gasp Several died throu the night from cold & hunger — blankets ropes & comfortables were eaten by them & my light over coat had one sleeve eaten off they were driven to the Camp of yesterday in hopes of finding a little grass & better shelter than in this bleak place — It was a day that tried the stoutest hearts & the whole party came very near to total destruction Many had their noses &c frozen and some became stupid from the cold — my eyelids stuck together from the cold and for a time I saw nothing but red — the snow continued all day the temperature somewhat milder towards night at least in camp we made ourselves comfortable by our fires & erected a shelter of blankets to save us from the snow & wind — what will a few days bring forth deliverance or destruction — B. J. Kern

[11] Dec. 17 — The trail was beaten thro 9 feet snow over the ridge very cold at night — B. J. Kern

camped in the snow in a small pine wood to the left —
Some of the animals were driven to the grass but the rest
were too feeble and died during the night —

Monday Dec 18 — Camped in same place — poudre
snow all day — mule first time —

Tuesday 19[12] — Still in same camp busy making moccasins —

Wednesday 20th Still in same camp. Men started to
find another camp but the snow drove them back —
Snowed all day and it was the most miserable one we had
yet passed — 59 animals alive

Thursday Dec 21st Still in same camp. Cold & windy
— men driven back again — Clear sunset but very
cold —

Friday Dec 22 Still in same place Men reached with
some baggage the opposite camp about 3 miles dist.

Saturday Dec 23rd Still in same camp — most of the
baggage removed to top of hill —

Sunday Dec 24 — Started for new camp — made it in
6 feet snow in pine woods — pleasanter than our last —
day cold but not unpleasant

Monday Dec 25 Morning[13] occupied in clearing camp
larger and making such preparations as possible for the

---

[12] *Dec* 19–24*th* during these days of horror desolation despair & almost
continued heavy winds intense cold & snowstorms we laid in camp fluctuating
between hope & despair half erected the tent & built a fire in front one after
another became smoke blind & sat under the drippings from the tent & their
backs coverd with the drifty snow — a situation making it a misery to exist —
   In the (morning) six inches had to (be) scraped off the bed with a pot lid
& 8 inches would be found there again in the morning — blankets coats &
ones hair frozen indiscriminately together — blankets packing of saddles manes
& mules tails were eagerly devoured by the starving animals. — B. J. Kern
[13] *Dec.* 25th — in the afternoon paid a visit to our last camp — a desolate
looking place a smouldering fire at scotts mess aided the effect — The remains
of the Cols dead mule butchered for our nourishment would readily have told
the condition of those camping there. A raven floating through the cold air
gave me music of its hoarse notes a perfect addition to camp dismal. — B. J.
Kern

day — Had Elk stew and pies, rice doughnuts, coffee biscuit & hot stuff passed very comfortable day — weather pleasant — Godey chief cook — [14]

Tuesday Dec 26 King, Old Bill, Creutzfeldt and Brackenbridge started for the settlements on the Rio del Norte to bring us relief — Godey went part of the way to explore a route — day pleasant [15]

Wednesday Dec 27th Camp employed in moving our mess to new camp on Creek — day pleasant

Thursday Dec 28th Packed up bedding & started for new camp — trail down hill and very glip [slipy] Camp

[14] Breckinridge's menu written years after read as follows —

CAMP DESOLATION
Dec. 25, 1848
M E N U
MULE

SOUP
MULE TAIL

FISH
BAKED WHITE MULE
BOILED GRAY MULE

MEAT

MULE STEAK	FRIED MULE	MULE CHOPS
BROILED MULE	STEWED MULE	BOILED MULE
SCRAMBLED MULE		SHIRRED MULE
FRENCH FRIED MULE		MINCED MULE

DAMNED MULE
MULE ON TOAST (WITHOUT THE TOAST)
SHORT RIBS OF MULE WITH APPLE SAUCE
(WITHOUT THE APPLE SAUCE)

RELISHES

BLACK MULE	BROWN MULE	YELLOW MULE
BAY MULE		ROAN MULE

TALLOW CANDLES

BEVERAGES

SNOW	SNOW-WATER	WATER

It is very evident that R. H. Kern was using his imagination to help out Christmas dinner of nothing but mule.

[15] *Dec.* 26 King Rusfelt, Breckinridge & old bill Williams started afoot down the River (which is from here about 8 miles) to get help — We all wished them a successful journey & speedy succour — the remaining packs were removed from the hill & brought into camp hope.   B. J. KERN

in beautiful valley about 2 miles dist — day being warm & pleasant

Friday Dec 29 — At yesterdays Camp beautiful warm and sunny with birds singing — Mule soup.

Sat. Dec 30 Same camp — day like yesterday [16]

Sunday Dec. 31 — Packed bedding back to where baggage was left on the hill — hauled our baggage to Col's camp of 29 on a fine plateau with a grove of pines — Creek very wild — Ned minced mule meat for pies — fired out the old year and passed the pleasantest night since our start — day pleasant with occasional summery clouds [17]

Jan 1st 1849 — Snowed when starting packed bedding beyond the next camp to the Cols, 3 miles distant — supped on meat pies — soup and coffee — Snowed during the night — passed immense piles of copper colored rocks — [18]

[16] *Dec. 30th* Started about 8 O clock to take a pack on the new trail got 1/4 mile from next camp & gave out left the load & crawled on my hands & knees back again very much exhausted got back at " Oclock had a good supper off my indian mule & coffee very tender and sweet expect to move bedding to-morrow & leave Camp disappointment behind us —   B. J. KERN

[17] *Sunday 31st Dec 1848* — a good supper out of mule & coffee our mess of Dick Ned Cathcart & the 2 indian boys made ourselves merry & sung several songs in our crude way — after supper Dick read Tom Hood & Ned minced boiled mule meat for pies to-morrows new years treat.   B. J. KERN

[18] It was California the land of plenty toward which these men were struggling. Some were destined to read such a menu after a few more months.

IN THE DAYS OF '49
An Old Bill of Fare Gives the Prices of Food in California During the Gold Excitement.
(*From the Nevada State Journal*)
MENU
SOUP

BEAN, 1.00	OX TAIL (short) , .50

ENTREES

SAUERKRAUT, 1.00	BACON FRIED, 1.00	BACON STUFFED, 1.50
HASH, Low-grade, .75	HASH, 18-karat, 1.00	

ROAST

BEEF, Mexican Prime Cut, 1.50	BEEF, Up-Long, 1.75	BEEF, Plain, 1.00
BEEF, with one potato (fair size) , 1.25	BEEF, Tame (from the states) , 1.50	

Photograph by Olive Baxter

Covered Wagons of 1925

Tuesday Jan 2 — Snowed all day until Sunset — Col moved to the river 7 miles distant — Ned Doc. Capt & the boys went to bring the baggage on — I staying in camp to fix and attend to matters erected the [shelter?] & slept alone — a perfect hermit but not Jerrolds Hermit of Bellyfull — cold night but clear

Wednesday Jan 3 [19] — Godey returned from the river & Cap & Gregorio from above — day pleasant with signs of snow —

Thursday Jan 4th [20] Doc & Ned returned with some of our things — burnt some — day cloudy & disagreeable — snowed during the night. —

Friday Jan 5 Snowed in the morning — cleared up during the afternoon pleasant but rather windy — night fine moonlight & clear.

Sat. Jan 6th [21] in same camp

GAME

CODFISH BALLS, double, .75	GRIZZLY ROAST, 1.00
GRIZZLY, Fried, .75	JACKASS RABBIT (whole), 1.00

VEGETABLES

BAKED BEANS, Plain, .75	BAKED BEANS, Greased, 1.00
TWO POTATOES (Medium Size), .50	TWO POTATOES (Peeled), .75

PASTRY

RICE PUDDING, Plain, .75	RICE PUDDING AND BRANDY PEACHES, 2.00
RICE PUDDING, with Molasses, 1.00	SQUARE MEAL WITH DESSERT, 3.00
Payable in advance	Gold scales at end of Bar

19 Wed Jan 3rd — cheered Ned up (Ned gave out during the day) & went to bed fine bright moonlight night & cold a good bed saw several mice looked at them with a hungry eye long for a mouse trap. — B. J. K.

20 Jan 4the Ned & I returned with a pack to our camp of Jan. 1st found Dick & Cathcart sitting by a digger fire they had erected a mean kind of a shanty over their beds — saw symptoms of approaching snow storm — supper of a little fat pork & macaroni. — B. J. K.

21 Jan 6th (last entry) — snowed & blowed till one Oclock employed all day in sewing Men passed on with loads & camped one mile below us — Col campd on the river, Jan 2 saw several snow birds, Ned shot at one in hopes of having something to eat — Hibbard came along about 3 oclock with some goats meat which he killed yesterday a very welcome addition to our provision No news from below Dick blowed his flute a little to cheer us up. — B. J. Kern.

Sunday Jan 7 Same camp

Monday Jan 8th Same camp

Tuesday Jan 9th Mr. Haylor went to the Col's camp on the river — on his way met Proulx, his legs frozen — helped him as much as possible — wrapped his blankets around him — On his return same night found him dead —

Wednesday Jan 10th Men occupied in bringing baggage from camp above and from our camp to Haylor's below —

Thursday Jan 11th Moved towards the Cols camp — We left early in the morning to meet and hurry the mules — day pleasant Cathcart & self met Andrews and Mc-Gehee, and camped with them under the shelving rock below the cave — Rolled down plenty of pinnes and passed a comfortable night — Boiled up some parflesh & raw hide tug rope for breakfast — night windy and snowing Godey [?] Preus Theodore & Saunders went with the Col — Ned and Doc camped further down with Shipperfeldt & Carver by a small grove of willows

Friday Jan 12th — Snowed all day — started and fell in the creek — returned to camp where we remained all day Cathcart luckily shot a small bird —

Saturday Jan 13th Clear — started for the river — had to break the trail until we met a party from the river Arrived at the river camp at 2 1/2 Oclk — Snowed during the night

Sunday Jan 14th — Cold windy and snowing — none of the party returned from above Cleared up at night

Monday Jan 15 — party returned from above

Tuesday Jan 16 started camp down river, moved about 2 miles & camped — near old Elk camp — Manuel turned back —

Wednesday Jan 17*th* — Moved down on the ice — stopped while Scott hunted — no luck — encamped a mile or 2 below the big rock — Wise remained behind — Move 6 miles

Thursday Jan 18*th* Moved about a mile and a half to let the hunters have a chance for the game — Carver remained

Friday Jan 19 made long [?] camp to near where we first struck the river — A deer was killed and 10 men received for their share 2 fore shoulders blades. It was the intention of Mr L D Vinsonhaler, who was left in command of Camp by Col Fremont to have said nothing about the deer but to have taken it and the strong men & pushed on to Albiquiu, and left the rest of us to perish — Our share of the meat was so unjustly small that it did us no good — Things indicated that the man left in charge was totally unfit, on account of want of tact and experience and correct principles. Besides his conversation did as much to discourage the men as our situation itself.

Saturday Jan 20 — Moved about 3 miles further down the river — Game signs almost disappeared — Instead of pushing on we should have remained a day to afford the hunters an opportunity of finding game — The man in charge was too big a coward and cared for self alone — Snow decreasing — Our boys left us to-day — snowy

Sunday Jan 21*st* Made 15 or 16 miles To those who had plenty it was no difficult job but it nearly used the rest of us up. Mr. Vinsonhaler — resigned all command of the party, declared it broken up and said each one must take care of himself — a piece of rascality almost without parallel — Moran & Sorel did not come to camp —

Monday Jan 22 — Mr. Vinsonhaler, Hibbard, Ducatel Martin Scott Bacon Ferguson & Beadle and the two indians Gregorio and Joachim started on ahead, determined to leave us — (Taplin Rhorer Andrews — McGehee Stepperfield A Cathcart. B. J. Kern E. M. Kern & R. H. Kern) to get along as we could or perish We made about 4 miles.

Tuesday Jan 23 — Remained in same camp — too weak to move Andrews & Roher both supposed to be dead — We looked for muscles & snails & earth worms — found none — Until the 28th these were days of Misery & death would soon have ended them.

Sunday 28th Godey came with Ferguson — almost missed us — F. returned to other camp and brought us some bread and corn meal on the 29th — Also a Spaniard & horses & mules — On the 28th Godey told us of King's death — Hibbards also — Beadle dead & Sorel, & Moran supposed to be the same.

Tuesday 30th Moved to where the rest of the provision & the remainder of the *strong* men were — 15 miles — fine day

Wednesday 31st S[t]ay in same camp eating Colt's meat — Other party pushed on — fine day.

Thursday Feb 1st Moved about 12 miles farther and camped among some willows — fine day

Friday 2nd Moved on about 6 miles — Forded Rabbit river — found Haylor's last camp — Ducatel other Spaniard & the two Indians left in it — fine day

Saturday 3rd — In same camp — fine day

Sunday 4th moved a few hundred yards to the finest camp we've had yet — killed other colt, fine day — little snow

Monday 5th Same camp — Fine day

Tuesday 6*th* Same camp — Godey came up in the Evening.

Wednesday 7*th* Moved about 10 miles and camped on the Conlerrur Creek — Snow very deep — Snowed 6 in. during the night —

Thursday 8*th* — Moved on to the Costea [22] Creek — Severe snow Storm on the prairie — nearly lost trail 15 miles we made 20 — plenty big timber

Monday 9*th* Moved on to the Rio Colorado — 15 miles — got there about sunset and slept in a house — Met Preuss and Creutzfeldt.

Saturday 10*th* Started for Rio Honda — After mile travelling my horse gave out. Returned to sa[me?]-forest and remained all day — The rest went on —

Sunday 11 — Godey sent a man & horse for me — Reached Rio Honda early in the afternoon. Found Doc. the rest had gone on to Taos in a wagon. Staid with Le Blanc; place formerly owned by Turley an American.

Monday 12*th* Went on to Taos with Doc & Le Blanc — Rode prairie

Tuesday 13 Col. and the rest except Cathcart, Shepperfield and ourselves went with

Wednesday 14*th* — Still at old Beaubiens — soup & weak coffee

Thursday 15 — Moved to quarters and had a supper fit for a human being.

Friday 16*th* — Same place — enjoying comforts long unknown.[23]

22 Costilla of to-day.

23 Kern made some notes on color and paint on the last page which included the mention of " asphaltum." He also wrote a list of the dates of the deaths of various members of the party. Richard Kern went with the Sitgraves expedition in 1851 and, in 1854, was with Captain Gunnison when he, as well as Kern, was killed by Indians, October 24th, near Lake Sevier, Colorado.

XVIII · COURTS

LIKE DIARIES AND STORIES, COURT RECORDS REFLECT IN part the life of any community. Scribbled in Spanish or English, the stamped, blotted pages of the heavy volumes kept in the Taos courthouse give glimpses, at times false, but in the main true, of the activities in turn of each generation. Most curious are those of the middle of the nineteenth century. Before that time there must have been some records but, if so, they were destroyed with other documents in 1847. The writing in the big books was always that of the alcalde or prefect who served without pay and acted as judge and even as military leader when necessary.

Most of the laws enacted in Spain made little impression on this far-away province, though a few of the early nineteenth century laws must have caused comment. On November 10, 1810, a decree forbade the publication of articles on religious subjects until approved by the local priest but this did not affect Taos country because there were no papers of any kind at that time. The law of April 22, 1811, may have been heralded with joy. All forms of torture, including stocks, were prohibited. The stocks were not all destroyed, however, and, as late as 1923 they were used at the pueblo but the younger Indians protested against this and their voice was heard. Now even the beams of the old stocks are gone.

Not until 1813 was a law passed abolishing the Inquisition, but it was repealed though later it came to stay. At one time all churches, convents and monasteries were ordered within three days to destroy all pictorial records of that awful institution.

By March 9, 1820, Spain lifted her head to the call of more modern thought and ordered all imprisoned for political or religious reasons to be freed. That same year the Indians were released from the payment of tribute, so long extorted by Spanish authorities for no other reason apparently than that of being alive within the confines of a Spanish province. In September of this year of 1820, there was a decree directed against gypsies. Apparently they came in fairly large numbers and the towns everywhere wanted them to move on. They still come to Taos but now they roll rapidly in automobiles and are unmolested if they travel on after a short stay.

By 1824, American whisky was being distilled near Taos and that brought trouble. By 1831, the first lawyer came to practice but not until 1854 do we have any description of courts in our community. With the establishment of American courts after 1847, there came the announcement that circuit courts would be held twice a year. News came that a United States District Attorney had been appointed. This fact links itself with the " tick tick " of a telegraph operator in Jefferson City, Missouri, who was given this message to send over the wires to Independence:

> " *Fink's stages are so rickety,*
> *His horses are so slow,*
> *His drivers are such drunken sots,*
> *They scarce can make them go.*
> *Then hold your horses, Billy,*
> *Just hold them for a day;*
> *I've crossed the River Jordan,*
> *And am bound for Santa Fe.*"

So Billy waited and Captain Reynolds caught the monthly stage and with him came W. H. H. Davis, the new attorney for New Mexico. They paid their fare of $150, deposited their allotted forty pounds of baggage and climbed into the seats in the mail coach which six sturdy mules pulled over the thousand miles or more to Santa Fe.

Once in the country, Davis was soon sworn in and began to look in vain for records of his predecessor. None were found, so he opened new books and pronounced his job a sinecure, barring the necessity for riding the circuit. Davis was to learn during the two and a half years he was in the territory that riding the circuit was, in fact, no easy job. The workings of an American court were little understood. Natives often wanted cases decided and punishment meted out at once. Trial by jury was too long. Why wait? The governor had always disposed of cases immediately.

The townsfolk were astonished that many cases were dismissed. This was new too. " In the year 1853," wrote Davis, " a man was arrested in Taos for this imagined offense (that of being a wizard) and bound over by an alcalde to answer at the next term of the United States District Court. When the case came up for trial it was at once dismissed and the prosecutor was made to understand that there were no such offenses under our laws."

In his " El Gringo," Davis tells of his first visit to Taos. Traveling on horse, he brought with him his trunk, none other than saddle bags in which he carried " a law library, wardrobe, and barber shop, which, being inventoried on the spot, amounted to two shirts, two law books, a small Bible, two pairs of socks, writing materials and shaving apparatus. These articles," continued Davis, " made up my outfit for a journey of near a thousand miles and an absence of three months."

Arriving in Taos after dark, the court were invited to a *baile* and were ushered into a dance hall where " we found all the fun-loving people of Don Fernandez assembled, including the *genta fina* and those that were anything else than *fina*. The floor was filled with merry dancers, and the two-handed orchestra was dealing out to them a terrific compound of catgut and rosin."

The next morning Davis went to the courthouse, " a low, rude building and less comfortable than the cow-stables in some of the states." The room within was about forty by fifteen and eight feet high, with earthen floor and two very small windows, covered with cotton cloth. Some old benches, three chairs, a sort of sentry-box for the judge and a pine table for clerk and lawyers were the furnishings of the place with the exception of a cage in which the prisoner sat. " I was not certain that I had not made a mistake and intruded into a sanctuary of the Grand Llama of Thibet, who was now seated in his box and about to receive the adoration of his subjects, instead of entering a court of justice," said Attorney Davis who had not failed to notice the large holes in the roof which suggested that he " was dealing out justice under a heavenly influence."

A small adjoining room was the jail where any prisoner would be about as safe as if he were lodged in the plaza for the door was well fastened with a string! During that term of court several miscreants were sentenced to stay behind that door or be rescued by some daring outsider who ventured to break into such a bastille.

Besides being entertained by Pascual Martinez, a brother of the priest, at another *baile* and having a fun-loving girl break an egg-shell filled with cologne over his head, a custom at lenten parties of the day, W. H. H. Davis had the good fortune to meet Kit Carson. " While in Taos," wrote Davis, " I saw for the first time and made the acquaintance of Kit Carson, the celebrated mountaineer. I was standing in front of Major Blake's quarters, when I saw a small-sized, modest looking person approaching, who, I was told, was the famous mountain-man of whom I had heard so much. He is about five feet eight inches in height, rather heavy set, and a little bowlegged; he is a mild, pleasant man in conversation, with a voice almost as soft as that of a woman. He has brown eyes and dark hair, with a face somewhat hard-featured from long exposure among the mountains. He was dressed plainly, and his whole personal appearance was entirely different from what I had imagined this celebrated trapper and hunter. There is nothing like a fire-eater in his manners, but, to the contrary, in all his actions he is quiet and unassuming."

Finally court was over and the whole party rode out of town toward Santa Fe, missing the road for several miles. Once on the main road, they were joined by three Mexicans traveling in the same direction and were glad of their company for the trail was too near the Jicarilla Apache Indians to be chosen for a pleasure trip. And so they went away from Taos in 1854.

During the same year which brought W. H. H. Davis to the Southwest there came another man as Associate Justice of the Supreme Court — Kirby Benedict. He lived in Taos for five years and through him Taos had a living link with Abraham Lincoln. No ordinary man was this judge, born in Connecticut but hailing from Decatur, Illinois. Brilliant in mind, quick to learn details, both legal and historic, he was a big man and yet a pigmy, for, living in the days when to get drunk was not considered unmanly, Benedict fell before any small decanter of whisky, which always held a persistent demon he could not resist.

This fault brought about a petition to have him removed as unfit to sit upon the bench. It was presented to President Lincoln who replied: " Well, gentlemen, I know Benedict. We have been friends for thirty years. He may imbibe to excess but Benedict drunk knows more law than all the others on the bench in New Mexico sober. I shall not disturb him." He further said that Benedict was too good and glorious a fellow for him to dismiss and he never would do so. After Lincoln was gone, another petition met with success. The press and enemies did their worst; Benedict's personal habits did the rest, and in 1871 he was suspended from practice. Broken-hearted, this splendid intellect, this glorious comrade and master of wit and humor, this man of rare gifts died a victim to whisky — a very giant undone!

His contributions to posterity do not include any account of his stay in Taos but they do contain some very unique legal opinions still read with eagerness by those who search the law. The most famous sentence which he ever pronounced was made at the close of a trial for murder held in Taos. It runs:

" José Maria Martín, stand up! José Maria Martín, you have been indicted, tried and convicted by a jury of your countrymen of the crime of murder, and the court is now about to pass upon you the dread sentence of the law. As a usual thing, José Maria Martín, it is a painful duty for a judge of a court of justice to pronounce upon a human being the sentence of death. There is something horrible about it, and the mind of the court naturally revolts from the performance of such duty. Happily, however, your case is relieved of all such unpleasant features and the court takes positive delight in sentencing you to death!

" You are a young man, José Maria Martín, apparently in good physical condition and robust health. Ordinarily you might have looked forward to many years of life, and the court has no doubt you have, and have expected to die at a ripe old age; but you are about to be cut off in consequence of your own act. José Maria Martín, it is now spring-time; in a little while the grass will be blooming; birds will be singing their sweet carols, and nature will be putting on her most gorgeous and most attractive robes, and life will be pleasant and men will want to stay; but none of this for you, José Maria Martín, the flowers will not bloom for you, José Maria Martín: the birds will not carol for you, José Maria Martín: when these things come to gladden the senses of men, you will be occupying a space about six feet by two beneath the sod, and green grass and those beautiful flowers will be growing above your lowly head.

" The sentence of the court is, that you be taken from this place to the county jail; that you be kept there safely and securely confined, in the custody of the sheriff, until the day appointed for your execution. (Be very careful, Mr. Sheriff, that he have no opportunity to escape and that you have him at the appointed place at the appointed time.) That you be so kept, José Maria Martín, until — (Mr. Clerk, on what day of the month does Friday, about two weeks from this time, come? ' March twenty-second, your Honor.') Very well — until Friday, the twenty-second of March, when you will be taken by the sheriff

from your place of confinement to some safe and convenient spot within the county (that is in your discretion,
Mr. Sheriff, you are only confined to the limits of this
county), and that you be hanged by the neck until you
are dead, and the court was about to add, José Maria
Martín, 'May God have mercy on your soul' but the
court will not assume the responsibility of asking an all-
wise Providence to do that which a jury of your peers
has refused to do. The Lord could not have mercy on
your soul, José Maria Martín! However, if you affect any
religious belief, or are connected with any religious or-
ganization, it might be well for you to send for your priest
or your minister and get from him — well — such con-
solation as you can: but the court advises you to place
no reliance upon anything of that kind! Mr. Sheriff,
remove the prisoner."

Here we have visions of a knife cutting a string! Tradition has it that Martín escaped but Teresina Bent Scheurich said she remembered that such was not the case. The
spring flowers in the breezes were not for José Maria
Martín.

To Kirby Benedict belongs the real honor of starting
a bomb rolling in New Mexico, through one of his decisions, which eventually crushed out peonage and freed
many who had been bound for life by debt. The curse
of such slavery was lifted forever.

XIX · MORE CASES

As the years went on, court records furnish more than one amusing commentary on the town life.

After this fashion they run, " Cattle stealing — carrying arms — murder — defacing brands — permitting gaming — ejectment ", etc. with the ever-recurring case, " Cattle stealing " until in 1874 we come upon " For stealing *a* cow! " Then as if discouraged at any attempt at holding court, the records cease entirely during the years 1877–1878–1879 and very little is written down until 1883.

During that year there came up a case for " breach of contract." A party of Mexicans had hired a young fellow of eighteen to go with them and procure food. The men traveled out on the plains but found no buffalo, so the boy decided to leave and go hunting on his own for bear and antelope. On his return to town he was hailed into court. On the jury sat our townsman, the late William McClure.

" We found for the boy," said McClure. " We expected to hunt buffalo too when Harry Arrowsmith and I crossed the plains in a covered wagon from Wichita, Kansas, to Taos in 1877. We didn't see any buffalo either. There was plenty of antelope and we had fresh meat all the way." This memory was too clear in the mind of the old man, once the young juror of 1883, to do other than declare, " It wasn't his fault that the meat had all gone north! "

Once, not very far from Taos, court was being held, and the following story of proceedings is vouched for by several reliable Taos men.

After hearing the case of an Italian who had knifed a companion, the justice of the peace solemnly pulled down from a shelf a paper-covered book. Turning to a page on which were several pictures of knives, the justice asked the prisoner, " Was the knife you used this size? "

The frightened culprit pointed out the size he thought was correct.

" Well, then," said the justice, " if that is the size of the knife you used, you are sentenced to bring in twelve kegs of beer and two boxes of crackers."

Then the justice, as sober as ever, put back on the shelf, —a Montgomery Ward catalogue!

It is probable that this sort of proceeding was not very unusual. Americans in town were wont to take sentences far from seriously.

During the eighties, Dr. William A. Kittredge was the only physician in town and apparently he was not a candidate for a first class halo. At one time a Mexican woman thought to get even with him and sued him for trespassing with his horse over land the doctor actually owned. A minor detail like this was overlooked and the case came up before the justice of the peace. At the proper time, the justice opened a book quite at random and declared, " Doc-tor! This On-er-ab-lie Courtie fines you fifty dollars and costs."

The doctor stalked up and down vigorously and then replied, " This On-er-ab-lie Courtie can go to H—. I'll appeal the case." But he never had to do so.

Once the famous gun-man Clay Allison was under bond to appear in the court house. On the day appointed, Allison came riding in with a group of men heavily armed. He halted at the door, dismounted, stalked into the room and walked straight up to the judge.

" Here I am, Judge. Does my coming release my bonds-man? "

" Yes," replied the judge.

" That's all. Good day," said Allison as he marched out of the place and, mounting his horse, rode away. No one dared to stop him or his armed comrades.

In the early nineties, there was an affair between the people of Arroyo Seco and the Taos Indians. The former had for some time been using a road through the Rio Lucero Cañon in order to get firewood. The people of Seco declared there was a road and that it was obstructed. The Indians gave testimony that there was only " a dim trail." The Indians won. The Seco people hauled wood from elsewhere.

During the controversy there came in some question-ing about the ditch which the Indians allowed the people of Arroyo Seco to build in the years 1817 to 1819. Under cross examination, the witness Juan G. Martinez decided he'd get the better of the man who was asking him so many questions.

" The Rio Lucero, out of which the ditch is taken, runs down through the Indian reservation and off again, does it not? "asked the lawyer, E. L. Bartlett.

" The river runs down; I never saw a river run up," answered Martinez.

" A gentleman of large observation evidently — now if you will answer my question," replied the lawyer.

When the questions were all answered it was found that the Indians had given the Mexicans as much water as would flow through the hub of a Mexican cart wheel placed in the river!

By 1838, the people of Arroyo Seco needed more water. They insisted on more and came ready to fight. On the other side of the ditch the Indians gathered, supported by some Taos people. Anger was growing when suddenly a cloud burst drove all to sheltering heights and there was more than enough water for all.

In 1893, there was no chance apparently of any heavenly interference and the same sort of trouble was brewing. Associate Justice Edward F. Seeds came to the rescue by deciding that 30 percent should go to Arroyo Seco, 35 to El Prado and 35 to the Indians and all was well and rifles stacked in corners again.

In 1918, came the last echo of the trade trails in the case of Guttman and Freadman vs. the United States. The men were long since dead but no decision had been given. The case related to damage done by Indians to a wagon train of the firm of Guttman and Freadman for which they had demanded redress. Alas, for the law's delay! Fifty years after the depredation the United States granted to the heir the sum of $2000 and the case of the sixties was cleared from the docket.

Still the law delays and, sometimes, juries meet for deliberation in the shady plaza. Politics and religion too often play a part in court decisions and the Anglo-Saxon continues to declare that he can not, as a rule, get justice in Taos courts.

XX · THE FIFTIES

DURING THE FIFTIES, A NEW LODESTAR ROSE HIGH IN THE Far West and stood over California. Very bright it was for a time and toward it struggled many a man and woman enduring much hardship while the golden light cheered them on. High with fever for gold and adventure went men from Taos. Some like Wootton in 1852 and Carson a year later took their gold with them in the shape of great numbers of sheep, which they drove over the northern route through the Salt Lake country.

When Carson returned he learned that he had been made Indian agent for Northern New Mexico. His appointment is one of the very rare examples of good judgment exhibited by the government in regard to Indian affairs during all the eighty odd years since 1847. Records of real understanding of the Indian problem in Washington are as hard to find as a needle would be among the piñons that top the hills of our Indian country.

During the years when, as the Indian agency, Kit Carson's one story adobe house on the west side of the plaza was beseiged by Indians of all tribes, the town was far from quiet in the undercurrents of life. New Mexicans could not easily forget 1847 and chafed under the knowledge that citizens of Old Mexico called them, " Little brothers that were sold."

Part of a letter of June 27, 1851, written in Santa Fe by the Rev. W. G. Kephart, gives the true status of affairs: " This is a conquered people and like all such, I have reason to believe that they secretly hate the Americans and would at any time gladly avail themselves of an opportunity to throw off the yoke. It was but a few days since that we had a rumored insurrection at Taos and a company of artillery went there from this city to quell it. The report turned out to be false; but every American feels as if such a thing *may be true* at almost any day.

" We live upon a volcano, which, but for the continual parade of arms, would burst out almost any moment. There is but little room to doubt that there are many disaffected Mexicans, who would at any time form a coalition with the savages against us, did they believe that, thus combined, they would be strong enough to rout an army.

" The conduct of many Americans toward the Mexican population " — and here Rev. Kephart strikes at the root of the matter — " is calculated greatly to increase that feeling. In all their intercourse with them, they put on airs of superiority and treat the Mexicans as a degraded and inferior people, feeling secure in the protection of our military force."

So much for the country at large as well as our town. Here there was also local strife between two parties of the Catholic Church over the treatment accorded Padre Martinez. His successor Taledrid was accused of being back of the effort to burn down the new church built by Martinez and furthermore he spent much time in the pulpit berating the deposed priest.

Finally, one Sunday morning, a brother, Pascual Martinez, felt he had had a little more than he could stand. He quietly waited for Taledrid at the church door and, catching up the priest's frock, threw it over his head and gave him the severe drubbing that he seems to have richly deserved. In spite of all the attacks on Padre Martinez, Taledrid was never able to break the power or spirit of the man who was so well beloved that he could continue to preach, marry and bury.

Meantime news came in that the Jicarilla Apaches over near the U. S. Hill to the southwest were becoming troublesome. They were starving because a change of administration in Washington had come and promises, previously made, were not kept in regard to food for these poor Indians. Governor Meriwether admitted he could do nothing and that the Indians were in a destitute condition. So the Jicarillas took to skulking on the trail of the Santa Fe traders and orders came to Cantonment Burgwin " to watch and restrain " this tribe.

One day, some twenty miles from Taos, in the rocky cañon of the Embudo Mountains, soldiers under a Lieutenant Davidson came upon some of the Indians who charged up the rugged slope and scattered among the boulders, joyful over the chance to fight in their own way. They soon routed the Americans, who, leaving twenty-two dead, made their painful way back to Fort Burgwin. Carson and Teresina Bent, on horseback, came upon the field a day or so later, and Carson stopped long enough to help bury the dead.

News of the disaster reached Fort Union at nine in the morning of March 31, 1854. Then that " peppery man with a language," Lieutenant Colonel Philip St. G. Cook who " talked through his nose so that you could hardly understand him, but you *had* to understand him," gave a decisive order and, by twelve, his men, though weary from a recent two hundred mile tramp, were again marching and this time toward Taos. Scouts under an Irishman James H. Quinn and a company of pueblo Indians under Carson soon joined the troops and proceeded to follow the Jicarillas across the cañon and on toward the timbered

Kit Carson House

Photograph by C. E. Lord

The Taos Armory

country around El Rito. Finally the Indian trail fanned out into twenty smaller trails and the white men knew they could follow them no longer.

A year later there came another call for volunteers to join the regulars. Trouble was brewing in the north. The Jicarillas had joined the Mohuache Utes and were ready to fight under the leadership of that splendid chief Blanco.

Seven hundred volunteers under Lieutenant Colonel Ceran St. Vrain, the well-known trader of an earlier day, went north and the Saguache campaign was on. Skirmish followed skirmish with heavy snow impeding progress on both sides. Nevertheless, although the Indians divided, they were followed, many slain and others taken captive, until they were ready to sue for peace. The pact, made then, was fairly well held though the whites still regarded the Jicarillas as dangerous.

By July, the volunteers were disbanded. One grand war dance of triumph took place in our plaza. Taos Indians gave vent to long pent-up feelings for to them the victory was over age-old enemies.

The choicest personal unpublished record of this campaign is a letter to be found in the addenda written by Colonel Dewitt Clinton Peters, the " fighting surgeon " and later the biographer of Carson. The original is in the possession of Charles L. Camp of Berkeley, California, who generously gave the writer the opportunity to use it.

Apropos of this account of Indian warfare, here it may be well to tell a few stories of that time which link themselves with Taos.

Probably one of the men whom Colonel Peters knew in our town was Richens or Dick Wootton, a one-time sheriff. He came with a wagon train in 1836 and became noted as a daring mountain man of many adventures. When Wootton was an old man he told the following tale:

One clear moonlight night in October (probably in 1849) a small party of men came to the Point of Rocks on the Santa Fe trail. Nearby they saw the ruins of a stage coach and ghastly remains of murdered men. The next day they learned from some Pueblo Indians who had just come from an Apache camp that a white woman and a child were there. The men believed that these were Mrs. White and child who had been members of the stage party which had met with such disaster. As soon as the mountaineers reached Las Vegas they sent forward by express the news, of what they had found on the trail, to the Indian Agent James S. Calhoun who sent out no less than four parties in the hopes of rescuing Mrs. White.

News of the catastrophe did not reach Taos for two weeks. Then, as soon as possible, Colonel Greer with some of his soldiers and the mountain men, Dick Wootton, Kit Carson, Tom Tobin, and Joaquin Leroux set out to assist, if possible, in the rescue of the white woman and her child, for the men knew only too well what it meant if help did not reach them.

Snow lay on the ground and it was intensely cold but the party found the trail of the savages and followed it for about four hundred miles. Then ravens were seen circling in the air not far ahead and to the experienced mountaineers that meant that the Indians were not more than a day ahead of them.

On the morning of the second day afterwards, the Indians were sighted. They had not seen the approaching white men and were thoroughly surprised when they heard a double quick advance upon them. Then came a fatal delay. Colonel Greer suddenly ordered a halt with the idea of asking for a parley with the Indians. To this, the mountaineers strongly objected, knowing full well that every second counted.

During those few moments of delay, the Indians reached their guns and began firing. Then, order or no, the men sprang forward, with their rifles popping. Some of the redskins made good their escape but not before three arrows had pierced the breast of poor Mrs. White. The rescuing party found her body still warm in the Indian village. No trace of her child or of the nurse was ever found. Wootton declared that about eighty Indians were killed during the fight but always regretted the fatal order which cost the life of the woman whom they had gone so far to save.

Sometime in the fifties or possibly a little later, there is an account of another interesting story which may fall here. A party which included an itinerant preacher, a Cumberland Presbyterian and a Mason by the name of Saschel Woods, drifted into Taos, possibly to trade. When their visit was over they traveled east and on the second or third day out suddenly found themselves surrounded by a large group of Indians. They had no chance to escape and were immediately made prisoners, disarmed and marched up into some small timber. Here the Indians tied each man to a tree, at the root of which dry brush was piled. The unfortunate men were to be tortured first and then burned to death.

Just before the ordeal was to begin, Woods managed to free his arms. It flashed across his mind in his dire trouble to give the Masonic sign of distress. He had no idea that this would be more than noticed. A chief near by, however, caught sight of Woods and he either knew the signal or thought it too powerful " medicine " for his men to cope with. Quickly he sprang toward Woods and im-

mediately unloosed his bonds and began a parley. The
chief told Woods that a member of his tribe had been
killed by some white men and they were out for vengeance. Woods replied that there must be a mistake as none
of his men had killed any Indian, that they had just come
from Taos where they had stayed at a certain hotel and
that they knew nothing of the murder of their tribesman.

" I will keep all of your men here prisoners," said the
chief. " I will send a small party with you to Taos. If the
owner of the hotel says that you and your men were at
that place on that day and that you know nothing of the
killing of one of my tribe, I will spare your lives. If you
have lied to me, it shall be worse for you and your men
than we intended."

After his comrades had been untied from the trees,
Woods and a few Indians left for Taos. Not far from the
town, two Indians went on ahead to ascertain if Woods
had told the truth and, finding that he had, returned and
conducted Woods back to the original camp where the
chief not only gave the men all their horses, guns and ammunition but sent with them a strong escort to protect
them against any other party of his tribe who should
also happen to be out on the white man's trail. They proceeded by a circuitous route and finally reached the main
trail east. There the Indians turned and left them.

Another story which probably belongs to the fifties is
that of hostile Indians circling around Kit Carson's home
on the Rayado, some miles east of Taos. Carson was there
with his niece, Teresina Bent. Fearlessly Carson walked
out to hold a parley with the Indians which resulted in
his asking them into his house to have food. Teresina
came in with a pot of coffee and was making the rounds
of the table when she noticed one brave looking far too

Mrs. Teresina Bent Scheurich, 1842–1918
Daughter of Gov. Charles Bent

eagerly at her. She dropped the pot and fled into the kitchen. Later the Indian asked Carson for the girl and he replied that her mother in Taos would have to give him his answer.

Knowing full well, that the Indians might attempt to force their way into his home and take his niece away with them in spite of anything he might be able to do, Carson, under cover of darkness, helped her to mount a sturdy horse, then mounted another and slipped away to Taos and safety.

Teresina Bent was for many years the pride of Taos. She was born November 15th, 1842, and, after the death of her father Governor Bent, was a member of the Carson family. In 1851, she was sent to the school of the Sisters of Loretto in Santa Fe. When her school days were over, she married an American teacher, named Locke, who soon left to join the Confederate forces and was never heard from thereafter nor did he ever return. Some years later, in 1865, she married Alois Scheurich, a trader on the old trails. For the earlier occasion she appeared dressed all in white and was the first so to meet a bridegroom. Before this time dismal black had always been worn by brides.

Except for five years when she lived with a sister at Greenhorn, Mrs. Scheurich spent her whole life in Taos and was known as a progressive, though quiet woman, as became a daughter of Charles Bent. She was the first to own a piano which was brought over the trails in 1856, first to have a lawn and cultivate choice flowers. A great reader, a lover of beauty, a most genial hostess, Teresina Bent Scheurich grew in grace with the years and, as a charitable, generous woman, was often sought by the village folk when they were in need.

Mrs. Scheurich passed away in 1918 but her kindly spirit lives on in the memory of her many friends. She will always be remembered especially as the best historian of Taos. No scholar seeking information about the old town ever failed to sit by her side and listen intently. All agreed that her memory was unusual, her mind keen and her personality splendid. Taos will never forget Charles Bent's daughter — Teresina Bent Scheurich.

XXI · THE CIVIL WAR

THE DECADE OF THE FIFTIES OVER, THERE CAME A YEAR
fraught with trouble — 1861. A flag was torn far to the
east. Cannon balls shrieked through the air with such
thunder that even the deserts and mountains of the Southwest gave them echo. A whole nation was awakened.

This was the time for quick action and the Americans
in Taos — probably there were not more than fifty —
knew it. To the mountains a few went and soon brought
back a cottonwood pole, bent at that for they had not
taken time to select a straight one. They *nailed* on the
flag of the Union and up it went with eight strong men
to support it. Carson helped put it there and with him
was a noted old-timer, the late Captain Smith H. Simpson,
who, fifty years after, said, " I am the only one left but the
flag is still there! " It was his boast that the flag always flew
in the plaza after 1861 and to-day Taos men carry on.

Captain Simpson and a friend with their guns went to
the old Bent and St. Vrain store on the south side of the
plaza and sat by a window watching to see that no attempt
was made to tear down the flag. They knew well that
probably half of the people in the town were for the
South. It was a divided community only for a short time,
however, for when the deserting Union officers from Fort
Massachusetts in Lower Colorado came through to join
the Confederate forces, the southern sympathizers rode
away with them.

By August of that year, the First Regiment of New
Mexico was being recruited " roundabout Taos " and
again the trading post won high honors. Ceran St. Vrain

was made its colonel but soon resigned and Lieutenant Colonel Kit Carson took his place.

The drilling of the more than raw recruits of native New Mexicans began here. A young lieutenant worked hard trying to make the men understand army orders. A superior officer came from Santa Fe to inspect the company and lustily gave commands but the soldiers stood stock still. Enraged at this, the officer was about to send the lieutenant to the guard house when some one ventured to suggest that Spanish be tried. So "Shoulder arms" came in the tongue the men knew and up went the guns. The company soon were ordered for further training at Albuquerque and by February were at Fort Craig where the Jornada del Muerto begins.

Below, marching from Fort Bliss, came slowly over the dull lava rocks and yellow sands a Confederate brigade under General Henry Hopkins Sibley. Their plan seemingly was to march through Santa Fe, then north to join the Mormons and possibly the terrible Apaches on the way. Had it been carried through, untold horror would have resulted but this was not to be.

While the men in gray were gaining the lower slopes to the river in order to use the ford, the men in blue were establishing their battery under the command of the brave but ill-starred Lieutenant McRae. The armies were in sight of each other, save where a bit of thick wood or sand hills interfered. Near by the deserted town of Valverde was being put on the map of New Mexico again for a battle was soon on and lost by the Yankees. The ford of the river was held by the men in gray who swept on to an easy capture of Santa Fe and Albuquerque. Only heavy snow kept the soldiers from marching north to take Taos.

Most of the New Mexican troops fought well though

there were some who ran in tumultuous haste when there fell, what Colonel Canby called, " a few harmless shells." Carson's men were commended in the press of the day.

Meantime down from Colorado were marching volunteers under Major J. M. Chivington. They were coming to retake Santa Fe and were forced to halt for battle in Apache Cañon near Pigeon's ranch. " Pigeon " was a nickname for a fiery little Frenchman by the name of Alexandre Valle whose report of the battle is at least unusual. " Zat Chivington, he poot 'is head down and foight like mad bull. Government mahns vas at my ranch and fill 'is cahnteen viz my viskey (and Government nevaire pay me for zat viskey) and Texas mahns coom oop and soorprise zem and sey foight six hours by my vatch and my vatch was slow! "

When Santa Fe was recaptured and the Confederates put to rout, Taos people were thenceforward only concerned with the Indian campaigns in which its men under Carson took part. They never left for eastern battle fields.

Kit Carson, with five companies, was sent south to reopen Fort Stanton in the heart of the Mescalero country where he soon brought the treaty-breaking Apaches to wish for peace. When a party of them reached Santa Fe, a chief made the following speech to General Carleton: " You are stronger than we. We have fought you so long as we had rifles and powder but your weapons are better than ours. Give us like weapons and turn us loose, we will fight you again but we are worn out. We have no more heart. We have no provisions, no means to live. Your troops are everywhere. Our springs and water-holes are either occupied or overlooked by your young men. You have driven us from our last and best stronghold and we have no more heart. Do with us as may seem good to you but do not forget we are men and braves." The Mescaleros were told to take their people to a reservation on the Pecos and for a time trouble with them was over or completely eclipsed by the activities of the Navajos, by far the most war-like tribe in the Southwest and so scattered that no treaty ever was considered by all of them, so the white man feared them most.

By 1863, Carson had received a letter from Abraham Lincoln, asking him to do all in his power to keep the Indians at peace. He let Tom Tobin of Taos know of the letter and told him to send him word at once of any trouble of which he might learn. Tobin was the one to do this for his ability as a scout was so remarkable that it was said of him that he could even " trail a grasshopper through sagebrush."

By June matters had become quite intolerable. It was no longer a matter of civil war in the East but a war with Navajos. Everywhere soldiers were guarding against or fighting Indians. No train could move nor a dispatch be sent without a guard. Among the company commanded by Captain Smith H. Simpson of Taos was a young lieutenant, Edward E. Ayer, now known as the founder of the great Newberry Library in Chicago. Ayer gives a glimpse of what was going on in his " Reminiscences " which are in manuscript form in the Bancroft Library in Berkeley, California. He says in part:

" Kit Carson's great fight with the Navajos was during this time, with part of his regiment and part of a regiment of California volunteers and then we cavalry were working on the outside, carrying dispatches and conducting Indians as they were captured in the Navajo country, down to their reservation on the Pecos River and of course working very hard; in fact I had been in the saddle nearly

all of the time, and once or twice I went on six to eight
hundred mile escorts, staying only one night and in Santa
Fe would get a fresh force and start out on another trip
the next morning. We never had any tents, sleeping on
the ground in snow and sleet, intensely hot in the summer
and very cold in the winter, especially nights."

Meanwhile in Northeastern Arizona, Carson established Fort Canby and sent out various companies after
the unruly Indians. It was from there that Carson went
through Keam's Cañon where today, one may find a stone
rudely cut with his name and the date, 1864.

The greatest feat of the whole campaign seems to have
been that of marching through Cañon de Chelly. While
Carson led heavy oxen teams with supplies through the
upper country, Captain Albert Pfieffer, well-known in
Taos, passed through the cañon from east to west without
a casualty — a feat which seemed hardly possible. One
paragraph from Captain Pfieffer's report will suffice to
give an idea with what he and his men had to contend:

"Here the Navajos sought refuge when pursued by
the invading force, whether of neighboring tribes or of
the arms of the government, and here they were enabled
to jump about on the ledges like mountain cats, hallooing
at me, swearing and cursing and threatening vengeance
on my command in every variety of Spanish they were
capable of mustering. A couple of shots from my soldiers
with their trusty rifles caused the red-skins to disperse instantly, and gave me a safe passage through this celebrated
Gibraltar of the Navajos. At the place where I encamped
the curl of the smoke from my fires ascended to where a
large body of Indians were resting over my head but the
height was so great that the Indians did not look larger
than crows and, as we were too far apart to injure each

other, no damage was done except with the tongue, the articulation of which was scarcely audible."

In February 1864, the wars of one hundred and eighty years with the Navajos came to an end. There were, of course, some outlying groups who continued to cause trouble but real war was over. About 5000 Navajos were supposed to be alive and most of these were sent down on the Pecos River. There they met their age-old enemies the Mescaleros but — that is another story.

The Apaches now demanded attention. Captain Simpson and one hundred Taos men started after them down on the Gila to the southwest while Carson was ordered to the east to find a large body of Kiowas, Comanches, Apaches and Arapahos on the Canadian River. There, at Adobe Walls, Carson all but lost to the Indians. He afterward admitted that it was a " scratch game " and that the fort and the howitzers had really saved the men before he gave the order to retreat. General Carleton was not disappointed in the news of this battle for he wrote to Carson: " This brilliant affair adds another green leaf to the laurel wreath which you have so nobly won in the services of your country."

Carson blamed the white man for the trouble with the red-skins. He repeatedly did so. Once on hearing of a massacre of Indians, he broke out with: " I tell ye what. I don't like a hostile red-skin any better than you du. And when they are hostile I've fit 'em, fit 'em hard as any man. But I never yit drew a bead on a squaw or a papoose, and I loathe and hate the man who would. 'Tain't nateral for brave men to kill women and little children and no one but a coward or a dog would du it. Of course, when we white men du sich awful things, why, these pore ignorant

Christopher Carson
From a photograph taken in Boston, Mass., about six months before his death

critters don't know no better, than to follow suit. Pore things! I've seen as much of 'em as any white man livin', and I can't but pity 'em. They'll all soon be gone, anyhow."

Carson's own days were numbered. When the Civil War ended so too did his fighting days. He turned his attention to doing what he could for the Indian. His home in Taos saw him but little for his travels in behalf of the Indian took him hither and yon. Honors came and sat but lightly on his shoulders. He was as of old the same good comrade who, Rusling said, "impressed you at once as a man of rare kindliness and charity, such as a truly brave man ought always to be. As simple as a child but as brave as a lion, he took our hearts by storm and grew upon our regard all the while we were with him." There are recorded many such expressions of love and esteem for our Taos man — Kit Carson.

One day in May 1868, the news came to town that Carson had died in the arms of his dear comrade Alois Scheurich. At Fort Lyon the end came, really as a result of falling from his horse several years before during the Indian campaigns. Kit Carson with his short span of but fifty-nine years was gone and with him went the days of the worst of Indian fighting. His body was finally brought to lie in the little cemetery in Taos and is now the goal to which many go to stand uncovered.

Not long ago here stood a tall slight man, dark and keen of eye and swarthy of skin, Christopher Carson, a son of William, the oldest son of Kit Carson. In his pocket was a piece of wrinkled parchment. On it were the insignia of the United States and the signatures of Andrew Johnson and Edwin M. Stanton under date of March 13, 1865.

Through this paper the country, which had once refused the minor title of lieutenant to this intrepid fighter and greater man, bestowed on Christopher Carson of Taos, the title of Brevet Brigadier General " for gallantry in the battle of Valverde and for distinguished services in New Mexico."

XXII · AFTER THE WAR

During the period following the civil war, Taos settled down to a steady easy-going life. There was little excitement save as, now and then, some plaza loafer or Texan desperado drifted in and "shot up the town."

Horses were stolen. Horses were swapped. Horses were raced. Crowds gathered together hurriedly in answer to moccasin telegrams — still subtly effective in the valley — and gambled and quarreled over their favorites. Such affairs undoubtedly brought over the mountains some of Quantrell's men who, during the war, were "soldiers all right and fought in the battles but didn't look up to Lee er any of them fellers." They had wandered into the West to become "good citizens" and with them came bad men as well.

Tales of the doings of desperadoes and of Indians who even yet occasionally stole, plundered and murdered were told in hushed breath in the dusk of lamp light throughout the valley. Many a lone sheep herder, meeting his kind, repeated the whispers.

One night, a group of Taos men found themselves in the Red or Canadian River cañon. They had traveled over much rough country during the day with their sheep and had driven them down for water. A rousing fire was built to dispel the gloom while one fellow who never could leave his beloved fiddle behind, rosined his bow and began sawing out a tune.

Suddenly up against the sky on the rim of the cañon appeared dark figures. Tall and thin they were and seemed to be wearing strange headgear of feathers, bundled in queer fashion over each ear. Down they came slowly, one by one.

"*Los Indios*," whispered some one in the crowd.

"*Por el amor de Dios, Patron, los Indios!*" came from other frightened lips as the men scurried away behind huge rocks which lie tumbled like refuse in the bed of the cañon.

The fire sputtered alone and no ray of light caught the outline of a single human being, not even the fiddler who, fiddle and all, had jumped into the water.

Breathlessly the men waited while down, down came the stealthy foe with double headgear bobbing.

"Help!" came a gurgling cry from the water, "Help!"

Creeping close to the ground, the men emerged from their rock shelters and quickly reached the water's edge. Help was surely needed. Into the cold water, the men waded to rescue the struggling fiddler and fiddle.

Still down the trail came the dark figures. Trouble a-plenty was brewing.

Suddenly the camp fire blazed a little in the night wind and disclosed not war-bonneted Indians but just — burros!

"*Por el amor de Dios*," shouted the men who now pulled with a will and dragged out the all but drowned musician who sought the fire and, shivering, dried himself and his loved fiddle and then went on with his fiddling.

Fears of sheep herders were shared by the masters of wagon trains which continued to come into the town. From the northwest, came Mormons seeking wheat seed for Taos held still its title of being the "granary of the West." Others came to buy the famous "Taos lightning

water " and brought with them jerked buffalo or pem-
mican, very finely ground dried buffalo meat for the plaza
market. Heavy oxen teams crawled in and out of town
carrying flour or wheat.

The electric cry, " Los Americanos " wakened the town
as it had in the forties. Señoritas, never pausing at the windows for they were, as of old, made of mica, crowded in
the doorways, called a greeting and disappeared to make
ready for the dance. Then they tripped their dainty way
under the portales of the plaza to the hall where no one
complained because the floor was hard mud.

Farewells were said for on the morrow some venturesome ones were leaving for St. Louis. Some would go to
Santa Fe and others travel eastward to catch the stage. The
fare was probably what it had been in the sixties, $250,
and gave the passengers the opportunity of two weeks'
travel with the nights for the most part spent sitting up
or hanging to straps and the meals consisting of hard tack,
coffee and sometimes beans!

A newspaper of the day advertised such travel by saying: "The stages are got up in elegant style and each arranged to convey eight passengers. The bodies are beautifully painted and made water tight with a view of using
them as boats in ferrying streams. The team consists of
six mules to each coach. The mail is guarded by eight
men with Colts. This is equal to a small army armed
as in ancient times, and from the looks of the escort
ready as they are either for offensive or defensive warfare with the savages we have no fear for the safety of
the mails."

Both wagons and coaches were soon to be out of date.
The railroad was coming. By 1871, the Denver and Rio
Grande was building south. Tres Piedras about forty or

more miles away was the first station to receive passengers
bound for Taos. They alighted there and took the stage
which hurried as fast as good horses could pull, across the
desert, down through the cañon and on to the flats leading to our village. The returning stage left at two in the
morning and never do old-timers tell of these trips to
catch the only train to Santa Fe or for the north but they
shiver mentally and physically.

To the east, the Atchinson, Topeka and Santa Fe rail-
way was forging ahead as a rival of the Denver road. Over
near Trinidad, there came the news, one night, that unless everybody was on the job early the Denver or " D.
and R. G." would get the better of the Santa Fe. Before
daylight, lantern in hand, our former townsman Dick
Wootton was at work in the dark and damp of the eastern-
most end of the now famous Raton tunnel. His allegiance
lay with the Santa Fe though as a result of its coming his
toll road would soon net him little income. Nevertheless
he knew the railroad must come, so he worked loyally for
the Santa Fe which did not forget him but gave him a
pension after the first train whistled its way into New
Mexico, the "bad medicine wagon," as the Indians
called it.

By 1880, Taos was fairly pushed off the map and all
but forgotten by the outside world. Mail stages continued
to run from Fort Garland and were always in danger of
hold-up men. The weekly mail made the last lap of its
journey on burros, fording the Rio Colorado, and often
was soaked so that letters had to be spread out on the
counter of the merchant who acted as postmaster. Sometimes weeks elapsed with no mail because the postal
clerks did not take the pains to throw off the sacks.

Service grew better as stations changed from Tres

North side of Taos Plaza before the fire of May 9, 1932

Piedras to Servilletta, Embudo, Taos Junction trying to get used to its recently acquired name of Stong and now Ute Park. The burro and stage gave way to the buckboard. Drivers were noted for their utter heartlessness toward their horses, often driving them when their backs were sore or even galloping them all the way. "We could hear the lashing before we could hear the stage," recalled an old-timer in Taos. Finally the government acted in the matter and horses had to be inspected by the station master. Then came the more kindly drivers like John Dunn who tried to show the Spanish American that animals have rights, a fact not yet understood by many in Taos Valley for cruelty still abounds.

Mail was made up at four o'clock in the morning here in town and doled out into boxes between seven and eight at night. William L. McClure was postmaster for several years at the princely salary of $30 a month. He secured tri-weekly mails and money order privileges and was the one who petitioned for the shorter name of Taos for the town. It took years for the new name, or rather the oldest of all, to come into its own.

Keeping a store in those days had its drawbacks as William McClure found after taking over the store his father had established in 1876 on the corner opposite the ruins of the new Don Fernando Hotel. Eleven years later he moved across the corner and kept everything that a general store can hold. Here came the Indian, Mexican and Anglo-Saxon to trade.

One morning, McClure was posting his books. A Mexican walked in, bought a pail of lard and asked permission to leave it on the counter while he attended to other errands. Meantime an Indian woman came in and took a drink from the common drinking bucket and, seeing the pail of lard handle up, slipped her arm under it and calmly walked out of the store.

Pedro, the Mexican, returned. The pail of lard was gone. Then McClure remembered. Pedro went to look for the Indian and soon returned saying, "She run like deer."

"Well," replied McClure, "We know who she is and we will get her when she comes into town again."

"The next week she died," said McClure. "The story is better than the lard was!"

Another time, an Indian woman came in to get the proofs of a photograph she had had taken. She thought them finished products. Pleased with her first picture she hurried along toward home when she suddenly saw her photograph growing darker and fainter, and in great fright took to her heels, sure she had seen the sign of her own approaching demise.

XXIII · SCHOOLS AND PROCESSIONS

DURING THE YEARS WHEN WILLIAM MC CLURE WAS HAVING his troubles, the matter of schools came under discussion. After the death of Padre Martinez, little or nothing had been done along the line of education. This accounts for the fact that to-day only the very old or the young speak English. The Mexican of middle life clings to his melodious Spanish at home or in the plaza and signs his X for his name.

About 1880, definite efforts were made toward establishing schools. The Presbyterian Board sent teachers into the valley, and rooms on the west side of the plaza served as a school house. Some years after, a fairly good building was erected on the loma which is now used as a Community Church.

Another school was and still is maintained at Ranchos de Taos, four miles away. Here came Alice Hyson, a remarkable woman, to whom much credit should go for arousing the town and county to its needs,— that county which cared so little for learning that its citizens voted, at one time, against public schools to the number of 2150 to 8!

While riding past this school in Ranchos de Taos, not long ago, a Spanish American friend of the writer said, with real feeling: " If there is one place in this world I love, it is that school. Every fellow who has really made something of himself in the valley got his start there. That's a fact."

A Catholic school was also established by a group of Sisters of Loretto, successors to those brave women who came over the trails from Kentucky in the fifties. Fine, good women they were and their school did its part in the belated awakening of an appreciation of education.

In the late seventies, there came to town a little giant. In stature he was about four and a half feet and he wore high-topped boots almost as tall as he was — a funny fellow with red hair, eyes crossed and face freckled. His was a fairly well educated mind, trained in Spain. The wide-spread ignorance which he found in the old town bothered him not a little. Finally he decided to try to move this Gibraltar of stupidity. So strutting around the plaza in his would-be seven league boots he announced that he was going to open a school.

Angel Carlos Labarta told the astonished men on the square that his school would be held in the one-roomed house where the court-house stood until the fire of 1932, in the middle of the north side. The jail and court-room were then in the rear. There, in 1878, Labarta opened his door and taught for two terms. Then teaching proved too great a task for the small man in high-topped boots. His temper had something to do with his failure no doubt. Over this he had little control as was shown, a year or so later, when he was engaged in freighting. He was stalled on a mountain road by a balky horse which could not be made to budge. Labarta walked around in front of the horse and looked him in the eye and then, in a flash, he whipped out his pistol and shot him dead in the traces. Then Labarta warmed his heels for two whole miles before he could get another horse. Later this temper of his and his power to act without thinking got him into further trouble and he left suddenly for Mexico, never to return.

A new century was to ring its way in and spend its

first quarter, almost to the full, before Labarta's dream of schools was to come true. The Taos High School graduated its first class in 1921!

As a result of this condition of affairs, superstition coupled with quaint religious ceremonies swayed many a home, during the last of the nineteenth century.

Perhaps the most unique of the public ceremonies, held even as late as 1904, was the procession attending fervent prayers for rain. One of these took place a short distance from La Loma, as the small hill in the western part of town is called. The people of Talpa, Ranchos and Ranchito set up three stations for their saints and brought images which were put in a row under the shelters, in front of a background of white sheets and bright colored ribbons. At each of the stations was held a " *velorio* " — a sort of wake for the saints, with much low singing and praying. The first day passed and the fields remained parched. The second night, the heavens opened and the rain fell in torrents so that on the following day the good folks were plowing through deep mud carrying their santos back to church and home.

The crops all flourished except in one field. This puzzled the people until some one recalled that never in their many processions with their santos had they set foot on that land. No! They were quite sure of that, hence the failure of the crop. No account was taken of the fact that planting had been done in that field long before the others and its crop was too far gone before the heavens were merciful and watered the sun-baked earth.

Another time, a long line of worshippers took their way along the road to Ranchos. It was a very hot day. They carried with them on a small platform, uncovered by a canopy, a waxen santo gay in purple and red. The priest offered prayers. At the fourth field they left their santo and returned to the Guadalupe church where they held service. After this they went again to the field and found that their santo was but a mass of white wax, red and purple. This was a sure sign to them that the saint was not pleased with the owner of that ground and that he was doomed to have no crop. This proved to be the case in spite of his paying for three such visitations to his unruly field.

Captain John G. Bourke, who traveled through this country about 1880, said, " I personally have marched in just such a procession at the pueblo of Taos " and further describes one he saw in town, in which apparently were only Mexican women. " They marched around the parched fields, praying for rain. Sure enough the rain came but in such torrents that it washed all the crops away. One of the men explained, in all seriousness, that they must have inadvertently made the rounds of the field once too often! "

Another disaster of a similar nature happened twenty years ago. An old-timer says: " We wuz almost et up by grasshoppers. One day I noticed out on the fields a group of Indians and went over to see what they were doing. I found they were placing on the ground the rain santo, San Isidro, which the priest at Ranchos had allowed them to bring out. I guess they put it there so that the grasshoppers would see it. They did all right." A few days later the Indians were asked what had become of their santo. " Oh," came the answer, " the darn grasshoppers et up all the dress and even the whiskers and left only the plaster."

Of this same San Isidro there is yet another tale dating from 1874. Rev. Thomas Harwood who had a wide parish in New Mexico was driving along in his one-horse buggy when a thunder storm came up. Since his rig had been struck by lightning two years before, Rev. Harwood decided to stop at a ranch house and seek shelter. Soon after he reached the house the storm broke in great fury.

" The old lady," he said, " took down one of her santos and asked a little boy to hold it at the door."

" It is San Isidro. It will keep the lightening out of the house," she said.

" Will it keep the lightening from me? " Harwood asked.

" Oh, yes! " came back the quick answer.

" I am a Protestant minister, you know, *señora.*"

" *No esta buena,*" was her reply, " it won't help you unless you pay two dollars! "

Harwood lived to laugh at the tale, however, and on reaching Taos went to the only hotel, the Dibble House, established in 1867 which stood on the northwest corner of the plaza where a general store stood until recently. This hotel continued in favor until 1890 when the present Columbian Hotel took its best patronage.

The proprietor of the earlier hotel was a Connecticut Yankee, always in his shirt sleeves and usually whittling on some small piece of wood when he glanced up to say, " Howdy " or " *Como le va* " to his guests. He seems never to have done anything more arduous. The real work of running the place fell on his Indian wife, Tomasita. Dibble was evidently fond of her and had more than one fight over her. Once Squire Hart induced Tomasita to come and work for him. Dibble went after her and paid for her release. He was evidently of the mind of the Californian who was recently asked, according to the radio, if he did not think it dreadful that in certain parts of the world a wife could be bought for five dollars? " Wal," he replied, " I reckon a good one is wuth it! "

About 1880, the artist, Montgomery Roosevelt, came to our town and a year later Colin Campbell Cooper. Some one rode into the plaza and fired. That was too much for Cooper and he left. Henry R. Poore also braved the rocky road to Taos in 1888. These men were among the last of passing travelers to see the old plaza with its *portales* running all around the square, for, about 1887, John Santistevan decided to open a store on the southwest corner across from the site of Don Fernando Hotel. He thought he would " improve " the corner and tore down the *portales*. After that, one by one, other merchants did the same thing and the picturesque plaza of the traders and trappers passed.

Ten years later, Mrs. J. E. Russell and " the Simpson girls," as Captain Simpson's daughters were always called, aroused civic pride and shortly a picket fence was built around the plaza and trees and hollyhocks appeared. The listless days of the eighties passed and with the nineties a change began to creep over the town.

XXIV · DIGGIN'S

GOLD! THE FEVER FOR GOLD HAS BEEN INTERMITTENT FOR centuries throughout the Southwest. It has never ceased since the days of the tale of a great peak of gold to the north or the yarns spun by El Turco who lied better than he knew. Gold has been found, is now found and will be as long as the prospector lives.

In the early nineties, Taos was aroused by many new tales of the finding of precious metals. Men knew gold had been discovered in quantity in Elizabethtown in 1866. In 1881, an Apache uprising checked the prospector for a while but by 1890, it was common for men to come into town and pay their bills with gold. T. Paul Martin, the young doctor from the East, always kept dainty Troy scales in his office for the valuable dust.

Undoubtedly all through the middle part of the century, in spite of Indians, there were lonely prospectors wandering all through the Sangre de Cristo range but the only Taos story available to-day of these mining ventures, begins in 1877 — the story of the Anderson brothers. In reality their tale begins some twenty odd years before that date on a farm in Canada, thirty miles west of London, Middlesex County. There, in a Scotch home lived two lads, William, some eight years older than Alexander who was born in 1852. When twenty, the younger brother followed William to Arkansas and spent several winters there, going back to Canada in the summers.

In the fall of 1876, the brothers went to Dakota and then took the burro trail for the Southwest which brought them some three miles west of Taos right through the land which was later Alex Anderson's garden. On to Copper Hill they went and then to Santa Fe where they put up at the old Herlow Hotel which had as an annex a row of little cabins and corrals for miners and their burros.

There the Andersons listened to the miners and especially to one Dorsey who told them of the Taos Valley and of the foothills which lie about eleven miles north at the mouth of the Rio Hondo. The men liked Dorsey's story best, so back up the trail they came with their burros. When they reached the rim of the Arroyo Hondo they could see far below a mill, a five stamp mill, which belonged to the Taos firm of Guttman and Freadman. The sight of a real mining camp and the looks of the mountains were enough for the young men. They went below to find a cabin home and begin prospecting.

" We found our mine, a gold mine," said Anderson. " Then we built an arrastre, you know, one of those small box affairs with heavy stones inside to crush the ore which we broke up as much as we could. We hitched one burro to it. Anybody would have laughed if he had come upon us two drivin' that burro round and round — two young men! "

While he was talking Alex Anderson was slowly undoing a small parcel done up in tissue paper. Smilingly he presented the contents to the writer for inspection with " That's all we got out of our arrastre. Twenty-one dollars in gold. We made it up in that button shape and I've kept it all these years. Burro power was too infernally slow.

" The next year we advanced a little. We built an arrastre with a water wheel. We went under writin' to the Mexicans to have the water we wanted. We agreed to keep the ditch in repair down as far as the old stamp mill. My

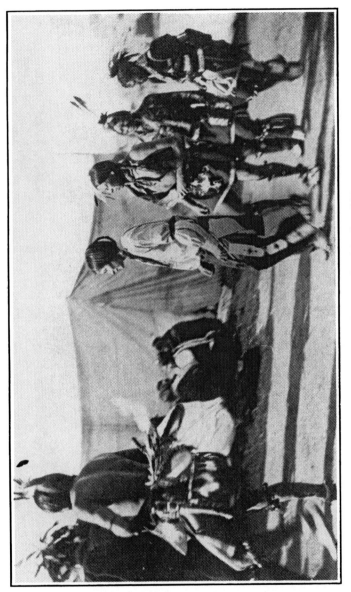

Taos Indians Dancing to the Music of Drums

brother did the freightin' down from the mine, a mile and a half away. I worked at the mill.

" After three days, the Mexicans came to me a-jabberin'. It was some time before I could make out that they wanted more water, though we were givin' them what we had promised. We had thought they might do that so we were prepared. I opened up the gate an inch. They wanted more. I called 'em names and just pulled up the whole gate and threw it into the water. It went floatin' away. We had stored up more water than their old ditch could hold. It broke in several places and flooded the fields. That was the end of the millin'. I went to minin', there and at Copper Hill. When we wanted ready cash we worked at our trade of carpentering." So it came about that a number of houses in Taos were built by Anderson brothers — miners.

In 1877, the Andersons in the little town of Arroyo Seco chanced upon two men, in a covered wagon, who had driven over the trail from Fort Garland. They were trading groceries, especially common molasses, for pelts. Suddenly one of the men, William Frazer, looked at William Anderson and each recognized the other as Highland Scotch. Then came the old familiar Gaelic greeting. Anderson was asked to spell the old words. " Though I'm Scotch," he said, " it beats me to spell it. You see father always held family prayers in Gaelic. I learned to read my verse by listenin' to the others but I didn't understand a word of it. We children talked English. When I went to church, I knew what the preacher was sayin' when he said ' God ' and ' Jerusalem ' but that was all."

The next morning, Frazer took a long look at the mountains and declared, " I'll quit tradin' and go a-minin'." So over the rim of the great arroyo he and his covered wagon started back to Fort Garland and the next spring he came in afoot with blankets strapped to his back. Again, on one fine Saturday night, in the Anderson cabin, the two older men jabbered away in Gaelic. True Scotch hospitality was there until the appearance of a red splotch on Fraser's cheek sent Alex hunting for a room. Frazer had small-pox and to that rented room he went and stayed while the Andersons carried his meals to his door. Small-pox raged through the whole valley that winter of 1877–78 and took a dreadful toll but Frazer was out after only three days and eager to be at work.

For a few weeks Frazer worked with the Andersons and then left for the mountains alone. It was not long before he had his own mine. Then came the hiring of helpers. With one of these, Pete Cromer, a carpenter friend of the Andersons, he had some hot words, probably over wages. No one was about. A shot rang out. Cromer fell. Frazer mounted his horse and rode into town with the short news, " Cromer was shot." A day or so later, Alex Anderson was about to ride his horse out to Arroyo Seco and beyond to see his friend for " he wasn't killed dead, you know," when again a horseman rode into the plaza. It was Frazer with the second terse bit of news, " He's dead." Nevertheless, Anderson took the road to the north.

A coroner's jury freed Frazer on his plea of self-defense. He accused the dead man of having stolen his tools and had a henchman of his bring in an old ax head which he said he had found in Cromer's pillow. " Well, I knew Cromer never stole an old ax without a handle. He was a carpenter and had plenty of tools, I spoke right out, ' It's a lie! ' I said. ' Frazer will die with his boots on. You'll see.' I hunted up the doctor and learned the truth. Cromer had been shot in the back! "

Craig, another friend of Cromer's met Anderson, one day, with " Alex, say the word and we'll hang Frazer in fifteen minutes." But Anderson did not say the word and Frazer soon felt it best to leave the neighborhood and went up the cañon where he kept on prospecting.

For three years after that, Anderson carried his pistol and narrowly watched Frazer when they chanced to meet. Finally, one day, he and some mining men pulled up at Frazer's home for he had now married a Mexican woman.

" Come in, Alex, and have dinner," was Frazer's greeting.

" I did so but I sat down at his table with that pistol still in my pocket," said Anderson; but that bit of hospitality convinced him that he need no longer burden himself with any weapon.

By 1892, Frazer had found lead or galena ore about eight miles up the cañon. Ill-feeling had worn away somewhat and he came down to Taos to tell of his find and talk loudly of the possibility of great wealth. Other men were needed now and he knew it. His enthusiastic tales had their effect so that there was much making of plans that winter of 1892 and 1893.

XXV · AMIZETT AND TWINING

When spring came in that year of 1893, al helphin-stine, his wife, Amizett and J. C. Hill went up the Hondo to prospect. Others followed. An old cabin was fitted up as a hotel and soon fifteen or twenty people were holding a meeting and deciding that the name of the place should be " Amizett," after the first woman following the trail up the cañon.

Among the first men arriving on horseback was Gerson Gusdorf of Taos, tired of his job of traveling salesman. He ordered the first wagon to make its way up by cutting down quaking aspen and forging ahead, thus making a rough road. A hardy team pulled up its load of lumber which became the small frame building known as " the store," topped by the sign " Gusdorf Bros."

One by one were pulled down the white tents which glistened half-hidden on the mountainsides where eager prospectors had been guarding their holes for, far below, was room for cabins and company. Saloons and dance halls sprang up like magic. On came the people, many of them lured thither by advertisements read in the Denver papers. An ore-sorter, Alex Schroeder, was asked how he happened to come to the place and replied, " I saw in the paper while I was ridin' along in a train, the story of a shootin' scrap up in the mountains over a claim and thought it must be a good place to come to."

No less than three hundred and fifty people came to live in Amizett while the " boom " was on. This lasted for a year. Meantime Denver men backed the Rio Hondo Placer Company and began to sell lots and advertise more extensively.

A daily stage driven by Bill Peete pulled in from Tres Piedras for about eight months. This stage brought many a greenhorn. One fellow, soon after his arrival, wandered over the cañon sides, looking for a chance to locate a claim. He came upon altogether too many signs marked " N.E.Cor," " S.E.Cor," and " N.W.Cor "! That was not all. There was still another rascal, " S.W.Cor." It was too much. Why, the whole slope was covered with such claim stakes! Down to the village he went and slammed into a saloon, angry clear through. " Who in H——— are these fellows, ' Cor '? Why, they have the place all staked out! There's no chance for anybody else."

Out came the pipes. The card game waited for a moment. The eyes of the old miners snapped and then came a wild whoop of laughter and the greenhorn made for the door. He outgrew his greenness, however, and, a few years later, made a fortune in the Klondike.

Yes, mines were worked. Ore was found. Then came the problem of getting it out of the cañon. Men had thought little of that. The Shoshone showed ore and was worked for four or five months and when the shaft was down about twenty feet, the Gusdorfs were offered, by no less a person than Governor John L. Route of Colorado, the sum of $20,000. " I wanted to sell," said Gerson Gusdorf, " but my brother didn't. We never got anything out of it. Nobody made any money. There was no transportation. But it's a good gold country. I still believe in it." So declared the one-time owner of the Shoshone, thirty years afterwards.

A second boom came to the cañon after 1895 when Amizett had shrunk to the point of being a deserted village. Gold was found up on Gold Hill and a great cry went up. Then a third boom struck the cañon at its head and

the town of Twining came into existence. This became a
fairly large place of log cabins, with a sizable hotel and
halls, all lighted by electricity. It thrived with people as
eager as had been those at Amizett three or four years
before. William Frazer had found copper on a near-by
slope and farther on was gold. He organized the Frazer
Mountain Copper Company and began selling stock.

Among the men lured to the new mines was Albert C.
Twining from New Jersey and, as president of a bank
in the East, he began investing other people's money. His
name was given to the place for he was probably the heaviest investor and later, in prison, he bemoaned his rashness
while the real rascal covered his tracks. Frazer was not
suspected of treachery when the mill was going up and
when men were working and being paid too.

Finally the day came when the great smelter was in
place. Outside were the ovens to make the charcoal fuel.
Coke had been brought over the wagon road from far-
away Trinidad at a cost of sixty dollars a ton. Huge piles
of wood stood by. Everything was ready. The place was
well equipped. The people were happy. The time for
success was at hand. The red-hot smelter was to bring in
gold — much gold.

By night the coke fires were burning merrily under the
huge crucible. Electric lights dispelled all gloom from the
mill. Men, in corduroy, strutted about in their high boots,
smoking, drinking and talking knowingly. Chemists were
busy with their compounds.

The raw product went into the cauldron. The flames
leaped gloriously. Hope was on probation!

Suddenly there came a hoarse whisper, " It isn't goin'
to work again. It will be all off for us if it freezes."

Frazer, drunk as a lord, made his unsteady way through

the crowd, declaring encouragingly, " No, it won't freeze, this time."

Midnight came. The two hundred men were more tense than ever when they strolled over near the smelter for a closer look. They offered suggestions. More of this or that should be used in the molten mass. Heads began to shake.

" It's goin' to freeze again " came in excited tones. Could it be possible that the molten ore and stone were to cling hard and unyielding to the sides of the great smelter? " No! Oh, no! It won't freeze," came again from Frazer's uncertain lips.

Between three and four in the morning, there came a very wail on the air. " She's froze, boys! "

" I can hear that yet," said Gerson Gusdorf who was one of those who spent that anxious night in the mill, watching, listening and waiting to learn the result of the final test.

" They prepared for a big thing and it blew up in one night," he continued. " The fires were never relighted. Frazer said it would be cleaned out the next morning and another effort made but the smelter never again was called into action. They just didn't know how to work it."

The news spread like a prairie fire through the village. It fell like a crushing blow. About $300,000 had been sunk in the struggle for success. Now, in one night, everybody knew that failure stalked their camp. Stunned, many sought the courage built by whisky. Then came depression. With heavy hearts, an exodus began.

" Mismanagement " came from the charitably inclined but more added the word " deliberate," as, wagon by wagon, the people moved down the cañon. Frazer seems to have played for failure in the hopes that the whole plant would swing into his hands. So the majority thought then and still think. He was accused of all sorts of misdoing, of the murder of that former employee Cromer, of knowing definitely the location of the lonely grave of the Swede, Guy Thomas, " the man who disappeared between sun-up and sun-down " because he was too attentive to the grass widow of the place.

Frazer paid little heed to the accusations and retained possession of his claims. Finally, years after, while rounding the corner of the cabin where lived his care-taker and about to lift his gun to fire, he himself fell dead from the shot of a quicker gun. Jack Bidwell, who lowered that gun, was brought to town and quickly cleared of any blame for the general consensus of opinion was that the country was better off. One old-timer recently wracked his brain to find something good to say of Frazer and finally recalled one instance of kindness done and ended by declaring: " He had a *few* good points."

For years the hotel stood unused. In 1922, dishes were still piled in the kitchen and bedsteads stood in most of the rooms. The post boxes looked new in the office but they held no letters. Without surrounding cabins were fairly well furnished but no fire burned in the once cheerful living rooms. Over in the red mill still stood the smelter. Little was disturbed until 1924 when a wrecker appeared and down came hotel and cabins. The mill was burned in June, 1932.

At Amizett log cabins were also standing in 1922 when a party of painters gathered around a fireplace where wood crackled and aided the candles to light a room in an old prospector's cabin. Outside the aspens were quivering yellow among darkening pines and their beauty had lured us with our brushes. We urged Bert G. Phillips, who had come to Taos in 1898 and had himself worked a mine, to tell us the story of the cañon. We listened intently. One story finished a question brought another in Phillips's inimitable manner. No one cared if the night was wearing away. Finally the tales done, an Indian model, Star Road, began beating his drum in dreamy fashion and songs, ages-old, broke the stillness. Then, one by one, out into moonlight went the guests. The log cabins gave out no welcome sign. They were but telling the truth. The day of the miner had long since gone. The day of the artist had come. Yet only twenty-five years had rolled away.

XXVI · LA BELLE AND ELIZABETHTOWN

WHEN THE AMIZETT MINER NO LONGER WAS NEEDED, Frank Staplin packed his printing press and moved across the mountains to set up *La Belle Cresset,* which began attacking its former home in a column headed, " Who killed Cock Robin or What busted Amizett? "

The editor let himself loose after this fashion: " They had a justice of the peace that could issue papers on Sunday and before the ink was dry, swear he did it on Saturday," and further declared: " Attachments were more profitable than gold mines. Men craned their necks down the road looking for the ship that never came. The newspaper committed suicide, the justice of the peace shot himself, the toll road grieved itself to death over this double disaster and the people have all moved to La Belle! "

The new mining town, 9200 feet high, enjoyed quick growth. By August 28th, 1894, a few men gathered in Garrison's cabin and drew up regulations and named their town. Log cabins and frame houses went up almost overnight. Three hotels began to do a surprising amount of business. One of these had been a $20,000 house but it was torn down and brought over the mountain for the big run of trade. No one then could guess that in a very few years it would be knocked down to the highest bidder for only fifty dollars!

Hopes were high. The Hamilton Mine of 1869 was not far away so there must be other good prospects. Low grade ore, however, was all the miners could discover, though they clung tenaciously to their various finds until forced to let go.

By the spring of 1898, *La Belle Cresset* began to gasp for breath and before it passed away, this came from its press which shows "what busted" La Belle:

April 14, 1898.

"The experiments now being made by Thomas A. Edison with low grade ores with a view to extracting the gold from such ores at a profit are being watched with much interest by the people of the Southwest. Mr. Edison expects to be able to work $3 ores of any character at a profit."

The watching proved too great a strain and La Belle fell asleep and for years only one lone man lived on guarding the place, hoping for a second boom, which never came.

Meantime Midnight and Red River also appeared on the map of the miners, while Elizabethtown of 1867 began to grow apace. Concerning the various towns the new *Taos Cresset* printed spicy items which lend the imagination the high-powered glasses to allow it to see how affairs stood in the mountains. One or two of these throw light:

Red River, July 4, 1895.

"W. W. Gaudy is still pegging away on the Sure Thing Lode up Bitter Creek. But W. W. saws wood and says nothing. He has a 'sure thing' and does not care to talk."

Elizabethtown, Dec. 22, 1898.

"The mill will be no experiment for the management know by actual tests what can be saved out of the ore exposed and what the profits will be."

So ran the news from the mines boasting of such titles as *The Puzzler, Paragon, Bull of the Woods, The Gold*

*Dollar, Black Joe, Iron Mask, The Only Chance, Heart of
the World, The O. K.* and —*Humbug Gulch!* The last
name takes us up over the mountains again to Elizabethtown, the most successful of all the mining villages. Its log
cabins, frame houses, hotels and bars with rows of bottles,
foot-rail, towels, counters and mirrors were photographed
for the Souvenir, published in 1901.

From the torn first page of the only copy of this pam-
phlet to be found in Taos we gather the story of the early
finds and the subsequent swift growth of Elizabethtown,
a little sister to our town, its nearest place for doctor,
lawyer, merchant, thief.

In the early sixties, Ute and Apache Indians roamed
the mountains and, one day, high up on Old Baldy, one
of them picked up a beautiful stone lovely in green and
blue. He felt fairly sure that there was something precious
hidden in his find and tucked it away in his blanket. Soon
he went over to Fort Union to trade and, that done, he
showed his pretty stone to the soldiers who were, at once,
on tip-toe, looking at the sample, turning it over and
over and weighing it. " Copper " was their decision. Two
of the men thought it wise to act immediately and dispatched one of their fellows with the Indian, somewhat
richer of pocket, to find the place from which the stone
had come. Straight to the ridge of Baldy they went and
a mine was located and marked.

The time for assessment work came in 1866 and Bron-
son, Kelly and Kinsinger took the trail for Baldy but they
camped, one night, on Willow Creek. While supper was
being cooked, Kelly took a pan and washed out some of
the gravel along the edge of the water and found — gold.
Then copper was forgotten and lively prospecting began.
Apparently they all found gold in such quantities as to

make them long to go to work at once. Only lack of proper tools forced them to return to the fort with the resolve that they would say nothing. The secret was, however, too much for the men and they soon began to talk wildly enough to arouse all New Mexico and Colorado.

Before snow had gone, prospectors were on the ground and the big pine, long known as " Discovery Tree " served as the starting point for measuring claims. So it was that Willow Gulch operations began. In fact all the gulches leading to Baldy, even Humbug Gulch, yielded good gold. Then, almost in a twinkling of an eye a town was there in the valley and named for the lovely daughter of John Moore, Elizabethtown, soon shortened to " Etown." This little place lured many from Taos for much money was made and more spent because there seemed to be no end to the riches roundabout.

Men did their part but so did the mules. Another news item ran: " When a mule chanced to run its leg deep in a bog hole, bringing up a quantity of gravel with its shoe, this too was tested and proved to be worth 75c. per pan. Great credit is due the mule for his part in the discovery which made Etown placer mines famous in a day."

It soon became evident that more water was needed so Captain N. S. Davis built a big ditch from Red River to Etown. The distance in airline was but eight miles but, as the engineer had to build, it was forty-two. The ditch was to allow six hundred inches of water but seepage and evaporation cut this amount sadly and the project failed to pay until 1875 when Matthew Lynch put the channel in better order. Then mining acticities increased perceptibly.

By 1897 greater ventures were to be tried. A huge dredge was pulled into town and set up on a flat boat

which could be moved up stream after the seventy-two
500 pound buckets had finished digging up " pay mud "
in one place and were needed in another.

When the dredge was ready, a christening was in order.
A Mrs. Mougey gave a welcome to all and "especially to
our esteemed friends who have braved the uncertainties
of the Sante Fe railroad and the dangers of the Hankins
Stage Line." Then, " stepping lightly forward with the
bottle of champagne to christen ' The Eleanor,' " she
added, " May thy wheels never turn without profit to
thy owners; may there be no loss in thy boxes; nor leakage
of water in thy seams." And there was very little. All
went well until the dredge had passed beyond Grouse
Gulch, then jealousy and greed allowed trickery to creep
in, if we read aright an award which came from the
courts giving one party the land and another the ma-
chinery. Then it was abandoned and even today the stout
wheel holds aloft several of the great buckets and could
they but talk they would say: "We cost all told about
$100,000 but we earned many thousands beyond our
cost."

As the gulches were worked out the miners began to
consider the whole mountain beyond. " They figur'd
with science — and some commonsense too," said an old-
timer, "that Baldy was probably a chimney." So they
decided to dig in and for thirty years or more a big tunnel has been eating its way into the very heart of Baldy
but as yet the chimney pot of gold has not been found.
The workers are now slightly to the left of the peak and
a side tunnel is being considered. Perhaps then may come
the great " strike." If so, the railroad will come for the
timber as well as the gold. There will be another big
boom and Etown will live again.

The Aztec mine and the town of Baldy still live on just over the divide. Much highgrading was done in days gone by and many a nugget of fine gold was slipped into the boots or jeans of miners in the Aztec. " All day Sunday one could hear the pounding in mortars all over the mountain," said Jack Ferguson, one old miner, while another broke in with, " You didn't have to wait 'til Sunday — just wait until the shift went off." Not much was done about this stealing of which the company officials knew perforce. Some one asked " Jim " Lynch once why more was not done to prevent theft. He looked up and said: " Well, they're advertising the place, aren't they? " So, in fact, did the name of the Aztec grow famous.

One of the highgraders was traced back to Chicago where he was found to have sold $15,000 worth of gold. Others were not so successful if we may believe the story told by a prospector who said when he was wandering over the mountain he stumbled on a skeleton beside which lay a large cow bell, stuffed with gold.

In 1887, Congress confirmed the immense Maxwell Land Grant and then began in the Etown country what is known as the Grant War. The company demanded twenty percent of all minerals found near Baldy. It allowed only one of two claims. This resulted in much bitterness. The full story of murders, clever stealing and profound discontent will never be told. Juries would not bring in verdicts for the company. Men drilled and practiced shooting openly. Finally, according to the miners, " bullies from up north " were brought in to clean out the country. They did their work well and, with the passage of the years the Maxwell Company must have lost millions by their policy.

XXVII · MINERS' TALES

Tales lend color to any mining town and etown is no exception to the rule.

The little town, once the home of 1500 people, looks today like a discarded movie set, falling where it is not burned down. A half dozen persons are about the place but they make no effort at building and show no signs of having any gold. That lies hidden in the rock which reaches to the sky.

No longer does the Irishman, old Jim Scully, leave to come over the divide to Taos — he who would quarrel over the boundary fence with his one-time pal, Tom Grainey, who finally felled him with a shovel. While he lay swaying between life and death the priest called and asked Scully to forgive his neighbor. The sick man looked up and replied, " Well, Father, I'll tell ye. Ef I die, I forgive 'im but ef I live, I'm the same old fightin' Scully." This he lived to be but with all his fighting he was not able to hold on to his wealth.

One dark night, a Taos man pulled up at Scully's barn and took all he wanted of grocery supplies and a harness. A few days later, the man who had so acquired the leather yelled out to Scully as he threw it over his horse, " Eh, Scully, yar's yer harness." But Scully went his way, learning the truth much later when he remarked, " Oh, he's such a darn'd old liar, I wouldn't believe him." So he remained the loser of the harness and some of that " Mocka and Javy " coffee, he liked, which came from " Muntgumery, Wird and Cumpany."

Some distance from Scully's ranch, along Willow Gulch, the gold aristocracy lived in its heyday. The miners and their wives fared well. Among them, " when everything went," was a negro woman whom Robinson, an early prospector, had brought out from Hot Springs, Arkansas, as his cook and subsequently married. He was a Yankee and she, a former slave, was wont to make him understand that Yankees were no good. At times when the whisky glass had been too full, she went yelling around their home, giving her Yankee a chase, crying out, " Hooray fer Ole Jeff Davis " and then went muttering to herself through the door, declaring that " no Yankee wuz a gem'mun."

This home of hers was built in 1879 by the Anderson brothers of Taos who spent many hours with the Robinsons. Alex Anderson said of her: " She couldn't help her color. She used to sit and play the banjo and sing by the hour — quite entertainin'. Every Sunday, I'd have an order on Montgomery, Ward Company to make out for her. She was layin' in lots of finery that didn't belong to a nigger, I knew. She'd do anything for anybody. She was very liberal and good-hearted. No human being ever had a better heart than that poor, old, black nigger. You can give her a better record than you could Frazer! "

The time came when her last man died and, little by little, her money oozed away. She was then reduced to taking in washing down in Chihuahua, the notorious suburb of Etown. She would sit in her rude shack after parting with her former finery and say bitterly: " When I wuz rich, I wuz ' Mrs. Robinson ' and now they call me ' Ole Nigger.' Why, the pore white trash, I want 'em to understan' I'se bin three times marri'd and had the pick o' the lan'. I wouldn't wipe ma feet on 'em." She did not knuckle to them either but held her head high until her never too strong mind suddenly snapped and she was taken away.

Another story of Chihuahua has often been told as true. Certainly, as characteristic of the miner town, it may have place. During the early days of this Mexican settlement adjoining Etown everybody lived a free and easy life. Finally there came from the East, an old wag by the name of Fortner who was promptly scandalized at conditions in general and living without benefit of clergy especially. He let this be known when he was made justice of the peace.

So, one night, Fortner was wanted at a marriage ceremony. He was hurriedly called from his " office " which was probably any bar where his foot could find a place on the rail. He was ready and with trousers well tucked into his high boots, his coat tails flying and his hat atilt, he walked along with the crowd to the wedding.

Once inside the poor hut and the people quieted, the justice performed the ceremony. Clearing his throat, he began,

> " *Unda this roof,*
> *In stawmy weatha,*
> *This buck and squaw*
> *I now join togetha.*
>
> *Let none but Him*
> *Who rules the thunda*
> *Put this buck and squaw asunda.*
> *Ye're married, be God, Sir."*

This brought down the house and the whole crowd burst into laughter. Thinking they were making fun of her, the bride quickly seized a frying pan and let it fly.

That diversion soon cleared the room and she was left in peace.

A story of a different kind comes from Harry Anderson, prospector, who was but a boy of nineteen in 1890 when he was made night watchman for the Moreno Gold Mining and Gravel Company. He had but lately read of the battle of Wounded Knee which took place to the north early that year and was much impressed by the fact that one young lieutenant had made a reputation for himself between sun-up and down. Anderson made up his mind he wanted a reputation too.

One night, as the president of the company, James E. Bloomer, walked out of the mine he gave Anderson strict orders to arrest any one who was seen entering the pit. So the boy who wanted a reputation thought possibly his chance had come. He kept sharp lookout. All went well until about eleven o'clock. Then down the way came a dark figure which Anderson recognized. He waited until the right second and stepped out from behind a bank, gun in hand.

" Hands up," he ordered.

" Oh, Heavens, Harry. It's a friend. It's a friend! " said the intruder.

" All look alike to me, to-night," said the guard with that reputation in mind.

" Are you going to put me in jail," came from the man who was evidently annoyed.

" No, I'll put you in the office so you will be there in the morning," Anderson replied and straightway marched his man away.

Finally the night surrendered to dawn and Anderson was about to be relieved when the superintendent met him with, " Well, what happened last night? "

" I arrested a fellow here in the pit," came the answer proudly since that reputation seemed now within his grasp.

" Is that so! Who? "

" Bloomer," came the laconic reply.

" Bloomer! I'd have given a hundred dollars if you had put him in jail," said the smiling superintendent.

" I figur'd I was fired," said Anderson telling of the affair, " and went home to bed." For the time being he was not so sure he wanted a reputation at all. The president, with his dignity a bit askew, was released but he was too good a sport to dismiss his night watchman for obeying orders.

Now the gravel pit lies open to all. Those days have gone but not the man who loves to talk about the gold still in the mountains. He may tell of frauds practiced, of the selling and re-selling of worked-out mines to " gullible parties back east." Perhaps he will relate the story of the mine in the Rio Hondo where $50,000 was sunk after some rascally Americans had planted ore brought from Etown. All, that was eventually saved, was brought into town and made by a Taos jeweler into the costliest watch chain in the world — a $50,000 gold chain.

More than one man right on the field learned to know the bitter sting of fraud. Once an Irishman Stevens drifted into Etown after he had searched the mountains, and told of a rich find, declaring, " I've a fine prospect. Now if I only had some one to go in with me — " The Swede Jacobson bit. Down to the office the two men went to make their deal. The next morning, Jack Ferguson, a miner, met Stevens on the road, bending under a good sized roll of blankets and belongings.

" I hear you have sold your prospect? " said Ferguson.

" Yes, and when I came to make out the papers, I found the d—— fool couldn't read. So I put the whole thing on to him. I'm headin' for Arizona," said Stevens who knew his part was to keep on headin' for Arizona too and away he went, never to be heard from afterwards.

Men in the mining towns were always sagely talking about their prospects and what they would do in the spring. Once, a group of them sat about a hotel fire when a buckboard drew up outside. The guests came in to register and among them was a preacher who soon joined the men around the stove.

The talking went on. The hour grew late and the whisky glasses too heavy to lift. The minister listened as long as he could and then he broke out with, " My dear brethern, I have a few words to say to you. You should be laying up your treasures in the New Jerusalem where the streets are paved with gold."

That last word reached a little fellow, Harry Majors, who was almost ready to fall under the table. He roused himself with effort, however, and flourishing a wavering hand in the air, exclaimed, " Where in H—— is that, Sir? Another big strike been found? Another *gold* strike? "

The more hardy men like Columbus Ferguson, already mentioned as " Jack " Ferguson, kept on tramping the mountainsides. Over thirty years ago he located the vein of copper which those earlier men of Fort Union failed to find and he named his mine the Mystic Lode. Then he cast about for partners. Two men stood ready to go in with him. " I soon realized I had two greenhorns," said Ferguson. " Wilkinson slid off an alfalfa stack back in Kansas and Stone, a Pennsylvania German, had worked in a soap factory in Cincinnati, I believe. They didn't know anything about mining. They didn't even know how to pack lumber on burros. After a year or so, each thought he was an expert miner.

"We packed the ore down on burros and had it arrastred and then sent the amalgam on to Denver. Lucien Maxwell sent some copper clear across the plains by ox teams to Westport but we sent ours to Colorado. Later we shipped to El Paso." Here Ferguson opened his little black tin box and took out an old paper. It was the smelter returns of the last load of copper ore he had shipped. Under date of October 6, 1913, the report gave $1950 for the car load.

Transportation facilities were too slight. The work was too heavy so Ferguson came to live in Taos but Wilkinson lived on in a little cabin high up above Baldy. In the winter of 1916, his heart troubled him and he went over the mountains to visit near Raton. On his return he drove to the Jackson ranch and from there started on foot to Baldy, taking the old Etown trail for his hut on the east side. After that there was a long silence.

Headlines of the newspapers read, "Aged Mine Owner Vanishes," and followed with the news of a searching party which tried to cut through the snows to the cabin but were forced to turn back. Hints of murder filled the air but nothing was ever proved. Years after a skull was found in the timber below the cabin, so small and odd in shape that it was quickly recognized as undoubtedly that of Frank E. Wilkinson, miner.

Murder, disappearance and fraud were often matters for comment but the search for gold did not cease. Once the lure brought men near to Taos. Lately some men asked permission to clean out William L. McClure's well. This took all summer! Then one man disappeared. In 1921, three Americans came from Raton and asked permission to use a divining rod in the home of Mrs. Gabila Vigil in Placita, a small suburb of Taos. The rod was used. Heads went up and down. Then came the spades and the hard mud floor of the widow's best front room was broken apart. Soon satisfied, the men went their way, leaving that floor in one fine mess. They had found only the remains of an old chest!

So the lure of gold still beckons. The day of the mining camp may be gone for the moment. The day of the prospector is always here. He never tires. He lives on forever!

XXVIII · 1898

BEFORE 1898, THE COMPASS OF TAOS SHOWED THE NEEDLE still pointing to the word "Spanish" but now another name was on the dial, for in the fall of that year the slender steel swung under powerful influence to the word "American." Even now when, on occasion, it quivers toward the old name, the magnet pulls it back for, since 1898, Taos has been a town of the United States.

During the late months of that year, far up in the mountains, three Americans sat reading a newspaper, many days old, and learned for the first time that there was real trouble between the States and Spain. It took but a few moments for a definite decision to be made and preparations for closing up business were soon under way. Then three young men started down the cañon on snowshoes, "going to war." "By the time we got down to Taos," said one of them, "Dewey had 'em all bottled up." So the three would-be soldiers did not get far on their way to battle.

From the town only a few men had gone. None, so far as the writer knows, rose from the ranks, except one Taos Indian.

The story of Joe C. Lujan stands alone. As a child, in spite of whippings, he would steal away to watch his father's sheep with a book hidden under his blanket. The little primer, which he had bought with a string of fish, he tried hard to read. He longed to go to school. Finally the governor of the Indian pueblo chose Joe as one who should be allowed to go to the government school and down to Santa Fe went a happy boy. He did well in his studies and became a leader among his friends. Then came the news that war had been declared. The boys talked it over. Joe insisted he wanted to enlist. Others followed him but Joe was the only one who really meant what he said.

"The Colonel was very nice to me," said Joe as we rode along pulling the precious two by fours needed for my new studio on the loma, for which we had gone many miles over the mountains.

"Yes, the Colonel was good to me. He asked me to come up to his room. He really wanted me to stay in school. I was catcher on the base-ball team by that time and I guess he thought I ought to keep on in school. He began by telling me all about what war meant. He had two boys of his own in the army and I guess he thought of them when he talked to me. He thought I did not understand what war was like. He told me all about the battles and the killing — all the worst side of it and then he asked me if I still wanted to go. I said, 'I know about that. I want to go!'"

"'All right, Joe,'" said the Colonel with feeling: "'You shall go.'"

So it was that Joe Lujan became a soldier and went to Fort Marcy and several other camps. He did his best in line of duty, and, hats off, you American men, to our Taos Indian who, with a background far different from yours, an education only begun along new lines, a young man who could stand his ground, make his own decision, go out into an unknown army life and come back — a corporal! Corporal Lujan!

This excursion into the white man's world led Joe east to Carlisle later. He went to work in a community, strange to him, and married a German-Swiss girl. For twenty

years Joe Lujan was, now a lead miner in Nevada and then
a carpenter in California. Down into Old Mexico he
wandered where he was appalled at the ignorance he encountered. Meantime his three daughters came and he
sent them to school. He played a man's part in a man's
world. He made. He lost. He was well. He was ill. Once
he fell hurting his head and had to be taken to the hospital
where he came under a surgeon's knife. As he lay there,
he looked up and smilingly said, " It's turn about now,
isn't it? "

Finally news came to Joe that his mother had died. An-
cestral fields awaited him. His Indian blood stirred. He
knew he must go back to his people. There was a council
and Joe left his family and came back to the pueblo. He
could stay away no longer.

Once at home, he did not want to put on the blanket
again nor let his hair grow long. For this he was perse-
cuted. He did not wish to obey the old men of the tribe
when they announced that wagons should not be used
throughout December. He harnessed his team, one cold
morning, and started for town when suddenly his wagon
fell apart. Every bolt had been removed! This angered
Joe and he appealed to the government for the right to
live his own life and wear what he wished and the Government stood by its former corporal.

Now as an older man he has more peace. He is called in
to the councils as an interpreter and a few years ago made
the welcoming speech to General Charles G. Dawes, then
Vice President. He is married to a charming Indian girl
and once in a while he heeds her importuning and stands
among his people muffled to the eyes in a blanket. Though
still not quite understood by them, he is yet one of them

and his greatest interest in life is to encourage all the little folk of the pueblo to go to school.

Joe Lujan is one of the outstanding Indians of his time but he is not the one who will reveal any secrets of his tribe though, be it said to his credit, he could not approve of a recent action of the council of the old men who burned in their presence the manuscript written with so much pains by the late Tony Romero — the only known attempt to tell the Taos Indians' own history by one of the tribe.

XXIX · AN ARTIST IN TROUBLE

SWINGING FROM THE PUEBLO BACK INTO TOWN AGAIN IN 1898, we find a Spanish flag displayed in one window of the house on the northeast corner of the plaza.

The older citizens of the town could not forget. They were not yet quite American. They rightly resented the fact that some Anglo-Saxons maintained an attitude which meant, "I am better than thou." Out on the distant ranches the resentment was undoubtedly much greater and there were rumors that the country folk intended to come in and clear out the Americans.

With ears to the ground, the Indians soon heard the mutterings. They sent word into town that they would stand by the Americans in case of trouble and added that their armed men numbered two hundred. They had not forgotten 1847 when they felt that the Mexicans had not sided with them. They were then and are now, in the main, for the Anglo-Saxons.

One after another the Indians came into town with guns under their blankets, when there was but a hint of an explosion. Several of them turned off Pueblo Road and sought the room of an artist, Bert G. Phillips. Many of them had posed for him or had raced with him and been beaten every time until they were quite sure he had owl feathers in this shoes! They were his friends, though he and Ernest Blumenschein had but recently come over the northern trail from Denver. The latter had gone back east and Phillips was to stay on until after Christmas, he thought, but, as a matter of fact, he has stayed here ever since, the first artist to make Taos his home and call for others who love brushes and color.

By December, snow had fallen and it was cold. The

twelfth came — Guadalupe Day, long celebrated by Taos folk. Bonfires lighted the way for the picturesque procession with its gorgeously arrayed santo under a canopy which was being carried through the streets.

Watching, Bert Phillips and his friend Lester Meyers stood quietly by. They were told to take off their hats. Something in the tone of voice used brought out the quick reply, " No, we wont. We have a right to stand here on the side and keep our hats on if we wish." That answer was given in challenging sound. Then some one attempted to snatch off the offending hats. In a trice, a tussle was on. Outnumbered the two had to submit to being marched off to jail where they were pushed into a cage that stood in the middle of the room. The gate was swung to and locked.

Outside anger was fed on whisky. A mob spirit was born and swept over a group of men sitting in a saloon and an adjoining room on the west side of the plaza. Luciano Trujillo, the sheriff, flourishing a gun, came unsteadily through the door. He caught sight of the boy Al Gifford and frowned as though he had a grudge against the young American. A rough remark was made. The sheriff's brother sprang on Gifford and falling under the table began firing. Snap, snap went triggers. The lights were shot out. Men fled from the room. When the smoke cleared, Trujillo lay on the floor badly wounded. Friendly hands lifted him up and carried him home.

Some one went for Dr. T. Paul Martin who soon came in. Later he was followed by the priest. Both knew the old antagonism against the American was at white heat.

" Have you got a gun? " asked the priest.

" No," replied the doctor in none too easy a voice.

" Well, I've got two," the priest said encouragingly and bulged out his pockets.

Some one in the plaza unjustly accused Gifford of having fired the probably fatal shot at the sheriff. True he had been in the room and armed. So away went the crowd bent on finding the young man.

Meantime, out from her home, had come Lina Scheurich. She was looking for her father who, she knew, had gone out with the purpose of demanding the release of the two men in jail. Fearing he had been shot she hurried along and came upon Gifford.

" I met her at the side door of the Espinosa house," said Gifford quite recently, " about forty feet up the alley, toward the Scheurich house, approximately ten minutes after the shooting took place. I took off my overcoat and hat and she and her sister threw capes over my head. I went out the back door as the mob came in the side door I had previously entered."

Sure that her young friend was safe, Lina Scheurich turned and calmly faced the angry crowd.

" What is the matter? " she asked quietly enough and waited, thereby hoping to gain a few moments for Gifford. The blood of the Bents stirred in her veins, while heedless of danger to herself she held back the mob by her questioning.

" Gifford shot the sheriff," yelled some one in the group. " We're going to search your house."

So sure was Miss Scheurich that Gifford was not there that she let them go through without a warrant urging them to help themselves to candles but the pie and cake on the dining room table caught their eye and taste. The sweets seemed to break their desire for revenge and after a mere pretense at searching they left the house.

Meantime Gifford was hiding out door and in, once under the dining room table with a washing spread out innocently enough over the near-by chairs. He remained in the house for several days unseen by any one even though at times some stranger would appear at the door on a trumped-up excuse.

Only once was there serious danger. A second mob came to search the place on that first night. Lina Scheurich heard them coming and tried frantically to find a safe place for the boy, for Gifford was but sixteen. Finally she whispered, " The well! "

Out he went into the yard and paused a moment. Then hearing a wild cry on the air, he took hold of the rope and without testing its strength slipped down into the darkness.

" I lowered myself," said Gifford, " into the well and hung suspended about ten feet above the water for twenty minutes until called. I answered and was pulled out, the well ropes holding my weight all this time."

Meanwhile over in the jail, shivering with the cold sat Phillips and Meyers in the cage. An appeal for their release, since there had been no warrant issued for their arrest, had been denied by the sheriff and it was not until he lay unconscious that the keys were taken from him. Then the cage door was swung open and the two men walked home accompanied by two Americans and one Spanish-American — Malaquis Martinez, a grandson of the padre who had befriended Americans in 1847! Does blood tell?

A few days of suppressed excitement wore away. Then came the news that Trujillo had died. He had begged those near him to accuse no one of causing his death for he said he alone was to blame. In spite of this, some of the Spanish-Americans — and at no time were the better element mixed up in this affair — declared they would find Gifford and " make sausage of the boy." A small group gathered in the plaza that night and were joined by others. With a low muttering the mob moved toward the Gusdorf store where almost all the Americans had hurried for safety.

Outside the door was a man named Harold Cobb, who, ready to lift his gun, yelled excitedly, " Shall I shoot? "

" No, you d—— fool," came quickly from Alex Gusdorf who reached his hand out and dragged him inside. This presence of mind saved the day. The mob turned as if suddenly of another mind and drifted up the dark street. Thinking that they meant to attack from the rear, the men in the store rushed back to defend that entrance. But the crowd minus a leader ceased their muttering and soon were lost in the streets.

By this time a courier, Albert Gusdorf, had ridden to the south to summon aid. United States Marshal Joe Sheldon soon arrived from Santa Fe and Gifford was safe in his hands. Then Lina Scheurich collapsed but she had lived up to the blood which flowed in her veins — this daughter of Teresina Bent Scheurich and granddaughter of the Governor Charles Bent of 1847.

Some days later the Americans demanded that two of that drunken mob known to be out on parole be returned to the penitentiary. Two others died. Bad men, both Mexican and American, left town. Law had shown its power and they fled in fear.

By January 1, 1899, a change was already perceptible. By summer, church processions came and went and no one gave orders. In a few years the saloons closed their doors. Down came the famous sign on the plaza. It was Gus Brazelton's sign with a huge snake coiled so as to make the word, " Saloon." With the passing of this came the day when men no longer carried guns and Taos became the safest small town in America.

XXX · FOREST FIRE

A NEW NATIONAL FOREST WAS CREATED IN 1906 AND IT too was to be made safe for man and beast. It was named the Carson Forest, and within its confines is the Glorieta Cañon of the Taos Indians which will remain theirs as long as the tribe lives. For this concession and the free grazing grounds allotted to them the Indians were told that they must promise aid in case of fire.

The next year, Forest Service men in bronze green uniforms rode up the cañon. One of them was stopped by the chief and told he could not proceed, but he looked the Indian squarely in the eye, wheeled on his horse and replied, " Yes, I will, I have a right to go and I will — now! " The Indian's face darkened with anger but never again did one try to molest or hinder a ranger.

It was an American who was the troublesome one. William Frazer was still living. He had for years issued spurious permits to Mexicans to go up the Hondo Cañon for wood and had thus kept the road in fairly good order for his own use as prospector. He met this same rider of the woods and demanded that he leave and desist from issuing any permits. He showed a hard face and the gun at his side hinted of trouble if he were not obeyed. But the forester listened to no such demands or covert threats. The man in green rode on and gave permits as he saw fit and carried a gun for several years, keeping a sharp lookout for the man who had threatened him and watched closely when they did chance to meet.

In all the years since there has been a Forest Service Office in Taos there has been but one fire that stirred both town and pueblo.

Late one afternoon in November 1917, a lookout, Harry
Anderson, once of the gravel pit at Etown, was high up
on Larkspur Peak which commands the Indians' cañon
for about eleven miles. He roused himself as he sat on
the rocks and squinted his eyes. One good look and he
knew that the distant thin line of wavering blue meant
smoke. Bending over a protractor near by on its rude
board table he moved the alidade until it pointed to the
fire spot. Then down the mountainside he hurried to a
telephone waiting securely in its booth. In the Taos office a bell rang. " Smoke bearing 231. Distance four
miles," came the call. " All right," came back the answer.
" We will send six men." " Six! " replied Anderson. " You
had better send sixty."

In a few moments, hurrying along Pueblo Road, went
Ranger Carroll R. Dwire on his good horse, tawny-colored
Buck. Reaching the pueblo, he sought out the war chief
who opened a huge chest of tools and three men were
equipped at once and with Dwire pushed up the cañon
for the fire, as announced, threatened the water supply
of the pueblo.

It was growing late but the men hurried up the cañon
searching for any sign of flame. For eight or ten miles they
rode. Still there was no smell of smoke nor glimpse of
the tiniest light. So the men rode back and the chief was
told twenty men would be needed in the morning. Meantime he called up the Taos office and learned that the
lonely lookout had rung in the news, " Fire spreading! "

Early, Dwire left the pueblo with five men. The others
were to follow. Into the cañon they plunged with the
knowledge that the same message was probably reaching
the home office again.

About three miles ahead at the mouth of what is now

called Burnt Ridge Cañon, smoke was seen. It was a
heavy cloud of threatening disaster, a challenge to the
five men who halted for a few words. Were there any trails
to the point? The Indians said there were none; so straight
toward the smoke the men rode breaking their own trail.

By noon, the small party were on the ground. Already
about 100 acres were ablaze or smoking where the fire
had spent its fury. A quick search was made for the cause.
Down on the creek the men found tell-tale moccasin tracks
and the remains of a camp fire where a truant spark had
started the whirlwind of red flame.

Then the fight began. Sharp orders were given. Men
hurried along clearing a fire line two or three feet wide.
From the creek eastward they worked. The group of
five was far too small. The lookout sensed what was the
matter and again he called in, " Fire spreading." The message was heeded. Forest Supervisor E. S. Barker saddled
his gray horse Chief waiting in the yard below. He found
Joe Gallegos and ordered him to gather pack mules and
find bedding, food and a cook. As soon as ready they
were to follow and make for No. 231 in the woods.

Sending ahead many tools, Barker finally dashed into
the pueblo grounds and asked, this time, for ninety men.
About four in the afternoon Barker arrived on the scene
and the fresh men took hold with a vim. Much had to be
done. Four or five miles of fire line were needed at once.
By nine o'clock, the tired men were called from their
work and the fire left to tear on its way. The men made
themselves as comfortable as possible and had to be content with the small amount of food each one carried;
the cook and supplies had not arrived and did not for
twenty-four hours, for they were lost in the thick woods
below.

Before rolling himself in his blankets that night, Dwire went out to make a survey of the whole area. He stopped at the Indian camp and asked for a volunteer to accompany him. No one moved. Then the chief passed a word or two, named an Indian and he rose quietly and left with the ranger. When plans were made for morning, all slept and the fire swept on tirelessly.

By morning, the men were up early and divided into two groups. A high wind was blowing and the need of even more men was soon evident. Over the trail to the lookout three miles away hurried a lone messenger with a note. Again the telephone wire quivered with the short message, " More men needed. Send forty or fifty by daylight."

Ira K. Cummings was a new man in the Taos office and he did not know where to get the men so sadly wanted in the mountains. He chanced to meet with the artist Herbert Dunton. He found the right man for there is none more willing to help in an emergency. The two men tried to get volunteers at a moving picture show but most of those present belonged to the stand-in-line and do-nothing brigade which prefer near-by fires. Dunton and Cummings were looking for red-blooded men. Out to Prado they went with the sheriff who, by this time, had decided to help. Here at a dance they found the men they wanted. The number required was soon counted and the time for starting named was three-thirty in the morning.

Some one mentioned the need of a guide. Then the sheriff recalled that he had locked up in the jail on some minor offense, Geronimo Mirabal, an Indian, known as Ruggles for he was wont to hunt bear with a man by that name, a so-called " hot air merchant on the plaza." Did Ruggles know the way? Of course, he did. What Indian would not? So it was agreed that the door of the jail should stand unlocked through the night. Geronimo was the first to be ready in the morning. By four-thirty the whole group were off.

On the fourth morning after the fire started these fresh men arrived just in the nick of time. The fire was gaining headway and the fighters were all but spent. Dwire said he never saw any men work harder than did the newly arrived group. Then the fire was held. The long clearing did its work. The wind subsided. The next day only a few on patrol were needed. It was not until the tenth day however that the patrol departed from the seven hundred acres of blackened tree trunks and smoldering ashes. A lazy smoke was fast being conquered by a gentle but persistent fall of snow which completed the work so many men had begun.

The Indians now understood as never before what the United States Forest Service means to them. Every year since then they have listened intently when a man in green comes to tell them what may be needed if there is another call to fight fire. They carry their tool chest over to the door of the newly elected war chief's home and he alone carries the key.

Since Taos men can fight as they did during those November days, it is small wonder that, when California called for help in its terrible fire of 1924, Taos men answered with a will.

Hard on the heels of such an event came news of the fighting overseas. Men were needed there and one after another, Taos citizens or mere boys left to join the ranks of the army sometimes with scarcely a good-by, sometimes after a dance given in their honor while people smiled to cover heartache. Now and then some one stirred the town with accusations which soberer days would never have allowed. One or two were watched and a few now regrettable affairs took place.

Red Cross work was done in the village. Artists painted range-finders and helped when the demon flu struck and carried off fifteen or twenty a day.

Out at the pueblo in July 1918, one lone Indian, back from work in an auto factory in Toledo, Ohio, visited his family before reporting at Camp Travis as a volunteer member of the 18th, the Cactus Division. After four months in the infantry Mirabal learned that there was a chance to try for the band. He made good with his clarinet and when discharged at Fort Bliss, left with the rank of second class musician. When he returned to his people he found a warm welcome but the older men did not like to see him in his uniform and Tony soon sought work in the white man's world as had Joe Lujan of an earlier day.

The whole matter of war was a good deal of a puzzle to both Indian and Mexican. One of the latter came back to discard the uniform. A "deserter," they called him but he was really only a homesick boy who could not adjust himself to the routine of army life. Without realizing exactly what it meant, no doubt, he had come home because he just could not stand it to be away. He declared he would rather die than go back.

Law is relentless in war time. So the sheriff called a posse and rode away to find the boy. They made for the desert with its clumps of sagebrush and shallow acequias.

The boy heard of the coming men and fled from his home. Hiding in the brush he could easily have picked off a half dozen men as they came toward him but he did no such thing. Instead he raised his own gun. A shot rang out and his lifeless body fell. It was death for him rather than the awful loneliness of life in the army.

Again and again, we, of Taos, have been told by the Indians that their wise men had long ago predicted the fight across the eastern water. They were not surprised when it came. One, at least, has told of guiding some Germans in the mountains years before the war and hearing them often use the word " front " after they had questioned him about the weather hereabouts.

One day, to give a personal experience, my Indian model sat wrapped in his red, black and white blanket with a gay Cheyenne war bonnet on his head. In his hands I had placed an American helmet, picked up, one raw March day in 1919, in Belleau Woods. I began to tell him about the helmet and of what had happened beyond the big water. Something too I told him of my own experiences in " Y " work down in Le Mans, Sarthe, in France when impatient men marked time waiting for boats to take them home.

A silence fell. I painted on. Finally the Indian stirred under his blanket and Joe Bernal began in broken English, " I was a boss-boss for Indians — fifty. We went to Tennessee. We work in munition plant. We stay two months and I think it helped some! "

" Yes, Joe," I answered choking a bit. " It surely did! " I knew full well that for Indians to go so far away from their pueblo, where some lost their lives with the flu, and work, day after day, meant far more sacrifice than it did for me to sail away when floating danger still lay on the high seas.

XXXI · EVENTS THE YEAR ROUND

THE STORY OF OLD TAOS MUST CLOSE WITH SOME ACCOUNT of the modern town, yet modern is not the word. It is ever an impelling age-old village, unincorporated,[1] governed by three commissioners, and still looking forward to the day when certain conveniences will be made possible in its homes.

Suppose we enter the village from the east. The wise traveler always leaves the train at Raton, takes the bus for the ninety-nine mile drive to Taos and then proceeds southward to Santa Fe. For diversity of beauty no road in the world can equal it and, thanks to the Highway Commission, it is safe and open throughout the year. Only under the most severe weather conditions in the middle of winter is the road ever closed and then for only a short period.

Flying over Taos has its thrills. Early one December day in 1923, I was skimming along overhead with the famous British ace Lowell Yerex and saw below the living map of our valley. " It's different," said the aviator, and so it really is. Straightaway runs the newly-made road to Ranchos de Taos where it bends as do all other roads leading from town. Fields lie like a great checkerboard, showing boundary lines of close red bushes or scarcely perceptible fence posts of cedar. Winding streams and irrigation ditches bind the valley with silver ribbons. Arroyos cut the distant sagebrush land into huge claws reaching up on the mountainsides which rise so intimately near and circle blue on the horizon.

[1] Taos was incorporated on January 24, 1934.

As we flew higher and higher we did not gain the level of the flat-topped hill to the east where once the sentinel watched for hostile Indians on the trail nor did we conquer old Taos Peak which seemed to lift itself with unwonted majesty, well-nigh sublime.

Below us lay the pueblo like a tiny pile of blocks, dull yellow and all but lost in the earth itself. Taos seemed but a tumbled down mass of blocks forming rectangles, disclosing placitas unknown. The pitched roofs, which mar the ancient lines of the town and loma suburb to the west, played little part in this bird's-eye view for flat roofs and squared walls mark persistent lines on the map of our village.

From Cañon, the first settlement in the valley to the east, the motorist catches sight of the long lines of the adobe town against the western sky cut with the red point of the new Catholic church which has so unfortunately replaced the fine old adobe structure of the centuries. Nearer and nearer draws the famous " mud town " — mud, it is true, but not the mud of the East. It looks like cement but much finer in surface and color, which may be broadly described as yellow.

The road takes the slight rise into town where once stood a round watch tower and a convent near by, now the studio home of E. Irving Couse. An old Spanish bell hangs over the door and flowers, wild and cultivated, half hide the place from view. Once up on Carson Street a heavy wooden door to the left attracts attention. It holds the name " Sharp." An old Penitente church shows a studio window. The cue is clear. This is a town beloved by artists.

A short distance to the right stands an old adobe house with a long portal where once Kit Carson greeted his Indian friends. Indians are even now on the road hiding under their blankets some treasures with which they mean to part across the street at the Mission Shop, built by the artist Ralph Meyers, in a yard once belonging to the Beaubien family of an earlier time.

On the plaza, the Indian is again in evidence with his face half hidden in his blanket as he watches closely the new-comers. When his errand in town is done, he unhitches his pony at the new stone wall which safeguards grass and trees of the square, mounts and is away for his home three miles northeast. Nearby, perhaps, with feet wide apart and hand holding a small paint box, an artist finishes his sketch of the now vanishing pony or some other horse patiently waiting for its owner to climb into the wagon loaded with firewood of pine and cedar or to step a bit higher into a light buggy of make forgotten in cities, with a gay striped blanket thrown over the seat.

If it chances to be a June day, perhaps the jury, through with debating in the shade, will rise and make its solemn procession back across the street to the new court-house, a two story adobe building, or a dance hall converted into a court-room. The children will pause for a moment at this strange proceeding and then call their dogs and romp again near the hollyhocks. Meanwhile, their elders will investigate the stores around the plaza, visit the curio shops or stand about the streets in the warm New Mexico sun which can sting with heat but never overwhelms for Taos is over a mile high in the air and every bit of shade affords cool relief.

If it is the Fourth of July, a horse race may be on the program. Out on the desert flats to the east the crowd will go. That over, they will gather in the plaza again where a foot race may be planned for Indian and American con-

testants. Nearby, Spanish-Americans, Indians, cowboys
in wide felt hats and leather chaps and Anglo-Saxon tourists, in the latest style or no style at all, shade their eyes
to see who wins. Then may follow an Indian dance on the
dusty street or in the grassy plot within the fence. At such
times, all sorts of vehicles line up in front of the stores
from the high powered car to the cart behind the burro.
People come and go, happy to be in town. The place is
alive. No wonder that on such a day a little girl who had
probably never been out of the valley in her life, was
heard to say " It's just like a *real* city, isn't it? "

So, too, is the town on the 29th of September, when the
San Geronimo Indian fiesta begins out at the pueblo.
Every available room in Taos, home or hotel, is made
ready and even then, car after car has to spread its tent
or make its way at night to the nearest inn in Moreno
Valley, twenty-seven miles away.

When the slanting rays of the sun play their last game
of light and shade over the irregular pile of adobe rooms
of the pueblo, Indian men, a hundred or more, come in
long lines from their estufas. One group crosses the old
bridge of squared logs down near the high yellow cottonwoods, hinting at the Midas wealth of Glorieta Cañon
just beyond. On they come to the beat of the drum and
form in double lines in front of the church door. In their
hands the dancers hold branches of green and yellow
signifying the full season of growth as well as their thanks
to the deity who made possible the harvest — the Sun,
their visible God. The drums begin to sound again and,
to the singing of the old men, the others dance their slow
up and down step out of the church gate. Around the Indian grounds they go, stopping now and then, to give
once more their " Sun-Down Dance." The stranger who

watches this age-old prayer without words, must be cal-
lous indeed if he does not join in thanksgiving, no matter
what his conception of God may be. Hard lines of belief
are swept away in a consciousness of a great unity, after
all, in what one terms, religion.

Varied are the thoughts which persist as one turns on
the headlights and runs, through the twilight, along the
road, where in the near-by bushes is here an Apache tepee
and there a supper camp fire which lights up the wheels of
a covered wagon.

At the pueblo on the morning of the thirtieth, hard
lines come to mind again as, to the tolling of the bell, a
procession moves from the church to a high leafy outdoor
shrine, where is placed an image of San Geronimo, the
patron saint of the day with its white canopy folded near.
In a flash, one is back in the days of the Spaniard with
his sword and the friar with his beads.

Below in front of the ladder which leads to the shrine,
drums sound again and aspen branches rustle gently while
runners form a semi-circle quite in the manner of the
days of the friars. Eager fellows, some young and some
older, sway their bodies, nude save for the breechclout.
Blotches of white mark their red-painted skins. Yucca is
tied to the ankles and feathers stick in the hair — feathers
for speed. Then the race begins. Away go two Indians.
Two others start at the other end of the quarter mile
course. The crowd cheers. Old men strike the runners
with eagle feathers and shout, " Om-mah-pah! " The
American translates, " Go to it! " Back and forth go the
relay racers until finally the north or the south pueblo
has won. East and west, they have run doing their " work
for the Sun," calling the Sun to do their bidding. Then in
two long lines the Indians face each other and slowly
step their way to the beat of the drums toward the eastern

Painting by Blanche C. Grant

The Sun-Down Dance

gateway in the old crumbling wall where the lines separate and the men make for their respective kivas.

Throughout the day the clan of clowns, the Chiffonetti,
clamber all over the pueblo walls and ladders, claiming
entertainment of some kind. They playfully seize some
youngster on the roofs, circle around him to his joy or
alarm, as he watches the strange fellows with faces gro-
tesquely marked with black and white and heads wreathed
with corn shucks which crackle in the wind. At three or
four in the afternoon, these men come out as a group to
laugh and cheer on one of their number who tries to
climb a huge pole at the top of which are a sheep and
bundles of vegetables which are to be used in the evening
meal. When the fellow finally makes the top, he amuses
his Indian friends with all sorts of humorous remarks
while below his clansmen go among the wagons and autos,
teasing and jollying the crowd of on-looking Anglo-Saxons
and Spanish-Americans. They argue angrily with any
greenhorn who has used his camera too freely. Once the
climbing and fun-making are over, the fiesta is at an
end for outsiders, though the Indian goes on with feasting
and singing far into the night.

As the San Geronimo crowd again fills the plaza, there
is much hunting for the tamale counter and wandering
along past the groups of visiting Indians gay in color and
jewelry or examining the temporary booths where nick-
nacks, Indian silver and pottery are for sale. Venturesome
ones try their luck at some throw which may mean possession of a gay blanket which now hangs high. This short-
lived outdoor market where people jabber in Spanish, Indian and English, is surely the echo of those fairs which
meant so much to Taos country two hundred years ago.

Some guests on San Geronimo Day seek out individual
artists. The paths lead hither and yon to the surprise of

those who have the strange idea that artists should submit
to segregation somewhere for the benefit of the traveling
public. It never seems to occur to them that doctors or
lawyers have no special joy in crowding themselves together. To those who choose the late afternoon for their
calls there is usually a welcome at the various studios
though a definite appointment always brings the best
results for both artist and visitor.

It must ever be remembered that Taos is the home of
the serious artist, not the art student or the dilettante, and
to him or her, the working hours of light are more than
precious. This, even the children know. Young and un-
taught, indeed, are they if they crowd around to watch
a painter at work, to which most artists object strenuously.
But if the artist's auto chances to get stalled on the homeward journey, they crowd around and peer in for a look
at the canvas and poke a little sly fun at him if asked,
" Well, where did all of you children come from? " by
replying, " New 'ork! "

October days bring much feverish haste in the studios
of artists who are soon to go east or west. News comes
every year that some one has won a prize. Then all Taos
plumes itself for, whether they call the artists " nuts "
or not, the townsfolk have after all a real pride in these
painter citizens.

West of the Mississippi there is no older colony of artists, and none which can boast of greater fame for some
of its number. Taos artists do not rest on their oars. They
work hard and their life business means more to them than
it does to most people. Some leave in the fall for other
painting fields and others stay on through part of the
winter when snow makes havoc with autumn color and
plays a game of its own. At rare intervals the mercury of
the thermometer goes a-mining, at night, down twenty or

The shrine at the Taos Pueblo — San Geronimo Fiesta

even forty degrees below zero for six weeks or more. Then wood fires burn constantly in the studios and work goes on just the same. Finally comes the time for boxing and expressing and on distant walls goes up a " one-man show."

" What brought you to Taos? " is often put to the artist. The valley gives the answer. Color, color everywhere! Taos Mountain is never done with its moods. Layman, as well as artist, will pause in his morning's chat to ask, " Did you see the mountain last night? It was superb! " One mood gives alpine rose while the sun sinks; another makes pure gold; another, soft in pink and blue, seems built for fairyland. When fall comes, aspen and oak give other hues, which later turn to mouse grays. Clouds hide its peak at times. Breaking lower, they drift in thin mist between the many hills and show the real design of what more often appears to be one massive mountain, guarding the valley with its adobe homes where shifting shadows mingle colors all their own.

Here are subjects with strong appeal to the matured artist — mountains, plains, deserts, Indians on horses, squaws with ollas above shawls now brilliant, now black, like those of their Spanish-American sisters in town. The younger girls have discarded the shawl, more's the pity. Then there is the low adobe house on the hillside or close to the small river where grow tall cottonwoods. Cañons abound in rocks, pines, oaks, and aspens and joy be! for the tired painter, streams there are, full of fish. Overhead is an ever-changing sky where clouds pile up in dramatic fashion, now threatening, now glorious in color. To these one must add the year-long run of picturesque events. Above all, however, is the very air vibrating with " the creative urge," the sense of the undiscovered, the time to think, to work on uninterruptedly, the time to give one's soul a chance and the time to dream!

XXXII · CHRISTMAS DAY

Dᴇᴄᴇᴍʙᴇʀ ʙʀɪɴɢs ᴏɴᴇ ᴏғ ᴛʜᴇ ᴍᴏsᴛ ᴜɴɪǫᴜᴇ ᴄʜʀɪsᴛᴍᴀs days in all the world. On Christmas Eve a crowd gathers at the pueblo. One by one many Indians go, candle in hand, to the little chapel as do the Spanish-Americans of the parish. When mass has been said, the bells toll. Around the bonfire without, boys pick up long fagots of branches and gracefully dip them in the blaze. Then they go to the dry wood piled neatly along the way of the procession which is to start in a moment from the church. Hurrying along, the boys bend their long flaming pennants and when all the piles are ablaze, they go to the river and slowly dip their torches into the water. This is hardly done before the procession, which varies somewhat every year, is on its way. First come the little ones dancing before their elders who, in turn, dance in front of the altar boys, priest and image of Mary, carried under a fluttering white sheet canopy. If it be the year for the Matachina dance, the older Indians are gaily dressed and wear high bishop-like hats decorated with all sorts of jewelry and a fringe of beads covering their faces.

This Matachina dance is far more vigorous in action than most Indian dances and at once suggests its Spanish origin in spite of the grotesque costumes. According to Dr. Edgar L. Hewett, this dance drama is " an old mystery play grafted upon an aboriginal Aztec drama which migrated north from Mexico and dramatizes the world-wide conception of the struggle between good and evil." In Taos, the Indians take three days to dance out the play.

As the Matachina dancers proceed, some who follow the procession discharge rifles, adding a real staccato to the music of the drums. Meantime, the bonfires reach their height and the air is filled with a luminous smoke, while on the top of some roofs across the river, flare up other fires. Down the old race course to the gate moves the double line and then back nearer the river and through the church gate lighted by candles placed in paper bags on each upward step of its outer form. When the santo is once again in place the church door closes. The Indians draw their blankets about them and, as the bonfires die away, scatter to their homes where feasting goes on to a late hour.

In the plaza in town, early in the evening, children gather around a community tree. The first of these was put in place in 1923. That night, up on a truck loaned by the Forest Service men, was lifted a small organ. Lamps and lanterns lighted the singers who represented everybody in town while the children munched on candy distributed at the foot of the tree. Later, a small group of the singers wandered over the town stopping here and there to give their Christmas greetings and sing old familiar carols. Others gathered for midnight mass to listen to ancient chants and, kneeling at the altar rail, kiss the small wooden image held by the priest. Above, in the snowy air, the bell rang in Christmas Day.

Very early the next morning children, bag in hand, knock at doors and expect to receive candy or fruit as presents. Occasionally some of them go about town giving *Los Pastores*, a morality play which harks back, at least, to the middle of the seventeenth century in its present language form. There are several versions of the play and undoubtedly that in Taos is one of the simplest.

It seems here to link itself immediately with the home. Good drives out bad from the very house where the players are. This, of course, appeals to the children most of whom in the role of shepherds carry flower-bedecked staffs. One little girl wears a crown and has two queer little wings on her back. She is the archangel. Two men accompany the children. One, all in red, is, of course, the Devil, while the other, with a blue coat thrown over his head, to suggest a cowl, is the good Hermit who wears a large crucifix with which he guards all from the advances of the Evil One.

One Christmas Day I stood with a small crowd outside of a neighbor's door and watched the players march back and forth to the rather mournful singing of their elders, most of whom were seated indoors. A little fellow, in a coat and hat borrowed from his older brother, no doubt, was Joseph. He carried carpenter tools strapped to his back. By his side walked the small Mary with a paper crown under her veil that refused to stay squarely in place. In her hand she carried a very small basket, in which were a few straws supporting a wee baby figure. When the singing was done, the children went inside. The Devil tried to follow but the Hermit held him back with his crucifix to the amusement of the audience who lingered without.

Indoors, the play itself began. The Good, represented as the Christ Child, was guarded by the Angel while the shepherds stood by. The Devil found a way into the home and began his pranks and mischief-making and was, of course, finally driven from the house, not, however, until he had received his pay in silver or, perhaps, a bag of flour. (Here in Taos, this part has been played again and again by the same man. He insists on his own original interpre-

Photograph by B. C. Grant

The Old Dolan Store

Photograph by B. C. Grant

Los Pastores Players

tation of his part and will not leave any house until he has what he thinks his due.) Shortly after the ejection of this Devil, the players came out and, in line, went along the streets to another home. So many years has the play been given on Christmas Day, that it creates little interest among the townsfolk, who only smile as the serious children go solemnly about their business of giving the old play. It is given first about one o'clock on December 24th but not every year.

While this is going on in town, out at the pueblo a crowd gathers to see the deer or buffalo dance. The choice of the dance is left to the governor who has announced, from the housetops some days previous, which one is to be given. The crowd is more colorful than at the fiesta in September and the dance seems more than ever Indian.

If it be the buffalo dance the Indians come from the kivas following the leaders who wear real shaggy buffalo head gear, while all the others wear horns, even to the little fellow of four or five who rejoices in wearing one horn tied over his ear. All are nude save for the clout, no matter how cold it may be. Their long black hair falls free over the back and over the face as well. In the midst of the dancers is one covered with a deer skin and head with branching horns. He is the Good Spirit come to run with the herd. Up and down the dancers move joyously with long arrows in their hands while the singers beat their drums loudly. The men are on the hunt. At a slight change in tune, the old men sing sorrowfully, while their eyes take on a far-away look of longing for the days of old. Then the dancers bend over and sway from side to side, for now they are the buffalo feeding on the plains.

The dance ended, the long lines form again and the men are away for their kivas while the Chiffonetti play

at horse with sticks shouting, " Go 'long Charlie," or
catch at some stray bit of paper. Once an old almanac
started one fellow singing " Abcd, Abcd! " So go these
funmakers at the end of the procession which is one of
the most brilliant, picturesque spectacles to be found anywhere. The Indians, gay in color and fine of figure, go
in single file, now with a background of the mountains,
now with the winter gray cottonwoods and then against
the sky until the line breaks and the different kivas claim
their men.

January sixth is King's Day at the pueblo and another
dance takes the interest. February has many dance days.
A few weeks later comes the first of the series of corn
.dances which are demands on the Sun to bless the seed,
the growing and the ripening of the corn. Meantime, in
the valley, now at Ranchos, Llano or at Talpa, usually
in February, is sometimes given a part of the old play
Los Comanchos which is above all a real New Mexico
drama. The last full performance seems to have been given
in 1923. Out on the flats beyond Llano is the place often
chosen for the play. Here is erected a square tent of sheets
attached to poles, the saint of the day enthroned within.
Near by sits a woman guarding two little children who
have been stolen by the Spaniards from the Comanches.
Their rescue is the motif of the play.

The townsfolk of the twin towns of Llano and Ranchos
take the parts of the Indians and the Spaniards, dress ac-
cordingly, and lead their horses to the field. After a series
of boastful speeches in which each chief tells how brave
he is and recites deeds of prowess, word is given for the
fight to begin. A rescue of the children is made as soon
as possible and then the Spaniards give chase to the Comanches, often racing for miles. When a capture is made,

the victor returns to the outdoor shrine. The despondent vanquished one bends over his saddle. The end of the play is always in doubt. That depends on the horses.

Then the players dance in the plaza in Ranchos and feast at night. The next day the return of the costumes, borrowed from the Indians at the pueblo, is made the occasion for a dance ceremony. So, closes the day of *Los Comanchos*, once given in many places in Northern Mexico, but now presented only at intervals in Taos Valley.

XXXIII · THE PENITENTES

MARCH BRINGS LENTEN DAYS. AGAIN INTEREST CENTERS in an old outdoor play and this time at Cañon, where a group, composed mostly of adults, presents *The Lost Child,* the story of Christ with the Doctors. Many of these actors are members of the sect known for centuries as *Penitentes.* Taos is considered the headquarters for these people who live, for the most part, in Northern New Mexico and Southern Colorado. Except for a few Indians to the south, the order is entirely of Mexicans or, as they now wish rightly to be called, Americans. They shun publicity. They are too sincere for that. They would prefer not to be mentioned in print yet they form too large a part of the present life in Taos for any historian to pass them by in silence.

No longer does the Old World, nor even Old Mexico, know the flagellantes. They exist only here — this third Order of St. Francis, the last of a long line of men who believed in public whipping and cross-bearing for self discipline. The story of the whip is a long one. Centuries ago, Egypt, Greece, Italy and Spain heard the awful swish of the rod laid on for punishment. In the Orient it is still heard. The first Christian to flog himself voluntarily seems to have been St. Pardulf, a Benedictine monk, in the year 737 A.D. Such a novelty impressed other fanatics so that by 1056 flagellation in Southern Europe was quite common.

About two centuries later the rules of the order were first published. Some of these still stand on their books. By 1349 A.D., Pope Clement VI and King Philip of

France threatened death to those who would persist in public demonstrations of their repentance. Such persecution bred converts. The sect grew. By 1535, there was a group of fanatical Protestants called Anabaptists who whipped frantically. In 1598, when Oñate started north from Old Mexico, he brought with him Franciscans who indulged in such self punishment. This has brought forth condemnation again and again from pope and bishop. Apparently, no threats of any kind from any source have ever had the slightest effect on the order in New Mexico. Taos has for many years maintained the most powerful *morado* or church.

The Easter season of the Penitentes has well been called "a carnival of penitential agony." Weight of opinion within the order itself will, in a few years, put an end to this as the real meaning of repentance comes to them. During the summer of 1924 there was sent out a command from the yearly council that there should be no scourging in public, unless it be done in the small hours of the night when no one is about. This was, of course, but the beginning of the end of this method of penance which results in several deaths every year.

In most places the Penitentes have already substituted the wooden image of the Christ for the man who used to be hung on the cross on Good Friday and often paid with his life for this honor. Even to-day, however, there are several places within a radius of one hundred miles of Taos where actual crucifixions do take place, privately as far as possible, but care is taken to spare the life of the man who impersonates the Christ. Here, in Taos, continues as in every lonely *morado*, the whipping with a scourge on backs cut with three crosses before the punishment begins. Here, too, the processions follow the penitents as they drag extremely heavy crosses along the road to the Calvary while the pito wails and rattles add to the strange music. So go these men and women who believe they should interpret literally Christ's words, " Take up thy cross and follow me."

Among the rules of the order published in 1221, A.D., most of which hold to-day, there is one which states that associates must be members of the Church (Roman Catholic), of good repute, and blameless life. Newly initiated members must restore all ill gotten goods, must renounce all evil practices and abandon all feuds and enmities with their neighbors. Wives can not be received without the consent of their husbands nor can husbands, who will not live with their families, belong to the order. There are several crimes, not often found on the court dockets, which bring condemnation and even expulsion from the ranks. The members of the order believe punishment lies in their hands and that accounts for the undeniable fact that Penitentes will rarely bring in a verdict against a fellow Penitente though he be proved beyond doubt guilty. In this, of course, they ignore the rights of the larger community. The members of the order do try to live up to their beliefs and endure much unjust, petty persecution. Far more sincere than most religious sects they surely have the right to live and believe as they will.

Among other tenets of these people is one that pain endured here helps eliminate agony in the hereafter. They believe they can vicariously assist their friends out of purgatory into heaven and accept as their duty, the care of their sick or their dead. They feel it is their privilege to present every year scenes from the Passion Week of the Christ. Some of these are given publicly. Not all are given at any one *morado*.

Penitentes

Painting by William Penhallow Henderson

On the afternoon of one Good Friday, I stood near the
Taos *morado,* out where only sage and lupins grow. From
the cross came one group of people, men with the skull
caps worn especially by Penitentes and women wearing
black shawls, while young girls added touches of brilliant
color here and there to the crowd. The leader carried an
image of Mary and paused only when the oncoming procession from the *morado* was met. Here was a slightly
larger figure of the Christ. At this meeting on the road,
the story of the journey to the cross was read in Spanish.
The one effort at dramatization was the pulling of the
string which controlled the head of the Christ figure
which then bent as if in the act of blessing Mary. Then
the two processions passed, the one continuing to the
morado and the other to the distant cross, standing bleak
against the mountain background.

To witness still another event of Passion Week, a group
of us went over to Valdez. We halted on the rim of the
deep, wide arroyo. Moonlight glinted here and there on
the patches of snow winter had left along the road which
winds down about five hundred feet. The group of adobe
houses so tiny, far below, made but a toy town. When we
approached the place, it seemed deserted. There were no
lights save at one home where the townsfolk had gathered
for a *velorio* or a wake for the saints. When they knew
who we were and that we had come in no light mood, we
were made welcome. Never will I forget the charming
courtesy shown us by the women, especially the older
mothers of the town — dear old ladies. We were invited
to enter the room where the saints were arranged against a
background of spotless white sheets — thirteen of them,
with the Christ figure in the center, richly dressed in red
satin. Before them were placed lamps which lighted up

the room and the group of women seated in silence on the floor. We, too, sat on the floor for a time, quiet and thoughtful. Without, in the next room, on benches against the wall, sat the men who sang low, sad songs.

After a while we left. No sooner were we outside than we were urged to partake of supper in an adjoining room. Here, coffee, cake and dishes rarely found on American tables, were given us and we ate, again impressed with the courtesy shown us. When the meal was over we took seats in a near-by room until it was time for us to go out into the moonlight again. About midnight, low singing came from the piñons beyond the Catholic church. Then a little yellow light showed us where a small group of initiates were slowly coming from the distant *morado*.

Once at the entrance to the room where the *velorio* was being held, they paused. The small lantern with peaked top and many holes in its rounding sides was held high and its door opened to let the light fall on the Good Book. Then was read the story of the arrest of Christ and, inside, went one man, who brought out the figure in dark red. He led the way as people walked to the near-by church. In front of the altar rail they stopped. Behind the light of only one or two lamps the large painting of Saint Anthony formed the center of the old altar decorations. Again the peaked lantern assisted the leader, who read the story of Christ's enduring the sneers of his enemies. Again only one action accompanied the reading. Christ was struck by a soldier. Slap went hands together and a Penitente leaned the Christ figure far over almost to the ground and back again. The reading finished, the crowd drifted out of the dimly lighted church which boasts of few if any seats but with odd lines suggesting the years upon years it has stood.

When out of the church yard, the people moved quietly away, some to their homes, others to the *velorio* for the rest of the night, while the small group of newly-made Penitentes disappeared among the piñons singing their way back to the *morado,* a half mile or more away. Months later I learned why those men had not come down whipping as is usual on this night. Word had been sent to the *morado* that an artist was in the group waiting for them in town. They know a painter often works from memory when back in his studio. I could not but be secretly glad that knowledge of my brushes had been the means of sparing these initiates that scourging at midnight on Good Friday, for I know something of what they had already endured — those quiet suffering fellows who went singing away into the dark.

Over to the east of Ranchos, stands another *morado,* quite alone by its graveyard. Here, on Good Friday, at three, takes place the Penitentes Passion Play. I had seen, in 1910, the beautiful conventional play at Oberammergau so falsely presented by moving picture concerns. I had seen the even more beautiful Pilgrimage Play which Los Angeles people have and do not appreciate. Here, on an American desert, I was to see the antithesis — a play that in primitive interpretation can be surpassed nowhere in the world. Again and again I looked about me. At my elbow stood a dark-skinned woman with her long, thin hand catching at her black shawl. Her lips moved in answer to the service. She was one of forty, listening to a long sermon summoning all to repentance. Finally, my thought would out and I whispered to a near-by friend, " Are we in the United States of America? "

In front of the half square which the building makes, was run a rope, supporting a sheet curtain, which did not hide from view the workers who brought out of the *morado* and placed in position a black cross, about seven feet high. On this they hung an old wooden figure of the Christ about the waist of which fluttered two aprons, pink beneath and white on top. On the head was the crown of thorns secured by corn-colored ribbon caught under the wooden beard. By its side stood a barefooted centurion, dressed in white and wearing over his cross-marked forehead, a colored turban into which was thrust a tiny American flag. He carried a spear, a pole topped with an old bayonet, with which he struck the figure in the side at the proper time in the reading. Again, this was the only effort at dramatization during the play which is in reality a service.

The reading ended, the figure was tenderly lifted from the cross and carried to the shrine of Mary, an image placed on a table near by covered with white oil-cloth. It was carried past three little girls, all in black, save for orange blossom wreaths over their flowing hair. They held a long cloth on which were three impressions of the thorn-crowned Christ head. Then the wooden figure of the Crucified One was laid in a coffin lined with artificial flowers and decorated on the outside with strips of white embroidery, which against the black suggested carving. When the peaked roof-like top was closed, the men lifted the coffin. Out from the *morado* came a young man who carried a crucifix on his shoulder. He led the whole procession. He was not in white surplice, but wore a regulation khaki army overcoat! Behind the coffin, held high on the shoulders of the bearers, followed and well-nigh staggered the fellows who had been inside the church and on whose bleeding backs we had heard the swish of the lash fall during the service. They wore their coats and bandaged their heads with colored kerchiefs. We followed after, stopped too at the cross and then watched the procession turn and wind its way back to the *morado*, singing as they went. The Passion Play of Taos Valley was over and we came back the four miles or more to town, with minds that fairly reeled and thoughts that fell back to the Middle Ages.

That night at twelve, the procession came out again. This time its members marched in single file over the mile to the Catholic church in Ranchos which is owned by them and was turned over to them for the midnight service of the *tinieblas*. On the altar are always twelve candles for the apostles. These are blown out, one by one, as the service proceeds. Then, in total darkness an unearthly noise begins, a rattling of chains, of sheets of tin, or anything that helps create a terrifying din. Moans of penitent ones add the human voice to the sound. To the outsider this is all inexplicable but to the Penitente it represents the earthquake which rocked the earth when Christ died on the cross. The Penitentes suffer with Him. The night wears away and morning hours bring peace to the agonizing ones. Easter Day closes the week with cheer and joy for, beyond the Hell made on earth lies Heaven. The wailing of the *pito* or the sad songs are heard no more save at such times as a wake is held for the dead or during a funeral procession when those standing in the wagon bearing the coffin, lift their voices again in a doleful cadence, unmistakably that of a Penitente song.

When the nights of the swaying lantern on the various Calvaries of the Penitentes are over, the days of long twilights begin. Spring air and rains give life to plum blossoms on the way to the pueblo and cottonwoods change their dull white for shimmering green. Out on the desert the sagebrush awakes and during a shower sends out over the country a delicious odor to assure all it is quite alive even though it lives on waste land. Lupin shows its green too. Arroyos fill with water coming down from reluctant mountains forced to part with snow. Once, in a great while, this water forms a wall which moves down these jagged cuts in the earth with great power, sweeping up unwary sagebrush and clearing away refuse and sometimes uncovering old ollas or arrowheads and stone axes which the Indians are sure rain down from heaven. Most beautiful of all desert plants, the wild rabbit-brush, often called incorrectly " greasewood," lifts its gray green and prepares for its lovely yellow blossoms. It is well named, for the days are coming when the rabbit will hide in its shade, hide for its life, for feast days are at hand.

Before the various saints' days, Indians mount their horses and, bow and arrow in hand, cheer as they leave the pueblo on a rabbit hunt. Out across the plains to the west they go. A shout soon tells of rabbits found. Then circling round and round, the Indian horsemen close on their game. When once they have what they want, they swing into town on the lower Ranchito road, whooping it up as they go, urging on their horses and fairly fly through the plaza with their rabbits bouncing against their saddles as they make for their pueblo homes.

When May third returns, the Indians repeat San Geronimo Day in reality, though another saint now has the honor. The men race again and, on this day, the very little fellows run too. Since there are fewer Americans about, the fiesta seems much more Indian.

A few weeks later, in town, the Corpus Cristi procession makes it way around the Guadalupe Church. Where once there were many such processions, this is now the only one which one sees in town. Sometimes small pine trees are brought from the hills and "planted" along the way of the people who form in a long double line after those who carry the host under an elaborate canopy followed by the priest, also under a canopy, clad in unusual vestments. A pause is made in front of three out-door shrines. These are usually on portals made ready with rugs, lace hangings and pine trees to receive the santo and supply an appropriate place for the priest to hold a short service while all along the line, one by one, each communicant sinks to the ground to pray.

June and July bring several corn dance days of the Indians when they pray for the success of their harvest and look forward to their annual fiesta again. The two remaining months of the year keep many of them posing for the artists for our summer clouds form a dramatic background for the mounted Indian while yellowing aspens against sloping mountainsides send the painter with his model far from the town.

So rolls the year around with ever-recurring, fascinating events.

XXXIV · THE CELEBRATION IN 1925

ONE EVENT WHICH BROKE THE ROUTINE OF LIFE IN THE old town was the celebration in 1925 of the centenary of the coming of the covered wagons.

The morning of the twenty-ninth of September of that year came sharply clear and sunny over the valley. The plaza, heart of the one-time trading post, was unusually quiet with the hush of expectancy. It was the day when wagons were again due over the old trails, one caravan from the north supposedly from the Old Taos Trail and the other from the Bent's Fort Trail to the east.

Just at nine, blue-coated, dark-skinned men mounted the bandstand in the midst of yellowing cottonwoods in the village square and with the sweep of the leader's baton the day of the covered wagons was on. Music held the eager, waiting crowd which began to gather and make inquiries. Still there was no news of the wagons. Would they end their supposedly long pull over the dangerous trails, to-day?

Shortly after ten, a runner, with the old valley name, Martinez, came rushing into town, breathlessly announcing that the wagons were coming!

Away went the crowd, band and all to stand under the long line of autumn-tinted trees shading the end of the trail from the north. Far down the old road, the wagons were curving in, one by one.

Through the flickering light and shade with a glimpse of blue mountains as a background, came the first caravan led by a horseman who was none other than Kit Carson, a grandson of the famous scout. He wore a fine, old buckskin suit, once the gift of Chipita, wife of Ouray, chief of the Utes, to Thomas Tobin, another Taos scout and maternal grandfather of the rider. Stuck in his belt were two pistols, one of Tobin's and the other, one of the now famous Brevoort pistols presented to the first Kit Carson for bravery on the trail. With splendid dignity, the Christopher Carson of to-day, not of Taos but of Walsenburg, Colorado, rode his proud horse. As he lifted his wide felt hat to the crowd, his face strikingly recalled that of his illustrious grandfather.

Behind the leader came swaying along the road a yoke of oxen, — only one, an ox however — drawing a two-wheeled cart with spoke sides, in which sat an old-timer who once knew the trails. Then followed wagon after wagon, made to look like those of old, as far as possible. A slow-moving caravan it was and, in spite of smaller wagons, so much more like the real trains of long ago that the memory of a famous moving picture featuring the covered wagons faded badly in the light and shade of the old Taos road.

High on its seat, a driver, in old clothes, brought in a real Conestoga, once actually used on the trails from Missouri. A wooden plow was tied on the side of a second wagon. A spinning wheel was in the darkened interior of another and a grindstone of make long forgotten was visible through the grimy sheets of still another wagon as it rattled along its way. Old guns played their part in the procession whether caught on the side ready for use or held on the lap of one lone woman driver with her cotton dress and sunbonnet or in the hands of several who, having caught the spirit of the day, trudged along as mountaineers.

Thrills there were a-plenty for the watching crowd but

greatest of all came from the sight of Lena Scheurich, granddaughter of the first American Governor of New Mexico, dressed in a beautiful old gown and crowned by a white mantilla. By her side sat Mrs. José Montaner, a granddaughter of old Padre Martinez, also in elegant dress and black mantilla. They were but two of many who peered out of the wagons at the crowd and helped them to live for the moment in the long ago.

To the Spanish and American music of the Santa Fe band, the first of the caravans moved slowly into the plaza. Old weather-beaten wagon sheets, lean horses, long swinging whips and the creaking of the wagons certainly bespoke the days of the trail trade, even if there were historic inaccuracies as far as the days of 1825 were concerned. There was much of the weary effort of tired followers of the trail about the whole train which gripped those who to-day may follow caravans only through books. There was enough of the picturesque to keep the artist alert and the man with a camera working overtime. The whole town awoke as out of a long Rip Van Winkle sleep.

About an hour later, the second train pulled in from the east, with a leader under an immense Mexican sombrero and gay serape hanging from his shoulder. Behind him came an even longer caravan than the first with special features, such as a burro-drawn wagon and groups of costumed townsfolk. Upon its arrival in the plaza, preceded by the band, it joined the other and thirty-seven wagons rolled around the plaza several times and then out the shady lane we know as Pueblo Road.

In the afternoon, the Santa Fe band, willingly working overtime, woke the town from its siesta. Then came the announcing of the winners of the best wagons. The judges, all old men who had actually driven across the plains in

Parade at the Centenary of the Coming of the Wagons, 1925

other years, gave the first place to the bull-whackers and their oxen, the second to the real Conestoga, the third to still another high-built wagon.

Again music broke the quiet of the plaza and to Indian music up went the first flag of the country, a deer-skin on a pole held by an Indian. To a change in tune, the yellow and red of the Spanish flag slowly unfolded, then the green, white and red of the Mexican banner. Next rose the red, white and blue of the flag of the United States and last of all, the recently made yellow and red state flag was pulled up under the stars and stripes to float against the blue of our southern sky as the band played, " My Fair New Mexico."

After a short intermission, the band led the way to the grassy base-ball grounds where automobiles formed a circle and within, the Santa Clara Indians in splendid costume gave their war dance, and as the Taos Indians failed to give one of their dances at the last moment, the Santa Clara Indians danced again. Then followed a dance by some little Taos girls under the direction of Leona Read.

Just as the sun was setting, the crowd gathered again and this time at the pueblo to see the Taos give the sundown dance, their old-age prayer to the God of the harvest. The full run of the seasons of that year of 1925, as of the year, one hundred years ago, was suggested by the green and yellow leaves of the aspen branches the Indians carried as they stepped through the church gate and danced around their grounds.

In the early evening, the band was again in the plaza, playing popular airs until the fandangos were to begin in the various halls. The most splendid of these, in point of costumes, was that held in the Montaner Hall. A gorgeous array of Spanish shawls and old-time brocades surprized the merry dancers as they sped their way through the last hours of " Covered Wagon Day."

The next day, the thirtieth, the usual Indian fiesta took place at the pueblo with races and dances after the manner of centuries ago. The story of a San Geronimo Day need not be told again here but that of the evening's event must be attempted. The word *attempted* is used advisedly for no account of that beautiful Indian encampment in Taos Cañon can be adequately given.

Against the darkening piñon-spotted, rocky side of our cañon, yet low by the Rio de Don Fernando, reflecting the flash of bonfires, were pitched three tepees soon lighted on their left by the rising moon. Here wandered Taos and Santa Clara Indians, gay in color, now eating from the great caldron of boiling meat, now throwing wood on the fires or standing inside a tepee, allowing their shadows to fall on walls yellow from an inner glow. Striped blankets and bright skirts caught high light from the bonfires or darkened softly against the farther tepees, while, now and then, flute notes broke the moon-lit silence of the cañon.

One fire fell to embers but two others flashed high. The light from one automobile was allowed to bring into silhouette the audience gathered across the stream, waiting.

On a natural stage near the tepees, where grew low *chamisa,* stepped out Tony Romero, a well-known Taos Indian, and announced the Eagle Dance by the Santa Clara men. One dance after another followed in this setting more perfect than words can tell. No motion picture has ever portrayed Indian life as picturesquely as this small encampment arranged by the Taos artist, Ralph Meyers, and carried out by New Mexico Indians.

Even after the Taos spokesman had told the audience, " Now you can go back to town and do as you please," many were reluctant to leave the blazing fires and the darkened tepees. They lingered on to watch the Indians throw their blankets about them and mount their ponies and splash through the little river or climb into wagons to start their homeward way. Then the hush of a sleeping camp stole over the deserted tepees and, though bonfires fell apart, glowed red and died, the moon kept faith high on its course and watched throughout the clear autumn night while gentle winds stirred the yellow aspen leaves in the midst of the stolid dark of pines on the hills.

So closed the last event of the fiesta of 1925 in Taos, which is still the land of the covered wagon, even though the full cycle of the years of a century is finished.

XXXV · THE TAOS ART COLONY

Now for one of the greatest factors in the development of the modern town of Taos, the art colony. It will be possible to write only of those who formed the real nucleus and limit our time by the year 1920.

We know of the coming of the Kern brothers in 1848. They hailed from Philadelphia. Earlier in the forties, Richard seems to have been an instructor at the Pennsylvania Academy. Of his own work there is apparently no record. Of his brother's, we have this from Richard when he wished to withdraw in favor of Edward as a member of an exploring party under John R. Bartlett, "Permit me to recommend my brother, Edward M. Kern," wrote Richard, "as one every way qualified to fill my place. In topographical, botanical and natural history delineation and portrait painting he is my superior."

From the time of that Fremont expedition on to 1880, there is no record of any artist having been at work in Taos, though there is a legend that a Frenchman with brushes found the place, before that year, which brought Montgomery Roosevelt. He did not tarry long. The following year Colin Campbell Cooper wandered into the village. During the one night he spent at an old inn, some men came riding in and shot up the town. That was too much for Cooper and he left. In 1888, Henry R. Poore was painting here. Five years later came Joseph Henry Sharp who was so entranced with the country and its possibilities for the American artist that, when he returned to Paris, he talked enthusiastically about the old adobe town in the Southwest of the States.

Henry Sharp did not stay in Taos in 1893 but did return in 1902 and, in 1908, purchased the old Penitente church and near-by house which he occupies to-day. Since he is the eldest of the colony we will write of him first.

Born in Bridgeport, Ohio, Henry Sharp's strongest childhood memories are not so much of that village as of a farm home, a few years later, near the Kanawha River in West Virginia, where he heard stories of Indian warfare and played at being Indian. It was here too, that he stood beside his mother's chair and watched her with her brushes. Though fascinated by this, he was also keenly interested in music and even made some of his instruments; but Henry Sharp was not to be a musician. His goal lay in another direction.

School days in Ironton, Ohio, were brought to an abrupt close on account of growing deafness. Then young Sharp boarded a steamer and went down to Cincinnati. He obtained work as a water boy during the day but evening found him trudging six miles to an art school where he was successful enough to warrant his leaving for Europe. He returned to Cincinnati but not for long for in 1886 he sailed again and, this time, to spend two years in Munich, where he studied with Carl Marr and Nicholas Gysis. On his home-coming, he was appointed a teacher in the school where he himself had studied but, after a few years, he was once more on the high seas and bound for Paris and classes under Laurens, Constant, Courtois, and Girardot. He was soon exhibiting at the Salon.

Tramping through Europe was a joy to him in those days as was also his visit to Spain with Frank Duveneck. Traveling through the States, up the coast to Alaska, as well as wandering over Indian country took much of his time. He lived and painted, however, among the Crow Indians for several years.

In 1892, Sharp married Addie Byram of Liberty, Indiana. She passed away in 1913 and two years later he married her sister, Louise Byram, who presides as a most genial hostess over the Sharp home, on Camino del Cañon in the eastern part of our village.

Many are the canvases of landscapes, as well as of Indians in ceremonials, at work, at play or signalling to others, which bear the name of J. H. Sharp, who paints on, though the years are many since he first felt the lure of paint and brushes.

Though Sharp saw Taos first, it was Bert G. Phillips who was first to stay and make the old town his home and set up a mental broadcasting station, urging others to come.

As a boy, in Hudson, New York, he stood by his father's side and watched eagerly while he drew all sorts of pictures for him and then gave him the pencil. By eleven, Bert Phillips knew he wanted to be an artist and, at sixteen, he was allowed to go down the river to study at the National Academy of Design and later he became a student of Benjamin Fitz at the Art Students League.

Phillips was already interested in Indians and when asked how that came about he replied, " It was that arrowhead more than anything else, I suppose." That treasure was found on an old battlefield and led to more reading of Fenimore Cooper's novels so that he was thrilled through and through and the love of Indian lore and romance has never left him.

After studying in New York, for a short while, Phillips left for Paris and the Academy Julien where he studied with Constant and Laurens with whom he worked in composition. Here he found there was another student bringing in pictures of American Indians. He sought him out and thus began a life-long friendship with Ernest L. Blumenschein.

On their return to New York, the two shared the same studio for two years and then, since both had the urge to go west, they started out. On reaching Denver, they bought a wagon and horses and began the long trek into the Southwest, expecting to go through to Old Mexico. An accident made a halt necessary. A coin was tossed and the lot fell to Blumenschein to ride on with the damaged wheel, " the heaviest wheel on record," to quote the man who brought it into town. When Blumenschein rejoined Phillips he had much to say for he had found a wonderland and soon they were slowly making the last lap of their journey into Taos.

Here the young men began to work feverishly for was there ever a land more inspiring? Three short months flew by and Blumenschein had to pack up and leave for the East but Phillips decided to stay on until after Christmas, little dreaming that he was to remain for decades, marry the young doctor's comely sister, establish a home by remodelling an old *morado* on Pueblo Road and become, by dint of staying, the founder of a famous art colony.

His work has ever been of Indians. One does not forget Star Road, perched on a rock, playing his flute in the moonlight nor the young Indian gazing at symbols of the past or standing under aspens, nor the Mexican musicians, in which the artist caught the rhythm of the old song, " Adelita." Fine in color and design, hundreds of Phillips's pictures attest to his love of his chosen motifs.

Now for his friend, Ernest L. Blumenschein. He was

born in Pittsburgh, Pennsylvania, and destined to be a violinist, had his father had his way, but a class in illustration made him hang his violin on the wall and begin serious work in art. This was not until he had finished high school.

During his teens he was especially interested in tennis and chess. In the latter, he nearly won the state championship when he was but seventeen. Then too he often sought an easy chair to laugh heartily over jokes he found in " Puck," " Judge " or " Life " taking special pleasure in the work of a certain artist called " Zim." Finally he established and illustrated a high school newspaper and, all who know Blumenschein's love of fun and keen sense of humor will smile when they learn that the name of that fifteen cent per annum paper was " *Tomfoolery*."

Study at the College of Music did not last long for Fernand Lungren had become Blumenschein's teacher in composition and the young man decided he wanted to be an artist. The father, a musician of note himself, was almost broken-hearted for he had longed to see his boy a violinist of the first rank but he wisely consented to send his doubly talented son to the Art Students League.

In New York, Ernest Blumenschein made good; then Paris beckoned. When the young artist was but twenty-two, he decided to return home and make his own living; so he came to New York. " Half an hour after I landed in New York," he said, " dressed in the corduroy suit and flowing tie of the style of the Paris art student, I had my first commission." This was from Scribner's and was the beginning of ten years' work as an illustrator, using only black and white until he almost lost his color sense. Surely no one who ever saw them will forget the illustrations made by Blumenschein for Jack

Group of Taos Artists

Upper — E. Martin Hennings, Bert G. Phillips, Victor Higgins, Ernest L. Blumenschein, Joseph Henry Sharp
Lower - Walter Ufer, E. Irving Couse, Oscar E. Berninghaus, W. Herbert Dunton, Kenneth Adams

London's story, "The Love of Life." These helped make both men.

"Every time I had $3000 saved, I went to Paris," said the artist and, by 1900, though he was still doing work for *Harper's*, *McClure's* and *The Century* magazines, he became intrigued with color. His interest was growing in 1904 when he met Mary Shepard Greene of Brooklyn, New York, who had already won laurels at the Paris Salon. A year later they were married and four happy years went by. Then the time came when, as Blumenschein puts it, "There seemed to be but two places in the world for me, Paris and Taos." In 1909, the latter place won. Blumenschein visited the friend he had left behind over ten years before. Then he went back to New York but each year saw him again coming in on the stage until, in 1919, he persuaded his wife to come to Taos to live and they bought a home on old Fernandez de Taos Street which overlooks the plains and mountains.

Blumenschein has painted many a now famous picture. He calls on the Indian and the Penitente to act as models and glories in giving his own reactions to landscapes.

Going back to the year after the arrival of Phillips and Blumenschein, we might have seen a young man riding on top of a freight car so as better to see the landscape. He came to Taos and was courteously received by Bert Phillips after he introduced himself as Oscar E. Berninghaus of St. Louis.

His is a colorful story of an odd boy — he says himself he was different from all his family — listening to tales of Indians and drawing them and even playing at pageantry on the floor. He now directs the great pageant of the "Veiled Prophet" every year in St. Louis. As a child he wandered down to the Mississippi River to kick his heels against a wharf while he watched men load the steamers and pull away, bound south.

As he grew older, there was much hard work for the boy. He learned to do lithographing and worked at all sorts of jobs, having but a term or two in an art school but being fortunate in knowing the artist, Richard Miller. The time finally came when the wanderlust was too strong upon him. Then he found Taos and every summer after 1899, Berninghaus came to paint during his vacation. It is about a dozen years since he purchased a house on the loma and now spends most of his time there.

Berninghaus is noted for paintings in which the mountains around Taos almost always play an important part and against this background are usually groups of Indians, colorful as any palette can make them.

Next to come and, in 1909, buy a home, the old convent rooms adjoining those of Sharp's home, was E. Irving Couse who hailed, as a boy, from Saginaw, Michigan.

Many were the hardships Couse had to endure as he strove toward his goal. Painting carriages and teaching drawing would net a few dollars which would be spent studying first at the Art Institute and then in New York with frequent visits to Saginaw to make more money. Finally he was bound for Paris and there lack of money brought distress but his indomitable will won out and Couse began to exhibit and sell. Then he married Virginia Walker, also a student in Paris.

One trip back to the States took him to Portland to paint but Europe called persistently and the young couple went across the water to France, this time to Etaples. Some years passed, and then Couse began to believe that Americans should paint in their own country and finally back to Oregon he came in 1895.

Now he began to paint Indians. " I always wanted to paint Indians," admitted the artist, " One of my earliest experiences was visiting the Chippewa near Saginaw and one of my first attempts at painting was of an Indian dance." This desire, so long dormant, came to the fore and Couse hunted out the Clickitat and Yakima Indians near the Columbia River.

After a period of constant trouble with the Indians over posing, Couse recalled hearing Blumenschein talk of northern New Mexico. He knew that Bert Phillips was there and so he set out to arrive at the nearest station about thirty five miles away in a wintry blizzard though it was late in June. This experience sent his spirits down to near the zero mark but they rose again when Phillips's genial welcome made Couse want to live in Taos and so down on Ranchito Road a house was found, a skylight put in and work begun.

" I still painted Brittany scenes and the like for the market for no one wanted Indian pictures then," Couse said as he recalled his earliest days in the village. Then an Indian stooping at his work by a fire-place caught Couse's eye and he began to make paintings of such. It was a happy fancy and success followed.

Couse says his first successful picture was " The Historian." For this he used a small boy as model and now he paints the same model as a man. He keeps his interest steady on the home life and traditions of the red man and his records in color will live on after the Indian, as a race, has disappeared forever.

When asked when he began to draw, Couse said quickly, " Oh, I always drew." So it was with W. Herbert Dunton who came to Taos in 1912. " Mother used to say I began making pictures before I could hold a spoon," and he went on to say that his mother had kept a book full of his childhood drawings. "You can always tell when I went to the circus. The drawings are most absurd with the man drawn bigger than the elephant."

His pencil was rarely out of his hand. At sixteen, Dunton decided he had had enough of school and so he announced, one day, that he was going to work at a store in his home town of Augusta, Maine. He added quite positively that he was later going to Montana. "Why Montana, I don't know," smiled Dunton.

After two years at the store, during which time Dunton had made extra money writing sporting notes for he knew wood-lore well and could make drawings to illustrate his work, the young man set out for Boston where he entered the Cowles Art School and came under the influence of Joseph De Camp and Walter L. Taylor. Later he studied with Fred Yohn and Frank Dumond.

Then the time actually came when Dunton " with a Winchester and a few things in a bag " started for Montana. "I went until my money gave out and got off the train at Livingstone, I believe. It was not long before I met a young hunter and was off into the wilds." Then followed the first of many experiences with cow out-fits which eventually took him into Old Mexico. Summer time was for such; winter called the young illustrator back to New York. At last, the day came when Dunton jumped into the limelight for cow-boy pictures were in demand and he knew that life better than any one in the metropolis.

Dunton was not destined to be an illustrator all his life. He was to be a painter. One day, he met Blumenschein at the old Salamagundi Club and received the encouragement he needed. He joined Blumenschein's class

at the Art Students League and the two often talked of
Taos. The following summer Dunton came into town to
stay and, through the years since, he has become noted
for his paintings of old-timers and especially of wild
animals in their forest haunts.

Two years after Dunton's arrival, in 1914, Victor Higgins bought a ticket in Chicago for the Southwest, not
knowing exactly where he would settle, but he too found
Taos.

Higgins was born near Shelbyville, Indiana, and was a
member of a large family. Fortunately his parents kept a
sharp look-out for the natural bent of each of their children and early found that the boy Victor loved to paint.

" I know my father must have been amused. I was always wanting to paint something. The smell of paint
electrified me. I was too small to paint the house so I
decided I wanted to paint the family carriage. So, father
said, if I must paint something I could begin on an old
buggy in the yard. That done, I painted everything even
to wheel barrows and the chicken coop. Everything to
which a coat of paint was not detrimental was painted,"
said Higgins smiling.

At school, having obtained some charcoal, he made
drawings from the wood-cuts he found in one of his
books and had the joy of seeing them hung on the wall,
a real event in any lad's life.

One day, on his way to school Higgins found a painter
at work on a huge signboard at the cross-roads. He forgot
about lessons and sat down to watch and later reported
his truancy to his parents, who, instead of scolding him,
allowed him to spend several days watching the painter.
Naturally, the man, John Cornelius of Indianapolis, began to take notice and finally talk with the boy and be-

came so much interested in him that when he came back from Indianapolis, one day, he brought a package. This he opened. It was a paint box and to the boy's surprise, the big man handed him the key and gave him the box, telling him to take care of it and remember him. Higgins of to-day has not forgotten that disappointed, would-be artist Cornelius and his message to him, " Art is a wonderful thing, my boy."

When the time came for Victor Higgins to leave home, he bought a ticket to Chicago, much to the surprise of his father, but that was where he wanted to go. Once in the great city, Higgins found the Holmes Art School, then the Academy of Fine Arts and finally the Art Institute. He had to earn money; so after school hours he sought out various theaters and timidly asked if he might have a chance to work. For several years he continued to do oleos and " front stuff " until a colleague asked him why he did not go to New York. That was enough. Higgins went to the greater city. There in turn he received another push forward by the famous draughtsman Bridgman and the young man was soon aboard a steamer bound for Europe. He wandered from place to place studying now under Rène Menard and then under Lucien Simon or Hans von Hyeck, ending by becoming a student in Munich and meeting the two men he was to know years after in Taos, Ufer and Hennings.

Upon coming to Chicago once again, Higgins knew that he wanted to go west. His chance came soon and so he rolled into Taos in the stage. Here he has remained, except for occasional trips east, and here his fame has grown.

Higgins' paintings show a great variety of subjects which belong to this country. Of his work, he once said,

" I try to get at the basic meaning of a picture. I know the old in art is a closed book. Cezanne opened a new book. I used to think they had overestimated Cezanne until, one day, in the Brooklyn Museum I saw a small still life, eight by ten, by that artist and then I knew in a flash what it was all about." Rhythmic form is one of his special aims in painting as well as fine color and Higgins gets both.

Not long after Victor Higgins had found this haven for artists, there came another, Walter Ufer.

His story begins back in the late sixties when, one fine day, a sturdy German of the Rhineland and his wife walked leisurely along a country road or in some such manner were safe across the Belgian border. Then Peter Ufer's knitted brow smoothed out. Like many another honest German, his ideas had clashed with those of the all-powerful Bismarck and he felt he could no longer breathe the same air. He sought freedom in the United States and was soon on his way across the water and on to Louisville, Kentucky. Here he found work as a gun-smith, and spent many hours cleverly decorating the long barrels and stocks of the guns he made. Here his son and chum Walter Ufer was born.

When only a very small boy, Walter Ufer began to draw on the backs of the handbills which, in that day, were tossed about the yards. Engines and steamboats he had seen and these he drew. Before his time to study geography he was making maps on the blackboards at school. In telling of the experience Ufer's hand went out as if to draw the maps again and glancing up over his glasses he said, "The funny line of Kentucky interested me."

Meantime the father had begun to give his young son lessons in drawing, " the first and, I believe, the best I ever had," said the artist. Later he spent his Sunday mornings studying the principles of perspective with William B. Clarke who had been a pupil of Meissonier in France.

By the time he was twelve, Walter Ufer was self-supporting. He lighted street lamps and carried newspapers as many a boy has done. Never too strong physically, the boy often had to visit a Dr. Schackner who became interested in him after he had seen his drawings and took him into his office to work for him. Soon a friend of the doctor's, A R. Sutton, noticed the young artist and wanted to send him to Europe but Peter Ufer could not consent to his son's leaving him quite so early. So Sutton remembered that he had many casts of famous marbles in his storeroom and these he ordered unpacked and put at the disposal of Walter Ufer whom a niece of Sutton's, a Miss Rawlston, gave strong, vigorous guidance and encouragement a-plenty.

Ufer entered high school but, after four months, he felt he should leave and make money. He found work in the lithograph department of the *Courier Journal*. Here he met a Johan Jergens, a very skilled workman, who later returned to Hamburg and wrote to Walter Ufer to come to Germany and study with him.

After many long arguments, the young man, now seventeen, was allowed to start out alone for New York and Hamburg. Five busy years went by but not all that time was spent in Hamburg for Ufer wandered south and finally settled in Dresden where he studied at the Royal Academy for three years. Then requests to return home which came from his parents were too many and he left for Louisville where he became special artist for the *Courier Journal*.

Real opportunity seemed to lie in Chicago, however,

and there he went and worked as a free lance, married Mary Frederickson, an artist of Danish parentage, and again left for Europe in 1911. This time, it was to Munich, he went and accomplished much. Two years later he returned to Chicago and opened a studio for himself. Not long after this his big chance came, as it had to Higgins and he set out for the Southwest and Taos. By 1916, Ufer began to win prizes with canvases presenting Indians, still life of strange things and subjects, symbolic and even ugly, but always painted well and drawn with great skill.

In 1917, Carter H. Harrison of Chicago, who had given both Higgins and Ufer the opportunity to come to the Southwest, hunted out the studio of E. Martin Hennings and showed him pictures of the country and soon this young man was on his way too.

Hennings was born on a small farm near Penn's Grove, New Jersey, of parents who had come across the ocean from Schleswig-Holstein. Two years later they all moved to Chicago. Here, as the young son grew, teachers gave encouragement and even called on his mother to tell her of her boy's talent and urge her to allow him to study art. She was more than willing and has remained through the years his stanchest ally.

One memorable afternoon, Hennings and a friend went to the Art Institute. The two boys wandered through one room after another. To one, the visit meant little; to the other it meant his very life. " It must have stirred me emotionally," said the artist, when speaking of that experience. " When we came to the desk I found folders about the art school and looked them over. When I left the Institute, that afternoon, I had already made up my mind to become an artist."

Hennings entered the Institute, gained special recognition in his classes, finally winning a traveling scholarship of which he did not avail himself as he wished to take up commercial work. This soon palled on him and in 1912 he presented himself as a candidate for the Prix de Rome. Eugene Savage won but Hennings was a close second. Not discouraged, he made ready to go to Europe at once and straight to Munich he went where he studied with Walter Thor and later entered the Royal Academy to be under Angelo Junk.

In the summer of 1914, Hennings set out on a tour of seventeen cities to visit museums and when he reached Frankfort he knew for a certainty that the war was on. Excitement was running high. Nightly in cafes, the national air was being sung with a vim. Hennings was warned to be on his way if he wanted to go any special place so he returned to Munich where he found the belief strong that the war would not last more than three months and so he settled down to study with Franz von Stuck. He worked on. The war was not exactly a real thing to him and, in 1915, Hennings decided he would like to go to Paris, little thinking that he would not be allowed to go and that, in a short time, he would be more than glad when the Washington authorities made it possible for him to return home by way of Holland.

When Hennings arrived in Chicago, the war was going strong and the work, at hand, for him was to assist the Red Cross with posters and wait for the second call for soldiers but that never came so in the summer of 1919 he was free to go a-painting and he went to Gloucester by the sea. The following winter, however, Hennings was given a second chance to come to the Southwest and by spring he was on his way to become a member of the art colony in Taos where, except for visits to Europe or Chicago, he has worked ever since, painting Indian subjects, fine in color as well as strong in drawing.

Such in brief are the stories of the artists, now living, who were here in 1920 and whom I have been privileged to know personally. There are, however, two others who should be mentioned. One is Frank Sauerwein who was here in the early days and lived on Pueblo Road for several years, though his health forced him to be away from the high altitude part of the year. He did some splendid work in both water color and oil. The other is Julius Rolshoven, who died in Florence, Italy, several years ago. He was living in Taos during the years around 1910 and painted many striking canvases of Indians with a princely sweep of his brush. Rolshoven was an active member of the Taos Society of Artists. As one of the members of the Society has said, the associate members did much, not only for the group but for Taos itself. Among them were the following well-known artists, John Sloan, Robert Henri, George Bellows, Albert Grolle, Gustav Baumann, J. B. O. Nordfelt, Birger Sandzen and Randall Davey.

The year 1920 turns on the calendar and with it a line must be drawn. It was that year which brought me to Taos with my brushes. Two years later, Bert G. Phillips, who had followed my work as editor for a brief period, of the local newspaper, still carrying the subtitle, *El Crepúsculo*, encouraged me to try my pen further. Now the temptation is strong to use that to write of my friend, Catharine Carter Critcher of Washington, who arrived soon after I did, and became, three seasons later, the only woman member of the Taos Society of Artists, formed in 1914 and disbanded some time ago.

All I may say of her is that her story is as colorful as any I have written — struggle, recognition in Paris as well as in this country, and final attainment of a rank, equal or beyond that of most men painters of whom Taos boasted in 1920.

Mindful one must now be of those who have passed on — Frank Sauerwein, lover of fine color, Julius Rolshoven, of the princely brush, Burt C. Harwood, vitally interested in good composition and the Indian motif, Linley M. Tonkins, collector as well as painter, and D. H. Lawrence, who spent most of his brief time in New Mexico, about eighteen miles away from Taos, and left records of both pen and brush which were inspired by this land of impelling beauty.

The list of well-known painters, other than those already mentioned, who live in the old village, is long and includes such as Nicolai Fechin, Leon Gaspard, Mary Greene Blumenschein and her daughter Helen, Mary Ufer, Elizabeth Harwood, who established the Harwood Foundation, Frank Townsend Hutchens, Joseph A. Imhof, Joseph Fleck, Kenneth Adams, Ward Lockwood, Charles Berninghaus, Elinora Kissel, Gene Kloss, Ila McFee Turner and Elmer P. Turner, Dorothy Brett, Evelyn E. Cheetham, Caroline Culbert, Mary Lou Thomas, Frank Hoffman, Ralph Meyers, Duane Van Vechten, La Verne N. Black and John Young Hunter. Occasionally, one sees color from the brush of Mabel Luhan, the writer. There are others who come and go. The latest to remain is Emil Bisttram, formerly of the Roerich Museum of New York who is bringing new life into the colony and has established an art school.

One word more before we leave the subject of the art colony, now the most noted in the West.

For years, the painters have kept their latch strings out for any who wished to visit their studios. Now they are inclined to prefer that appointments be made if one reads aright such signs on doors as "*Indian model posing. Look out for your scalp!*" or better still, "*Dynamite!*" There are many reasons for this which will be obvious to the intelligent tourists in Taos, of whom there are many but there is the other class as well.

How many laughs we have all had over the boy who yells to his playmate, "Eh, Jim, here is a *hand painter,*" or the visitor, looking at a picture of graceful aspens in yellow leaf, who exclaimed, "Oh, look at the *quacking asps!*" My right hand is up for that is true. Then there was another transient, gazing at a panel of Egyptian appliqué work. An Indian had quickly asked, "What tribe?" but, this time, the question took this form, "*Did Miss Grant paint that when she was in the war?*"

Truly the laughs have been many. Save for controlling courtesy, this would have brought a shout. An elderly woman, used to hearing what is often called artists' *lingo,* was riding along the Ranchito Road and seeing Holstein cattle in the distance exclaimed, "*See the Holbeins!*" Again my hand is up!

My pen could scratch along and keep my readers laughing and even turn the laughs on the artists themselves but it must do no such thing. Not now! The present story of the growth of the justly famous art colony is finished.

XXXVI · TAOS TO–DAY

ONLY A FEW YEARS NEED PASS AND FULL FOUR CENTURIES will have rolled away since the first white man saw Taos Valley where none but Indians lived. The village of Taos itself nears its three hundred and fiftieth anniversary. Would that we could name a definite date!

About two thousand people claim Taos as home, to-day. That number includes all the out-lying *placitas* but not the pueblo where six or seven hundred Indians — not more than that, we believe, in spite of a recent census — carry on in much the same manner as they did when Alvarado visited them in 1540.

Probably the town of Taos is more prosperous than it was one hundred years ago but that may not be true. No one can tell. Our streets and roads are better kept and our adobe houses are plastered more often. A few modern roofs have changed the skyline somewhat but civic pride now holds the thoughtful builder to a plan of flat roofs and fairly low walls.

The plaza was widened for traffic and a new stone wall built around the green with its bandstand, flagpole, cottonwoods and hollyhocks, in 1929. New hitching posts for Indian ponies were put up at the same time. Two years before, the fine new hotel *Don Fernando* [1] was opened on the southwest corner of the plaza and a definite attempt was made to build once more a portal all around the square, somewhat after the manner of years gone by, though larger and more substantial. Such plans have been forced into the discard for a time by the great fire of May

---

[1] This hotel was burned to the ground on Dec. 15, 1933.

Photograph by C. E. Lord

Taos

View toward the west

9, 1932, which swept away the whole north side of the plaza, as had the eastern side disappeared about twenty years before. The latter, now an up-to-date filling station and grounds, was never rebuilt. The former has risen into a beautiful line of business houses.

Tourist camps and two outlying lodges, San Geronimo and El Chamiso, tend to give the town a new atmosphere but the main part of Taos is still so strange and different that more than one traveler has asked if he were not suddenly in Old Mexico.

That, which is most regretted by all, is the passing of many old customs. There are fewer processions and fiestas than there were a decade ago. Outwardly the town is becoming American but within the homes of Spanish-Americans do yet hang *santos* and tales of long ago are told, such as that of the woman of Cordoba who rose from her grave and appeared all decked in her jewelry to the consternation of her family, or, of the portrait of a beautiful young woman, which was brought over the trails and later was found struck through by an Indian lance! Then there is another, or many perhaps, related about the ruins of a settlement once called Buena Vista and lying about four miles to the west, where live the little people! Did some keen eye once see fairies?

Politically, our town is honored, now and then, but on the whole, this amounts to less than a politician's promise. Once in a while its poll books take on unusual value. Not long ago, an election was in doubt. A telephone bell rang in Taos and a prominent citizen received the message that a big car was starting north and in it was a man who undoubtedly would try to secure the poll books of Taos County. The news was quietly told to six men who decided those books were not to be stolen. The men secured a key to the office in the old court-house where the safe was and silently took their places around the room in the dark.

Hours wore away and in due time the big car halted at the hotel. Not long after, the waiting men heard the click of an opening door. In came a Taos man followed by two men who were armed. He carried a lighted candle and stooped down to unlock the safe. Suddenly, he caught sight of a face in the darkness and asked, quickly, " What are you doing here? "

" I'm here to see that you do not steal the poll books of Taos County," came the answer, calmly enough.

The man straightened up, astonished. His candle flashed on another face, another and yet another until the henchman of the man in the big car realized the game was over. His armed companions had been asked to lay down their guns. There were few words spoken. The two men withdrew. The big car rolled out of town. The watchers in the night left and all was well. The poll books were safe!

Trickery succeeded once, some years before, and the books were actually stolen. Unfortunately this is not the only tale of such a nature which clouds the political history of our town and county. All one may say is that, in such matters, Taos keeps abreast of the larger cities.

When the election booths are open, our townsfolk elect inefficient men to the legislature, more often than not. The office of sheriff and treasurer have rarely been held by men who were equal to their jobs, hence shortages in accounts and many a murder problem left unsolved, notably that of Arthur R. Manby whose decapitated body was found in his home on Pueblo Road on July 3, 1929. Fortunately for the town, such hideous crimes are rare but such is not true of the county districts. Taos, itself, is noted as a safe town and deserves its reputation, on the whole, even if there have been many robberies during the past years of distress due to the depression, no doubt, and to newer elements coming into the village.

Socially, the town is somewhat divided. There are the bridge-playing group, the community worker group, the small number of people interested in eastern philosophy or modern art. The artists form no main social company, perhaps due to the fact that they are very individualistic and they live in all parts of the village. Since the coming of Bert G. Phillips, in 1898, there has been a steady growth in the number of artists, until to-day there are about twenty-five who drag anchor and call Taos home. The summer time brings many more and usually there are one or two who linger and eventually belong here.

Instead of being the paradise of the mountaineer, now Taos is that for the artist and if there has been any fundamental change during the years since the days of the fur trade, it may be that it is one of climate. Easy to live in, it certainly is but during the past five years the summer months have brought an undue amount of rain. Scientists tell us that four centuries ago, the whole Southwest was passing through its most arid period. It may be we are swinging toward the establishment of a rainy season, as such, though Taos is too high ever to be free from the four definite seasons. The autumn is always a glorious time, in the valley, but winters vary a good deal. Sometimes it is possible to paint out of doors all winter and, at others, like the winter of 1931–32, one suffers with cold. This winter was the most severe and the most prolonged ever known by the inhabitants of Taos though old-timers insist there was such a winter in 1885. Storm clouds, heavy with snow, hit the mountains instead of passing over the divide as usual and the result was much distress partly due to the intense cold and partly to the fact that the depression, begun in the East in 1929, had, at last, become felt in this far-away town. Nevertheless, most of the days of the year in Taos, are bright, sunny and cool for our altitude is almost 7000 feet above the sea.

Whatever the weather, Taos holds a persistent charm. It is never devoid of interest. Around its plaza and through its winding streets go men and women who represent three distinct types of civilization — the Indian, the Spanish-American and the Anglo-Saxon.

The Indian, shrouded in a blanket, moves quietly about in moccasined feet and rarely gives more than a glimpse of his real self or his philosophy which is based on natural phenomena. He clings to his ancient customs and religion varied but slightly through the years. He is Catholic, in name only, Indian in truth. His home comforts and his clothes are, alas! becoming modern. He studies the white man and his learning but actually banks on the wisdom of the old men of the tribe. At times, the Anglo-Saxon stands aghast at the knowledge of the red man as, for instance, with the coming of what is undoubtedly that of a new age of thought, we are told that both Taos and Santa Fe are destined to be the centers of culture beyond that ever before known and that *our* guiding spirit dwells on Taos Mountain. The strange fact is that the Indians have known such things for years. This gives the pale face pause.

The Spanish-Americans, now only slightly akin to the Indian, have grouped themselves into two classes; the one reaching out for learning and better home conditions, the other content to cling to the past. The latter

Photograph by W. L. McClure

Northwest corner of Taos Plaza about 1883
Dibble Hotel in the distance

Photograph by C. E. Lord

North side of Taos Plaza in 1933

have their fiestas, neighborhood banquets and *velorios* and, on funeral occasions, turn all mirrors to the wall. They care naught for change, will not send their children to school for more than three or four years and love to dream away an easy life. Both groups are noted for an innate courtesy and kindliness which puts to shame every Anglo-Saxon in the valley. They dislike the name Mexican because to them that means people of Old Mexico. They prefer to drop the word Spanish and be known simply as Americans.

The Anglo-Saxon, with his skepticism, his iconoclastic tendencies and love of learning contacts both Indian and Spaniard and profits far too little. Crude in manner and often possessing only the dangerous amount of knowledge, the American, as he loftily refers to himself, often appears ludicrous and makes many unfair deals. On the other hand, there is the type of Anglo-Saxon who appreciates his fellows, strives for higher ideals, develops schools, calls loudly for good roads and better conditions generally and to him credit is due, along with the progressive Spanish-American, for the general trend upward in the town.

The plaza of Taos will continue to be the center of life for centuries to come. It will ever be the meeting place for the three peoples to whom will cling their fundamental differences for, it seems now as if true amalgamation will never come. Everlasting will be its charm for over it will always lie the memory of the days when Indians howled to the war drum and Spaniards, in shining armor, pushed in, bent on discovery and settlement, and easterners prodded their burros or rumbled along in their covered wagons searching for trade and adventure.

Old trails will ever be new as they run from the plaza

though they may fall into line with modern highways. They will never wholly yield up all their treasures to the archæologist, no matter how persistent he may be. Neither will they ever prove uninviting to the artist for millions of brushes can not wear out the wealth of Taos Valley.

The story must end though much more could be written about our village in its land of dramatic clouds, vast stillness and earth-bound homes. Echoing the Past, Taos grows steadily into a more modern town and salutes the Future, knowing full well that its beauty can not wholly fade nor its history ever prove other than its most valuable talisman.

ADDENDA

I. MANUSCRIPTS AND LETTERS

OÑATE'S SOLDIER–COLONISTS

Here are the names of some of Oñate's associates,[1] first settlers in New Mexico, which exist to-day in the state, and are to be found in and around Taos.

Captain PABLO DE AGUILAR	HERNAN MARTIN
ASCENCIO DE ARCHULETA	JUAN MARTINEZ
ESTEVAN CARABAJAL	—— MEDINA
ALF. JUAN CORTÉS	JUAN DE ORTEGA
JUAN FERNANDEZ	—— ORTIZ
ALVARO GARCÍA	SIMON PEREZ
BARTOLOMÉ GONZÁLES	PEDRO DE RIBERA
JUAN GRIEGO	PEDRO RODRIGUEZ
ANTONIO GUTIERREZ	BARTOLOMÉ ROMEROS
ANTONIO HERNANDEZ	ALONZO SANCHEZ
CRISTOBAL DE HERRARA	*Captain* FRANCISCO VACA
ALF. JUAN DE LEÓN	VERALA
CRISTOBAL LÓPEZ	*Sec.* JUAN VELARDE
FRANCISCO MARQUEZ	*Captain* JUAN DE ZALDIVAR
ALF. LEON ZAPATA	

[1] Bancroft, History of New Mexico. Vol. XVII. p. 125.

VISITA DEL OBISPADO DE DURANGO POR EL SEÑOR DON PEDRO TAMARON, OBISPO DE SU DIOCESIS — TAOS, 1760

[From the H. E. Bolton Collection in Berkeley, California. Translated by Nellie V. Sanchez]

To REACH this Indian pueblo, whose patron saint is San Geronimo, one traveled over pine covered mountains until making the descent to the spacious and beautiful valley called Taos, in which were encountered villages of peaceable heathen Apaches, who are gathered under the protection of the Spaniards for defense against the Comanches. Then a river was encountered which they call Las Trampas, which has a good flow of water. Half a day was spent in a large house of a rich Indian of Taos, very intelligent and well off. His house and lands are surrounded by (armas) for defense. In the afternoon the journey was continued through that valley. Three rivers were crossed, of the same current and amount of water as the first; all have plenty of water for irrigating, and are distant from one another about a league and a half. After passing the last one, the pueblo of Taos was entered, where a Franciscan missionary curate resides. It is twelve leagues distant from Picuris to the north, and is the last and most retired pueblo of that kingdom in this direction. It is situated at the foot of a very high mountain range, in 40 degrees. The pueblo has 159 Indian families numbering 505 persons, and has as neighbors 36 white families numbering 160 persons. It has a very good, capacious church.

I worked with all possible strength there to induce the educated ones to make the act of contrition and confess. For this reason I left them until later, confirming the children first; and, in fact, some of them confessed, and strengthened by contrition, unless it is in Castilian, I was not as well satisfied as I could wish, so I reproved the missionary father and charged him with his duty, charging him to continue confessing them.

This pueblo is divided into three sections with many stories, and it would be better, as I told them, if they had a common door; for one of them is on the other side of the river about 200 yards from the crossing of the river. It has a wooden bridge and it freezes over every year. When it is thus frozen up, they told me, the Indian women came with their children, naked, broke the ice with a stone, and bathed them in those waters, putting them in and taking them out. They say it is done so they may become hard and strong.

While I was in this pueblo two villages of friendly, but heathen, Ute Indians arrived with a captive, who had fled from the Comanches. They said the Comanches remained on the Las Animas River hunting buffalo, in order to come to the fairs; every year they come to the fairs. The governor comes with a great part of his presidio and people from all over the kingdom to those fairs, which they call ransoms. They bring captives to sell, buckskins, many buffalo hides, and booty that they have taken in other parts — horses, guns, muskets, ammunition, knives, meat, and various other things. No money circulates in these fairs but articles are traded for each other and in this way those people provide themselves.

I left Taos on June 12, and a few days afterwards 17 tents of Comanches arrived. They make these tents of buffalo skins, and they say they are good protection, each one being occupied by a family. At the end of the said month of June 70 of these field tents arrived, making the big fair.

These Comanches are of such a nature that while some of them are peacefully trading in Taos, others of the nation are at war with some retired pueblo, and those who are peacefully engaged in trading say to the governor: " Put no faith in them, for among us there are rascals, the same as among you, and if you catch any of them, hang them."

This year of '60, in the early part of July, I left that kingdom and on the 6th of August, there came in war, so they say, nearly 3,000 Comanche men, with the intention of making an end of this pueblo of Taos. They (the people of Taos) attacked and provoked them from a very large house, the largest in all that valley, belonging to an Indian called Villapando, who, luckily for him, went away that day on business that came up. Seeing so many Comanches coming, because his house was the strongest, many women and men of that neighborhood took refuge in it, trusting in the circumstance that that house had four towers, and a large provision of muskets, powder and ball, it is said that they fired on them. At this the Comanches became infuriated to such a horrible extent that they broke down the house in several places and killed all the men and some of the women, who also fought. The mistress of the house, seeing that they were breaking in the outside door, taking up a lance, went to defend it, and they killed her fighting, 56 women and children were carried off, and a large number of horses which the owner of the house had there. Of the Comanches 49 dead bodies were counted, and others running with blood.

The governor Don Francisco Maxin del Valle, as soon as he learned of the affairs, convoked the people as rapidly as possible, and setting out with a thousand men on their trail, followed them almost 200 leagues, when the Apaches, being tired and the food giving out, lost heart and returned, 40 days were spent in this, in which they explored good country, but accomplished nothing else. This large and warlike nation of Comanches, it is said, and so they told me, came and showed itself on the frontier of New Mexico in the years 1717 and 1718, and they said they had been traveling from their country for twelve moons; from which may be inferred how immense that unpopulated country is. In the following year of '61 happened what is related in the letter written to me by the temporary governor, Don Manuel Portillo Urrisola, which runs as follows:

MOST ILLUSTRIOUS SIR:

Sir, with general pleasure I received your letters of the 27th of last October, in which you deign to inform me of your important health, and although I suppose that your illustrious highness is very much occupied in the care of the sheep of that wide-spread flock, my duty compels me to molest you with the reiteration of this, believing that your illustrious highness will appreciate the information.

As a result of not admitting the Comanches in the month of August of last year, until they should fulfill their promise to bring in the captives, on the 18th of the month of December I received a letter from the Alcalde Mayor of Taos in which he informs me that eleven captains of that nation had arrived, with them their principal man named Onacama, and they said that within three days their village would arrive, which was composed of 40 tents, and that they were bringing seven captives, so that they might be given the ransom. I immediately gathered together the few people that there were in this town and La Cañada, and with the soldiers that I had which were very few, 22 of them being in the north, waiting for my successor, I set out on the road, arriving at Taos on the 31st at 8 in the morning. Two hours afterwards the Comanches arrived, and going out to receive them, after they had saluted us, I accompanied them to a point in front of the Pueblo, where I made them encamp near the Sierras. 68 tents were counted, which made me distrust them, fearing some treason. For this reason I kept all the soldiers on horseback, with their arms in their hands. Having retired to the pueblo, at two in the afternoon ten captains came to see me, with them Onacama, who haughtily told me they were bringing seven captives — three women and four boys, for whom I would have to pay well and to their satisfaction, and grant them the ransom, and if not they would see if I were man enough to make them, as I had done in the month of August. This proposal I refused, making them confess that what they had done at the house of Pablo Villapando was false treason, since they were at peace with us, I told them I would not pay them for the seven captives they had brought, nor would I grant them peace or ransom until they brought all the captives whom they had carried off. They then broke into an uproar and tried to go, but I stopped them and disarmed seven of them, whereupon they wished to kill me. Having allowed one of them to go to bring the captives whom he had in his village when he arrived there he sent them to me by another captain, remaining himself to prepare his people, making them mount their horses and urging them to kill me first. As soon as I learned this, leaving six soldiers to guard the ten captains, with orders that if they should attempt to take flight to kill them, I mounted my horse and went to join my men. Reaching the village, I found all the Comanches on horseback, formed in three files, threatening a fight, notwithstanding the small number of people that I had, ignoring the large number of the enemy, confiding in the protection of the Holy Virgin and the justice of our cause, with a broadsword in my hand, I went among them and asked them what all this uproar was about. They replied that it was nothing, that all was now finished, that we were comrades. My man seeing me in this danger, begged me, weeping, to withdraw, which I did not wish to do, until I was compelled to do so, on account of hearing shots in the pueblos, although I had left all my men on horseback with Lieutenant Don Thomas Madrid, surrounding their villages, with orders not to allow one of them to go out, nor one of our men to alight. I returned to the pueblo and found out what had happened, which was that the ten captains, as soon as they saw that I had gone, forced the guard in a rush, and having got possession of two firearms, they ran out by the stairways, and the soldiers seeing that he could not stop them, fired. One of them fell dead, and most of the rest wounded, and not having been able to reach the open country because the door of the house was held by the cavalry, who had come up on learning of the shots, they fortified themselves in the stable and some rooms from which they kept firing all night. They killed the horses of the soldiers of the guard, and made pieces of the saddles. We remained so all night with our arms in our hands, and the same outside, until the dawn of the 22nd, when the lieutenant sent word to me that they had come out in front of their village with a cross and a white flag, asking for peace, and that their captains should be delivered up to them, and that the ransom be granted them, I caused them to be told that in order to give them what they asked they would have to give up their horses to me and remain on foot, and when the affair was over and the business adjusted, they would be given back to them so they could go away. This they refused, breaking into an uproar again and shouted " War! " Seeing it now to be necessary and invoking the Queen of the Angels and Men, I fired a small field cannon charged with cartridges and a volley from the muskets — and although they put up a considerable fire and resistance, but on the second volley given them, and being able to endure this blow from heaven, discharged upon them. They abandoned their villages, and with their women and children took to flight. The heathen Indians called Yutas, who had promised me they would fight in our favor to death, took no hand in any of it, and as soon as they saw us occupied in pursuit of the fugitives they sacked the village. They carried off more than a thousand horses and mules and more than 300 Comanches, old and young, going without stopping until they reached their country. Although I saw them I could not prevent it on account of lack of men. Continuing in pursuit of the fugitives until a place was reached which it was impossible to pass. Comanches were killed until the fields were covered with them, not one being willing to yield himself alive; this glorious action was concluded in less than an hour, with such evident signs that the All-Powerful fought for us, that, although I had but 80 men, counting soldiers and citizens, more than 400 Comanches died, and only two of ours, one an Indian, the other a citizen, and ten more wounded, but so slightly that they are all now well.

Returning to the community houses and seeing that the captains who were in it did not wish to yield to either side, fire was set to it; but as it did not burn with sufficient violence, when night came four of the captains who had been left alone came out armed with two guns which they had and attempted to escape, but only one of them succeeded. On account of the darkness of the night he succeeded in getting away, but, although when his trail was followed the next day he could not be overtaken, on account of the bloody tracks that he left it was believed that he had died.

Through a Yuta, who was a captain in the power of this village and succeeding in making his escape, it has been learned for certain that all that escaped from this affair of the whole village were 33 men and women, and that as soon as they learned of their disaster they set fire to everything they had, killed all their horses, and loosed the sheep, and took to flight, and that the nation was going in pursuit of them.

From this glorious victory I hoped for the complete pacification of this kingdom, on account of the terror which it has caused to all the heathen nations, and at the same time, the gratitude which they have shown; but I believe it will be frustrated with the arrival of my successor, who took possession on February 1, for it seems he has a mind to call the Comanches, by sending to them some of their captives. If he should do so I fear, and with reason, that in some one of the fairs they will put an end to the kingdom, for it (what) has been done by this bellicose and false nation have (has) always happened when they were at peace with us. May God remedy it, and grant me the favor of leaving this kingdom as soon as possible, for I am no longer of any use in it.

I trust that your Illustrious Highness is enjoying perfect and excellent health, which I trust that the Lord will do me the favor to put (me) at the disposition of your Illustrious Highness with the highest good will, and I pray the Most High to preserve the very important life of your Illustrious Highness for many happy years.

Villa of Santa Fe, February 24, 1762.

Most Illustrious Sir, your most humble servant prostrates himself at the feet of your Illustrious Highness.

MANUEL PARTILLO URRISOLA

LIST OF SETTLERS

[Citizens who were given grants of land in 1796–99 at Fernando de Taos. Archive 883, U. S. Surveyor General's office in Santa Fe, N. M.]

TOMAS MONTOYA
ANTONIO JOSÉ ROMERO
JOSÉ MIERA
PABLO BACA
MIGUEL BARCLA
JUAN BAUTISTA MARTIN
JOSÉ CORTEZ
JUAN PEDRO PACHECO
PAULIN DE ERARA
JUAN CRISTOVAL
    MONDRAGON
MARIANO MONDRAGON
DOMINGO LOVATO
SANTIAGO SILVA
IGNACIO MEDINA
BENANCIO ORTEGA

MARIA TOMASA ORTEGA
FRANCISCO BRITO
JOSÉ JUAQUIN BLEA
ANTONIO BLEA
ORTA MIERA
MIGUEL COCA
MATEO COCA
MANUEL COCA
MANUEL TAFOYA
LAZARO ROMERO
ANASTASIO VIGIL
JUAN DEL CARMEN
    MARTINEZ
JOSÉ MARIA CHAVES
ANTONIO JOSÉ MARTINEZ
MANUEL ORTEGA

José Montoya
Pascual Aragon
Roque Martinez
Patricio Aragon
Pablo Lujan
Ignacio Gonzales
Juan José de la Cruz
José Rafael Montoya
Juan Cristoval Medina
Francisco Fresquis
Juan Angel Pando
Juan Antonio Casados
Nicolas Montaño
José Joaquin Blea
Estevan Bargas
Salvador Martinez
Manuel Ramos Martinez

Isidro Arquello
Cristoval Corteis
Domingo Maese
Francisco Lovato
Josepha Lovato
Cruz Cortes
Polonio Sisneros
José Maria Cortes
José Ramos Sandoval
Nicolas Barela
Manuel Suaso
Juan Angel Garcia
Estevan Baca
Lugarda Torres
Manuel Baca
Juan Gonzales
Lazaro Rael

Juan Nicolas Duran

LETTER BY CERAN ST. VRAIN

[Chittenden, Hiram M., The American Fur Trade of the Far West, pp. 520–521.]

San Fernando del Taos
Sept. 14, 1830

Messrs. B. Pratte & Co.

Gentlemen: It is with pleasure that I inform you of my last arrival at Santefe which was the 4th of August. We were met at Red River by General Biscsa, the custom-house officer, and a few soldiers; the object being in coming out so far to meet us was to prevent smuggling and it had the desired effek, there was a guard placed around our wagons until we entered Santefe, we had all to pay

full dutys which amounts to about 60 percent on cost. I
was the first that put goods in the Customhouse and I
opened immediately, but goods sold very slow, so slow
that it was discouraging. I found that it was impossible
to meet my payments if I continued retaling. I there fore
thought it best to hole Saile & I have done so. I send
you by Mr. Andru Carson and Lavoise Ruel one wagon
eleven mules, one horse and 653 skins of Beaver 961 lbs.
nine hundred and sixty one pounds, which you will have
sold for my account. I do not wish the mules sold unless
they sell for a good price.

I am with much respect
Your obdt. servant,
Ceran St. Vrain

GEORGE NIDEVER'S VISIT. 1831

[Mss. in Bancroft Library at Berkeley, California. Date 1878]

After entering New Mexico, in 1831 and just before we
reached Arroyo Seco, a small Mexican town and our point
of destination, we met the first signs of civilization, in a
herd of to me cattle which we saw quietly grazing off at
the right of our line of march; soon after we met a band
of sheep driven by a young Mexican on horseback.

When we struck the head of the band they parted, allowing us to ride in among them and without showing
any fear at our presence. Not so with their herder, whose
attention being diverted did not discover our presence
until we were quite close to him, and then with a startled
glance saw only that a party of horsemen were upon him.
His fright prevented him from distinguishing us. He ut-

tered a yell and put off for the neighboring mountains as fast as his horse could carry him. He took us for a war party of Arapahoes, as these Indians made frequent incursions into New Mexico in those times. The Arapahoes and Mexicans were deadly enemies and although they would trade freely with each other, woe betide the poor Mexican who was sought by these savages and the Mexicans spared no Arapahoe who might fall into their hands.

A few miles farther on we came to a shepherd's hut, its sole occupants being an old man and boy. The old man was the first to see us and he, like the young herder, took us for Arapahoes. He gave us one look and turning ran at the top of his speed to a ravine nearby. He was some distance from the hut and had no time to call to the boy. By this time we were close to the hut, when the boy, hearing us, came out and recognizing us as white men, advanced towards us and held out his hand, showing great pleasure at seeing us. The old man had by this time reached the opposite side of the ravine where he stopped to look back. Seeing the boy among us and realizing that we could not be Indians, he came back almost as fast as he had run away. He ran up to us, caught hold of our hands and could hardly contain himself with joy. He proceeded to kill a sheep for us and brought us out milk and corn cakes, which we ate with the greatest of relish.

Arroyo Seco was about fifty miles distant and we arrived there three days later. Here, as at the shepherd's hut, we received every hospitality, and in fact, everywhere in New Mexico we always met with the same treatment. This seemed to be a great wheat country and flour was in consequence quite cheap. Upon our arrival at Arroyo Seco they brought us a cart load of bread. There were quite a number of flour mills in and around Arroyo Seco.

About twelve miles from Arroyo Seco was situated the town of San Fernando de Taos, quite a large place. The fur traders who came out annually from St. Louis had permanent trading posts established here. We went to San Fernando very often but made our headquarters at Arroyo Seco. Having arrived here, our party separated but fourteen or fifteen of the original company remained together.

Those who left us here, as far as I can remember, were Col. Bean, who by this time was looked upon by all the company as the most insignificant among us. We had made a great mistake in choosing him for our leader, but the high estimation in which he was held by all, and his rank as colonel of the militia, led us to suppose him the best man. His brothers were well known to my family, my father having been with them in the early Indian wars. They owned the saltworks on the Arkansas and were men of very good standing.

William Bean also left us here with his father. He was a quite sensible young man with none of his father's cowardice, and was very much liked by all. They both returned to Arkansas with the first annual trading train that left San Fernando. Dr. Craig went into Sonora. About nine or ten joined Young's party at San Fernando and came to California by the lower route via Fort Yuma. Among these were Austin, a wild young fellow, Weaver, Hace, Wilkinson, the two Greens, Anderson and Basey. The names of the others I do not remember. Anderson was killed by one of the Greens, not far from Los Angeles, and just after they had entered California. While with us, Anderson, who was a large man, had imposed to a great extent upon Green, who was a small man, by continually throwing his traps into the river and setting his own on Green's beaver signs. Green had warned him that if he continued to treat him in that manner he would certainly kill him. To this threat, however, Anderson paid no heed, nor to the repeated warnings of others of the company that Green would carry out his threat into execution. He continued to illtreat him until Green put an end to him.

Near the place where he killed Anderson, he had set his traps for beaver when Anderson, having come across them, threw them into the water, as he had repeatedly done before and set his own traps in their place. Shortly after Green visited his traps and finding Anderson's, returned quietly to camp, walked up to him and shot him through the heart. Capt. Young gave Green up to the authorities at Los Angeles but nothing was done with him, I believe, and he was allowed to leave the country.

At San Fernando, Rowland and Workman, of the Puento Ranch, Los Angeles County, California, were living. They had already been there I think nearly fifteen years. Rowland had a flour mill in that town. He was married to a Mexican woman and they had three or four children. I was well acquainted with the family, having often visited their home while I was in San Fernando. With Workman I had less acquaintance. I was told that he, too, was married to a Mexican woman but I never visited his house. They afterwards removed to California and settled in Los Angeles County. Workman had a store in San Fernando. He sold clothing, provisions, etc. We did most of our trading with him. Besides these foreigners there were two brothers Kincaid and an old man by the name of Chambers living in San Fernando.

Our party had arrived at Arroyo Seco early in March of '31. A few weeks later, Graham, Sinclair, Alex and I decided to make at attempt to get the traps we had left on the Arkansas. Having secured the services of three Mexicans with their mules and procured fresh animals for ourselves, we lost no time in starting on our trip. A few days brought us within a short distance of our traps but we found the snow still too deep on the mountain that lay between us and the river.

At the same time an event occurred that caused us to retrace our steps with all possible haste. This was the presence in the vicinity of a large party of Arapahoes. We discovered them on a neighboring hill early one morning while we were in camp. Fortunately, they did not see us and as soon as possible we packed up and made our way back to New Mexico, traveling day and night, until we were well out of the Indian country. The Mexicans who accompanied us were very much frightened when they saw the Indians and needed no urging to keep up with us on our retreat. We were somewhat disappointed in our failure to get the traps, as they were very dear at San Fernando.

Having sold the few skins we brought with us on our first arrival, we laid in a few supplies and in March, '31, our whole party, now reduced to fourteen or fifteen men, set out for the Platte. On the North Fork we found a valley with beaver and we remained until we trapped them out. On July 4 of '31 we arrived at Arroyo Seco again with about two packs of skins of 60 each. These we sold in San Fernando at $4 per pound, or an average of $10 per skin. In those days although there was a heavy duty on all beaver skins brought into New Mexico, no one ever thought of paying it and, as in our case, they would be smuggled into town in the night.

We fitted ourselves out a second time and in Sept. 1831

again started for the headquarters of the Arkansas. Our party had been increased by the addition of three or four Mexicans who had been hired by different members of our company.

From Arroyo Seco to the Arkansas we kept company with a band of trappers composed of French and Mexicans, about a dozen in all. On our way we saw a few Crow Indians and had several horses stolen by them. We also saw numbers of the Snake Indians, who were then very friendly with the pale faces.

Just before we reached the Arkansas our camp was alarmed one night by the appearance in our midst of a young woman of the Snake tribe. An old Mexican who was sleeping near me was awakened in the night by some one passing near him and reaching out his hand caught hold of her and held her fast, calling out at the same time, " I got one woman! "

We were all on our feet in an instant and, with our arms in our hands, ready to meet the expected attack, but no more Indians appeared. We gave the poor woman plenty to eat and the next day she left us for her village not far away. We were able to learn that she had made her escape from the Kiowas, who had taken her prisoner and had found the buffalo road which ran through our camp and followed it until she was caught in our midst. She had passed our guard without being seen.

We reached the headwaters of the Arkansas in October without any further adventure. A few days more brought us to the " Platte."

LIST OF MEN WHO LEFT TAOS IN 1841

WILLIAM WORKMAN *and family*
WILLIAM GORDON *and family*
JAMES D. MEADE, *Physician*
BENJAMIN D. WILSON
—— KNIGHT
JACOB FRANKFORT, *Tailor*
WILLIAM CAMPBELL, *Naturalist*
THOMAS LINDSAY, *Mineralogist*
HIRAM TAYLOR, *Musician*
WADE HAMPTON, *Gunsmith*
ISAAC GIVENZ, *Engineer*
JOHN MCCLURE
JAMES DOKES
L. LYMAN, *Physician*
DANIEL SINTON, *Carpenter*
ALBERT G. TIBIANA
—— BACHELDER, *Cooper*
FRANCIS BADEBRY, *Carpenter*
FRANCIS GWINN, *Blacksmith*
MICHAEL WHITE
JUAN MANUEL BARA *and family*
LORENZO TRUJILLO *and family*
YGNACIO SALAZAR *and servants*
—— TOMAS, *Carpenter*
WILLIAM MOON, *Cooper*

William Workman was born January 16, 1802, at Clifton, Westmoreland County, England, and died May 17, 1876, at Puente, California. His wife was Nicolasa Uriarte of Taos, New Mexico.

John Rowland was born in 1791 in Boston, Massachusetts. He married Maria de la Encarnaction Martinez of

Taos. She died and he then married Mrs. Charlotte Maril-lia Gray. It was John Rowland who made the above list which was published in 1880 by Messrs. Thompson and West.

GENERAL STATISTICS OF THE SANTA FE TRADE
as made by Dr. Josiah Gregg in 1844

[Probable amounts]

Years	Amt. Mdse.	Wagons	Men	Proprietors	To Chihuahua	Remarks
1822	15,000		70	60		Pack animals only used
1823	12,000		50	30		Do.
1824	35,000	26	100	80	3000	Do. and wagons
1825	65,000	37	130	90	5000	Do. and wagons
1826	90,000	60	100	70	7000	Wagons only henceforth
1827	85,000	55	90	50	8000	
1828	150,000	100	200	80	20,000	3 men killed being the first
1829	60,000	30	50	20	5,000	1st U. S. escort 1 trader killed
1830	120,000	70	140	60	20,000	First oxen used by traders
1831	250,000	130	320	80	80,000	Two men killed
1832	140,000	70	150	40	50,000	Party defeated on Canadian 2 men killed
1833	180,000	105	185	60	80,000	3 perished
1834	150,000	80	160	50	70,000	2nd U. S. escort
1835	140,000	75	140	40	70,000	
1836	130,000	70	135	35	60,000	
1837	150,000	80	160	35	80,000	
1838	90,000	50	100	20	40,000	
1839	250,000	130	250	40	100,000	Arkansas expedition
1840	50,000	30	60	5	10,000	Chihuahua expedition
1841	150,000	60	100	12	80,000	Texas-Santa Fe expedition
1842	160,000	70	120	15	90,000	
1843	450,000	230	350	30	300,000	3rd U. S. escort Ports closed

Note. The trade was resumed in the spring of 1844 and continued in good form until 1880.

"UNCLE DICK" WOOTTON'S STORY OF THE TAOS MASSACRE. 1847

[Conard, Howard Louis, " Uncle Dick " Wootton, pp. 178–186]

I was there (Pueblo, Colorado) at the time of the Taos massacre and about five days later John Albert, who had managed some way or other to make his escape from Arroyo Honda, came into Pueblo, bringing the news of the Mexican uprising and its bloody sequel. He had traveled the whole distance on foot and was almost exhausted when he reached us.

When Albert had laid before us all the details of the tragedy, our little band of trappers held a council of war, to determine what we should do. The situation was as perplexing as it was distressing. The friendships of the mountain men were warm friendships. We had never seen the time when we were not ready to attempt the rescue of a friend whose life was in danger and it was seldom indeed that the killing or wounding of one of our number had gone unavenged.

Among those who had been so brutally murdered at Taos and Arroyo Honda, were men who had been my warmest and best friends, ever since I came to the country and I felt that I should, if possible, do something toward securing punishment of their murderers and protecting the property which they had left, for use of those who were entitled to it. What to do, however, was the question. We should not have hesitated much about attacking an ordinary band of roving Indians but to undertake to put down what seemed a formidable rebellion was, of course, out of our Line. We did not know what might be going on at Santa Fe or how long it would be, before we could expect any help from the government forces and without assistance, the small party of volunteers that we should have been able to muster, could have accomplished nothing.

We parleyed over the matter awhile and reached the conclusion that there were soldiers enough at Santa Fe to put down the rebellion, and having agreed on this point we reached the further conclusion, that it was our duty to render them all the assistance possible.

This determined our action and five of us mounted our horses and started across the country toward Taos. It took us several days to make the trip and we approached the place very carefully. We made our way into the high mountains east of Taos and from there we could look down on the town and see pretty well what was going on, without being discovered ourselves. As we could discover no signs of the arrival of the soldiers, we knew that it was not safe for us to venture further.

In the meantime, Thomas Tobin, the messenger who had left Arroyo Honda with the news of the massacre at that place and at Taos, had reached Santa Fé and Colonel Price had lost no time in marching against the rebels. He met the first force of Mexicans and Indians at La Cañada, some distance out on the Taos road from Santa Fé and soon had them on the run. He then sent Captain Burgwin, with two companies of troops on toward Taos. Colonel St. Vrain, Governor Bent's partner, accompanied Captain Burgwin, with about sixty volunteers, picked up in Santa Fé. At Embudo they had another skirmish with the insurgents and did not reach Taos until the third of February.

We were watching for them and saw them when they marched into the town. The hostiles had all gathered at the Pueblo de Taos and fortified themselves in and about the old church. The soldiers marched to the Pueblo and fired a few shots, but as night was coming on they returned to Fernandez de Taos and went into camp for the night.

The Americans were by no means certain that the entire force of the enemy had gathered at the Pueblo, but half suspected that a force was secreted in the town of Taos. Before going into camp they made a careful reconnoissance, inspecting every building in the town, to find out who was inside. Where the doors were closed they were broken down and a thorough search made of the buildings but where they stood open it was taken as a guarantee of a friendly feeling on the part of the occupants and their residences were not disturbed.

While the soldiers were in camp that night, I made my way down to where they were, along with my four companions and joining the Santa Fé volunteers, was ready for the storming of the Pueblo and the fight which was to commence in the morning. It commenced early, and the battle which followed was a bloody one, considering the number of men engaged in it. It lasted until sundown and I think we were resisted as stoutly as were the American soldiers upon any battlefield of the Mexican War.

We soon drove our enemies out of the pueblo building proper but their position in La Iglesia de Taos — the old church — was a strong one and we found it difficult to dislodge them. We had three small howitzers and one six-pound cannon, but the walls of the church were so thick that the shells from the howitzers would not go through them, and the solid shot from the cannon only made a round hole. As we were short of ammunition, we could not afford to waste any, and for that reason volunteers were called for to breach the walls with axes. This was a hazardous business, as the work had to be done while a hot fire was being kept up from the inside of the building.

Thirty-five of us, however, volunteered to make the attempt and we gained the cover of the walls with a loss of only three or four men. It took us but a short time to accomplish what we had started out to do and when a few shells were thown through the holes we had made and exploded in the building, they created a fearful havoc. We lighted the fuses, and threw some of these shells into the church with our hands, in order that they might be sure to explode at the proper time and place.

This made it altogether too hot for the besieged party and bursting open the doors and windows they undertook to make their escape to the mountains. James Q. Quinn, of Illinois, a cousin of Stephen Douglas, planted the American flag on the old church, but as the Mexicans were retreating, they stopped long enough to shoot it down.

The last stand made by the insurgents was at the old church. When they were driven out of there, they fled in every direction. Of course, we pursued them and not much quarter was asked or given. There was considerable hand-to-hand fighting, Colonel St. Vrain, himself, I remember, engaging in a contest which, in spite of the peril of the situation, was amusing. The colonel was riding along with myself and two or three others, who were about to join in a pursuit of one party of fugitives, when he observed an Indian whom he had seen a great many times and knew very well, lying stretched out on the ground, apparently dead. Knowing that this Indian had taken a prominent part in the massacre, Colonel St. Vrain dismounted and walked a few feet from where we were, to see whether the red skin was really dead or only shamming. That the latter and not the former, was the proper diagnosis of the Indian's case, the colonel was soon very thoroughly convinced. He had scarcely reached the side of the apparently dead Indian, when the latter sprang up and grappling with him undertook to thrust into his body a long steel-pointed arrow. Both the Indian and the colonel were large, powerful men and as each managed to keep the other from using a weapon, a wrestling match followed the Indian's attack, which, it seemed to me lasted several minutes before outside help terminated it in the colonel's favor. I sprang to his assistance as soon as I saw the struggle commence but the Indian managed to keep the colonel between him and me and was so active in his movements, that I found it difficult to strike a lick which would be sure to hit the right head. I managed after a little, however, to deal him a blow with my tomahawk which had the effect of causing him to relax his hold upon the colonel and when he stretched out on the ground again, there was no doubt about his being a dead Indian.

We lost thirty-five men out of the comparatively small number we had engaged in this battle and among them was Captain Burgwin, who was as brave a soldier as I have ever seen on the frontier. We buried him at Taos in a grave by himself, while the other thirty-four who were killed, were buried side by side in a long trench near where they fell.

We never knew exactly what the Mexican and Indian loss was, but it must have been in the neighborhood of two hundred.

This battle ended the Taos rebellion, as it is generally

called, although the conspirators had their plans laid to bring about a general uprising of Mexicans and Indians in New Mexico and they evidently thought with this combination of forces, they would be able to drive the Americans out of the territory and keep them out.

A detachment of soldiers remained at Taos, after that, and the work of hunting down and punishing those who had stirred up and been prominently connected with the insurrection, commenced.

Pablo Montoya and El Tomacito were both captured. El Tomacito, the Indian leader, was placed under guard and we proposed to give him along with the rest a formal trial but a dragoon by the name of Fitzgerald was allowed to go into the room where the Indian was confined, along with others who wanted to take a look at him. The soldier looked at the savage a few minutes and then, quick as a flash, drew a pistol and shot him in the head, killing him instantly. Fitzgerald then made his escape from the building and succeeded in getting away out of the country. If he had been caught, he would, of course, have been punished. The Indian deserved to be killed and would have been hanged anyhow, but we objected to the informal manner of his taking off.

Pablo Montoya was tried and hanged and twelve others (the best record gives sixteen as the number) were disposed of in the same way.

They were all tried by drum-head court-martial and there was no unnecessary delay about reaching the climax of the proceedings. The twelve that I have spoken of, were hanged at the same time and dangled from the same pole. I acted as marshal in making arrests under the military authority and was kept busy for some days. The only law we had was military law but that was just what we wanted and it was not long before order was restored and the rebellion experiment has never been tried there since.

The traders who had been absent from Taos when the massacre occurred, that is, those who lived there, found upon their return that their stores had been sacked and burned and most of their property destroyed, but they congratulated themselves upon having escaped with their lives, and after the fashion of pioneers, set about building up other fortunes to take the place of those they had lost.

LETTER² WRITTEN TO HIS FAMILY BY COLONEL DEWITT CLINTON PETERS

Surgeon of the U. S. Army

Fort Massachusetts, New Mexico.
April 5th, 1855.

WE started from this Post 500 strong, on the 14th of April and encamped on the River Trinchera (called so from being formed by 3 rivers) about twelve miles distant from the Fort. The next morning Feverlee awoke us at 4 o'clock and soon our forces were in line and marching. This day we travelled about 20 miles westwardly and encamped on the Trinchera again near where it empties into the Rio Grande. We found that day where the Indians had killed some stolen sheep, but no trail was discovered. We encamped after travelling some 23 miles and again next day we put out early and travelled about 21 miles before encamping being obliged to rest here, at the mouth of the cañon through which the head waters

² Edited only as to paragraphing by the author. Courtesy of Charles L. Camp, Berkeley, California. It deals with the Saguache campaign against the Indians.

of the Rio Grande flows, and where Col. Fremont lost so many men and animals, while attempting to discover a new pass to California, some 2 or 3 years since, the men having frozen to death. Our spies 50 in number were dispatched to examine it in reference to discovering if they could see any signs of Indian. Late in the evening they returned reporting in the negative.

The next day we made another early start when Kit Carson our guide soon struck upon a large fresh trail of Indians and their stolen stock. We travelled along the range of mountains laying on the west side of the great valley of St. Louis (Luis) — Col. Benton's backbone of America where he contemplates having the Pacific Rail Road pass in order to get through the Rocky Mountains. This valley is about 100 miles long — level as a floor — it can be easily watered from the mountain streams and can be made instead of a pasture for game and the roaming ground for wild Indians the garden of New Mexico. We kept the trail for about 25 miles and encamped on a small stream near where the Utahs had been summering — which place they were obliged to leave on account of the small pox. The bones of the victims fallen by this scourge were lying scattered about on the surface of the earth bleaching, having been well cleaned by the wolves. This night we were not allowed fires, on account of the supposed proximity of the Indians — which was cold comfort, but with frozen bacon, cold water and a little bread we appeased our appetites and went to sleep.

The next day we got out early and all began to fix our war instruments, for Kit Carson had prophesied we were to have a fight today between 1 and 2 o'clock, when we left the fort and his word on such affairs is as good as wheat.

We pushed on to the pass leading to Grand River and California, where (travelled) poor Capt. Gunnison who was subsequently killed at Salt Lake [8] by the Utahs. This place has an Indian name (but not spelled) Sow watchey; here we hoped to find the Indians, but everyone began to despond as the trail appeared to grow less on account of the late snow storms — it being some days old.

At about 10 o'clock we turned into the pass, Kit Carson and our Quartermaster being a little ahead reached the top of a mound so they could look up the valley, when they beheld about 150 warriors one mile off coming down as we supposed to go out on another plundering expedition — Kit gave us the alarm, by riding his horse around a ring — our command was necessarily stretched for a long way back, as the pass is narrow, and the soldiers advanced by couples.

The Indians soon discovered us. Supposing we were but few in number, as they could not see our whole party on account of the mound and the hills and being prevented from discovering us, while crossing the prairie the days previous by the snow storms, they formed in line for a fight. Orders were sent back for the companies to hurry up — Belonging to the commanding officer's staff I remained on the mound with the rest of the party composing it while this order was completed, the Indians during this time crying out to us in Spanish to come on and their chiefs riding up and down encouraging them to fight well. Some 200 Dragoons charged over the mound, having stopped to throw off their overcoats etc. I picked out my place for the wounded and ordered my steward there, with my medicines, so as to give immediate relief to the wounded.

[8] Capt. Gunnison was killed near Lake Sevier Oct. 26, '54.

The order was to surround them (and wipe out the whole party) but the Indians seeing the immense force coming, broke like sheep and ran for the mountains, not however until the Dragoons had reached them on their tired horses, and had broken them up in squads. For a time arrows, balls and spears were used freely. I had myself a hand to hand encounter with one of these red men — being at the rear of one of the advance companies, as it swung around to him then me, we went right through a small party of them separated from the rest — when I found myself within ten steps of a fellow who saluted me with an arrow which passed between me and my animals' heads. I let go my revolver at him until its five barrels were expended and being excited I then threw the pistol at him (in the hopes I suppose now of giving him a black eye, for that I find is the best way I can fight). The buck exchanged three arrows with me, for my five balls, (these balls were not larger than buck shot, as the pistol was small) — we then parted, I riding about 20 steps to get down, and tie the bleeding vessel of a poor horse's neck wounded by an arrow, just ahead of me.

The Indians fled in every direction, leaving bloody trails as they vamosed. Two companies during the fight charged on their village, but not until the women and children had taken french leave. Musicians were dismounted and also Dragoons and put after them in the mountains and firing was kept up for an hour or so — when the recall was sounded. We had two men wounded and lost two horses, while the Indians lost 2 chiefs and six men killed and a good number wounded.

It being nearly night — our animals broken down, with but little to eat, we encamped nearby. As we were seated around our camp fires chatting two persons were seen coming towards us from the mountains opposite to those into which the Indians had taken refuge but a few hours before; these two people proved to be two Indians returning from the chase or a visit to some other village. They approached unconscious of their danger, as our waggons etc. were hidden from them by the trees on the creek. Two of our men mounted quickly and if ever a race was pretty this was, for they had two miles to run to get in the woods and we sat where we could see the performance distinctly. The Indians reached the timber however where they left their animals, two fine horses. Our men fired and wounded one but he managed to get away as did his companion.

The next morning we were up bright and early ready to pursue the Indians at a quick pace. Our waggons, two cannon, provision and most of our pack mules were left behind, under guard of 150 men, commanded by Lt. Beall, while we took 7 days' rations on our pack mules and 1/2 bushel of corn on our horses. These preparations were necessary for forced marches over mountains and trails almost defying even a foot traveller to oppose them. There being an Asst. Surgeon of the Volunteers along, who of course was my subaltern, he was ordered to remain with the sick and wounded, while I pushed on with the chief command.

We soon struck the Indian trail as they had come together again with their families. We travelled as fast as we could, being obliged most of the time to lead our animals, for the Indians were taking us over the worst places they could pick out in order to break us down, for no white man can travel with them over these mountains. The air is so light that you must necessarily give up to fatigue. We exerted ourselves to the utmost travelling most of the time to the northeast. We gained daily on them and captured one and killed another. On the fourth day we overhauled them again, killed some of them, took from them a great number of horses, meat, camp utensils, and some prisoners. One woman told us she destroyed her own child and a niece and that others did the same to prevent our capturing them — In the fight they separated in all directions. We had men out all night and the next day, but they could not find a trail to follow, but brought in a few more animals. Our prisoners tell us this band is entirely destitute now of everything and must starve as the snow is so deep that they cannot join other portions of their tribe. Probably they will make peace now and stop murdering and stealing.

We had one wounded man to carry back to our fort. The process of this may be novel to you as it was to me. By it a man can ride as easy as if in a carriage; it is an Indian practice. A litter is made with two long poles with shafts at each end, while the man rides in a buffalo robe tied on its sides to the poles. He has a mule before him and one behind; in other words he is in a common litter; instead of a man at each end to carry him he has two mules. You would be surprised at the places these portable beds can travel and how easy the wounded can travel in them. Lt. Col. St. Vrain who " brought up " Kit Carson, and is the oldest mountaineer in this country and who is attached with the above command to the volunteers assured me he had carried a man six weeks in this way, until his thigh united, and that he travelled himself in this way all the time he was suffering from small pox.

Our provisions were nearly out and we were now on half rations our animals were also broken down, and we were obliged to kill 5 or 6 fine dragoon horses that gave out daily to prevent the Indians from getting them. So an express was started back for our wagons to meet us and we turned on the back track to recruit. After six days we reached our post again, where we stay a few days and then put out again after another band or bands as it may happen.

2/3rds of the time we were out it stormed furiously. We missed our waggons which we wished to meet to get provisions, and were a day finding them, they having passed within a few miles of us during a storm. We went where no white man or Mexican had been before, for we had the oldest hunters, trappers and guides in the country along and they said so. I have had the honor of seeing the headwaters of the Arkansas, which but few men who live on it can say, I doubt if any. Altho' I froze both of my feet slightly and nearly perished with the cold every night yet I must say I had some enjoyments and return with a wolfish appetite. We saw Geese, Elk, Ducks, Partridges, Rocky Mountain Goats, Antelope and Deer in abundance and were living on bacon at the time, for the order was, no firing from the ranks.

Kit Carson amused us, by his description of his travels, of trapping and hunting, while Col. St. Vrain who is very wealthy, described to us his (and) Carson's visits to the states, and of his being Col. Benton's guest and his impressions. He has a head as good as Daniel Webster's and had he been educated, would have made the greatest explorer and engineer living. He has been offered a commission in the army but refused it. I never was so greatly deceived in a man in life — I took him for a bragadocia, but he is modest, says but little, does not drink, is kind hearted and brave as a lion. He has not an enemy here.

Some Mexicans killed a young squaw, in one of our

fights, mistaking her for a man. When Kit heard of it he jumped on his feet and said he would give 500 dollars. I never saw so tender hearted a man. A poor dog was drowning at one of our camps — being unable to get out of the river. If it had been a human being he could not have exerted himself more.

One beautiful sight I saw while passing thro' a deep gorge in the mountains. My horse was carefully picking his path over the rocks; beneath ran a stream whose course was dammed up every now and then by the work of the beaver who inhabited it. Some of these works were on an immense scale. On the banks of the ponds there were the stumps of fallen trees which were decaying. The beaver cuts these trees down, (and some were at least a foot thro) felling them into the water, where he keeps the tops for the winter, eating the bark of the trunk during the summer. They tell me beavers will fell a tree whichever way he pleases them. The cut surfaces of these trees looked as smooth as if it had been done with a knife. The beaver has a great propensity for damming. There was an old trapper who lived in Taos who had one who was pretty tame. Whenever the family would go out Mr. Beaver would set to work, lug pillows etc. and make a complete dam across the room.

On the opposite side of the pass I was describing there were hot springs that were sending their fumes to heaven — the day was beautiful and this lent its aid to the grandeur of the scenery which I assure you I enjoyed much. I should say the Territory of Utah from the little I saw of it must be much more valuable than that of New Mexico.

You may think from what I have written about fighting and killing Indians, that it is a very cruel process, but were you here and heard of the murders and depredations they have committed on the inhabitants you would think differently. These bands of Apaches and Utahs have broken treaty after treaty and they now hold in bondage several Spanish women and children whom they treat most cruelly.

II · AUTHORITIES

PAGE 1

Sangre de Cristo. There is a tradition that Spaniards believed that the blood of Christ was white and that they first saw our mountains covered with snow and hence the name but the red glow of the summer sunsets on our range seems to give a far better reason for the name — Sangre de Cristo or Blood of Christ. Oñate came in July. It is possible that the name does not date as far back as his time.

Táos. Doc. de Indias, Vol. XVI, p. 257. " Esta dia, depues se missa, pasomos à la provincia de los Táos, que tambien llaman Tayberon, y otras; ay seis leguas por ser mal camino — "

Tao. In 1909, John P. Harrington discovered that the Picuris Indians still refer to their relatives, the Taos, as the *Tao*, a name which was apparently here before the Spaniards came.

PAGE 2

It is a land — Ayer, Mrs. Edward E. The Memorial of Fray Alonzo de Benavides, 1630, p. 26.

PAGE 3

Solemn scholars — Smithsonian Institute men.

PAGE 4

Cabeza — For all historical studies of the Southwest, it is necessary to consult, Twitchell, Leading Facts in New Mexican History; Bancroft, H. H. Vol. XVII, Arizona and New Mexico, and American Ethnological Annual Reports, as fundamental sources. — How far Cabeza came north will be forever a mooted question. Prince, L. B. History of New Mexico, p. 92, " Just how far up the Rio Grande Cabeza de Vaca came we shall probably never know; but evidently not further than central New Mexico, as the turquoises which were presented to him and which certainly came from the great Chalchuitl mountains in the Cerrillos, south of Santa Fe, he mentions as coming from the north." Adolph Bandelier, the great scholar of the southwest, believed that Cabeza was never on New Mexican soil while Twitchell says there is no way of ascertaining whether he was or not. Leading Facts, Vol. I, p. 122. See Bishop, Morris, Cabeza de Vaca, The Century Co. 1933.

PAGE 5

Treatment — Crude osteopathy — Bandelier, A. Southwestern Contributions, Arch. Inst. Series V, 1890, p. 33.

Hawks-bell. Winship, George Parker, The Coronado Expedition. Am. Eth. Ann. No. 14, p. 350.

PAGE 6

A mighty kick — Winship, George Parker, The Coronado Expedition, 1540–42. Am. Eth. Ann. No. 14, p. 361.

Marcos, a liar. Whether Fray Marcos deserved his reputation of being a " lying monk " has never been definitely settled. That he was so called in his day can not be disputed but his detractors seem to have not been without known flaws as far as veracity is concerned. Scholars of our day have tried to believe that Marcos was a much maligned person, on whom others may have wished to hang reasons for their failure, etc.

PAGE 7

Alvarado, Hernando de. Captain Alvarado was evidently a strong leader. He was chosen by Coronado to travel toward the east. It was he, with his party, who first came to the Taos pueblo and saw the land on which much later our town of Taos was to stand. According to one of the most reliable Taos Indians of to-day, his people, when they saw the Spaniards riding in on burros, with white faces showing under their metal helmets, believed these strange men to be gods. They were friendly to Alvarado and his soldiers.

Alvarado, in his own account, does not give a name to Taos but his description tallies with that of others who referred to the place as Uraba, Braba and Valladolid. His own words are, after referring to various villages, " Among them is one which is located on some streams; it is divided into twenty divisions, which is something remarkable; the houses have three stories of mud walls and three others made of small wooden boards, and on the outside of the three stories with the mud wall they have three balconies; it seemed to us that there were nearly 15,000 persons in this village. The country is very cold; they do not raise fowls nor cotton; they worship the sun and water. We found mounds of dirt outside of the place, where they are buried." Report of Alvarado, Am. Eth. Ann. No. 14, p. 595.

A Juan Jaramillo, evidently a companion of Alvarado, speaks of Uraba (Taos) as well worth seeing, of *two* story houses, of corn, beans, melons, skins, long robes of feathers, cloaks of cotton of plain weaving and also of their kivas or " hot rooms." Narrative of Jaramillo, Am. Eth. Ann. No. 14, p. 587.

Yet another, who seems to have been with Alvarado but whose name we do not know says, " This river (Rio Grande, no doubt) rises where these settlements end at the north, on the slope of the mountains there, where there is a larger village different from the others, called Yuraba (called by the natives, Tüatá, probably even at that time) . It is settled in this fashion; It has 18 divisions; each one has a situation as if for two ground plots; the houses are very close together, and have five or six stories, three of them with mud walls and two or three with thin wooden walls, which become smaller as they go up, and each has its little balcony outside of the mud walls, one above the other, all around, of wood. In this village, as it is in the mountains, they do not raise cotton nor breed fowls; they wear the skins of deer and cows entirely. It is the most populous village of all that country; we estimated there were 15,000 souls in it." Relacion del Suceso, Am. Eth. Ann. No. 14, p. 575.

Again we have Casteñada's account, " There was a large and powerful river, I mean village, which was called Braba, 20 leagues farther up the river, which our men called Valladolid. The river flowed through the middle of it. The natives crossed it by wooden bridges, made of very long, large, squared pines. At this village they saw the largest and finest hot rooms or estufas that there were in the entire country, for they had a dozen pillars, each one of which was twice as large around as one could reach and twice as tall as a man. Hernando de Alvarado visited this village when he discovered Cicuye. The country is very high and very cold. The river is deep and very swift, without any ford. Captain Barrionuevo returned from here, leaving the province at peace." (1542) Am. Eth. Ann. No. 14, p. 511.

While Alvarado was, undoubtedly, a brave, daring man, he was also ruthless and unfair. At one time, the Indian guide El Turco declared some gold bracelets had been stolen from him at Cicuye. Alvarado was sent to get these. When he reached the village, he demanded them and they said they knew nothing of them and that the Turk was lying. " Captain Alvarado, seeing that there were no other means, got the (Indian) captain Whiskers and the governor to come to his tent, and when they had come he put them in chains. The villagers prepared to fight, and let fly their arrows, denouncing Hernando de Alvarado, and saying that he was a man who had no respect for peace and friendship. Hernando de Alvarado started back to Tiguex, where the general kept them prisoners more than six months. This began the want of confidence in the word of the Spaniards whenever there was talk of peace from this time on, as will be seen by what happened afterward." Am. Eth. Ann. No. 14, p. 493.

The pueblo buildings which Alvarado saw stood a few rods to the east of the present structures. Scholars agree that, except Acoma, no pueblo stands exactly where it stood in 1540. Taos pueblo was sacked by the Spaniards but not burned according to their records. It was burned later in some manner, not now known. The Indians know this. Their new buildings were probably built, after De Vargas entered the country, perhaps about 1700. The present chapel stands on the site of the earliest church. The fine old mission church was destroyed in 1847 by the Americans.

PAGE 7

Spaniards of 1540–42 — John P. Rinker, who has lived in Tres Piedras, N. M., for many years as U. S. Land Commissioner, found a coat of mail and a stone on which is the date, 1541.

Eighty wagons — Oñate reported such a number in a letter to the king, March 15, 1598. Bandelier, Vol. I, p. 395. Historical Documents Relating to New Mexico, Neuva Vizcaya and Approaches Thereto to 1773. Carnegie Inst. Washington. 1923.

Soldier colonists — Records vary. 205 — Col. Doc. Ind. Vol. XVI, p. 196, Hammond, George P., Don Juan de Oñate and the Founding of New Mexico. El Palacio Press. Vol. II, p. 19. 200 — Oñate was under contract to take that number, Gregg, Josiah, Commerce of the Prairies, 1849, pub. by J. W. Moore, Vol. I, p. 117. 400 — the number given by the historian of the expedition Gaspar Villagrá. 130 — Bancroft, H. H. Arizona and New Mexico, Vol. XVII,

PAGE 8

What reckoning will you give — Translation of Villagrá by Fayette Curtis, Jr. Unpublished.

For God, the King and himself — Twitchell, Leading Facts, Vol. I, p. 311.

PAGE 9

Founding of Santa Fe — 1610 is now the recognized date. Bloom-Donnelly, New Mexico. History and Civics, 1933, p. 86.

Mission at Taos — 1617. Bancroft, XVII, p. 159.

PAGE 10

Killed soldiers and priest — Fray Pedro de Miranda; guards were Louis Pacheco and Juan de Estrada. F. W. Hodge. Note in Benavides Memorial.

Twenty years swung by. — Taos Indian tradition.

Finally the time came — Wallace, Susan B. Land of the Pueblos, p. 87.

PAGE 11

Popé — His tricks were many. The following will be of interest though of a date almost two centuries later. Letter written by Father de Smet. (Chittenden and Richardson, Father de Smet's Life and Travels among the Indians, Vol. I, p. 250.)

University of St. Louis, 7th Feb. 1841

" The following is one of the most singular of the tricks and one which the Indian sorcerer was unwilling to perform in my presence, because my *medicine* (meaning my religion) *was superior to his.* He had his hands, arms, legs and feet tied with well-knotted cords; he was then enclosed in a net, and again in a buffalo's skin. The person who tied him had promised him a horse if he extricated himself from his bond. In a minute after, the savage, to the amazement of the spectators, stood before him perfectly free."

PAGE 12

Herrera and Chaves. Bolton, H. E. Collection, MSS., Berkeley, California.

Pope's associate — Tupatu. Volanté, Mercurio. MSS. in John Carter Library, Providence, R. I. Photostat copy in Bolton Collection, Berkeley, California. In 1693, Volanté wrote, " In the town of San Juan, situated not very far from Santa Fe lived an Indian, Don Luis Tupatu, middle aged, whose splendid qualities and greater valor won for him the confidence of the people and he was appointed governor of that Kingdom with general approval after the death of Alfonso Catiti and Popé."

De Vargas. Don Diego de Vargas was accused of misuse of funds, of being responsible for the famine of 1695 and was thrown into jail in Santa Fe where he stayed three years. His case was tried in old Mexico and the result was a thorough white-washing. He was reinstated as governor in 1703 and died six months later. He never regained popular favor. This is suggested in his will in which he said, " I order that on said day [his funeral day] be distributed among the poor of said town fifty measures of corn and twelve head of cattle. — I want and it is my will to have five hundred masses said, two hundred applied to the Holy Virgin of Remedies, my protector for the benefit of my soul, and three hundred for the souls of the poor who died in the conquest of this kingdom and may have died to the present day." De Vargas Will, archive in Surveyor General's Office, Santa Fe, N. M.

PAGE 15

De la Serna. 1710. Archive 830, Surveyor General's Office. Translation by William M. Tipton.

San Geronimo de Taos. Name used for Taos by Governor Valle in 1761. Archive 719. Surveyor General's Office, Santa Fe, N. M. This gives color to the belief that Don Fernando de Taos was chosen as a name after this date.

PAGE 17

The alcalde's own report — Archive 883, Santa Fe.

PAGE 19

The papers of said ranch — Archive 23, File 109, Spanish Doc. 10, Santa Fe.
Catarina Romero sold — Archive 3, File 120, Santa Fe.
Dividing line — Archive 6, File 109, Santa Fe.

PAGE 20

Nerio Sisneros — Archive 159, File 81, Santa Fe.

PAGE 22

Gnawed his head off — Bancroft, Vol. XVII, p. 257. Note 4.

PAGE 23

The Bishop wrote — H. E. Bolton Collection, Berkeley, California. MSS. Translation by Nellie V. Sanchez. See addenda.

Señorita Villapando — St. Louis, Mo. Archives, Vol. III, p. 137. " Madame Sala dit Lajoie (La Señorita Villapando) had a most adventurous life. She was born at Taos, New Mexico. Her parents were killed and she was married off by the Comanches. She came to St. Louis about 1770 and died here 27, July, 1830, said to be of the age of one hundred and seven years."

PAGE 24

When his little daughter was — Gregg, Josiah, Commerce of the Prairies, 1844, p. 146.
Singing as they went — Taos Indian tradition.

PAGE 25

Urrisola letter. See addenda.

PAGE 26

One other glimpse — Archive in City of Mexico. Translation by Ettie M. Healy in thesis, The New Mexico Missions in the Middle Eighteenth Century, Univ. of California. Berkeley, California.

PAGE 30

Imaginary pesos — The use of false money continued in the valley. Not until 1921 was a law passed against the use of " chips " or metal pieces which had been given for many years to Indians and Mexicans by Taos merchants. These were marked so that buyers were forced to trade with the merchant whose name the pieces bore.

PAGE 32

No record of Taos fairs — A neighbor of mine, the late Sostenos Trujillo, when he was 92 years of age, told me that he remembered the last of the Taos fairs in the early forties. If they existed as late as that they were but the faintest echoes of the real, busy fairs for which Taos was noted.

PAGE 33

A brave Mexican girl — Mariana Jaramillo, N. M. Reports, 1857, Jaramillo Vs. Romero. Vol. I, p. 194. Test case.

PAGE 34

Bautiste La Lande. Juan Bautiste La Lande, the French Canadian from Kaskaskia, Illinois, was refused the right to return to the east and went down to Chihuahua. On his return to Santa Fe he became a guide as Albert Pike in his " Poems and Prose Sketches " says. La Lande married Maria Rita Abeyta of Los Luceros. Their children were Tomas, Juan D., Dolores, Guadalupe and Josepha. Later he went to live in La Cueva where his wife died and he married a Polonia — by whom he had a daughter, Maria Rita. Again he moved and this time to Ranchos de Taos.

La Lande's daughter Josepha married Ignacio Gonzales. Among her children were two boys named, Bautiste La Lande Gonzales and Francisco Gonzales. The latter became a famous Indian fighter and, when fighting during the Civil War, was wounded at Valverde. He married Andrea Montoya. Their daughter married Agapito Martinez, a nephew of Padre Martinez. These were the parents of our townsman, L. Pascual Martinez of to-day, from whom I have this information.

Family tradition insists that La Lande lived and died in Ranchos de Taos and was buried there. The home of his daughter Josepha was for many years pointed out as that of " La Francesa " or " The French Woman."

PAGE 37

To acquire the title of ' Villa' — Archive 1168, Surveyor General's Office, Santa Fe. The original request is not on file but the following answer is. " This deputation has received your official letter of the 18th of last July, with the enclosed solicitude from the inhabitants of Taos requesting to grant the title of village to that place and at the same time the one of the same date relative to the reluctance of the members of that provincial junta to assist in the proceedings, (So!) all of which account will be rendered to the Honorable Congress of this State at its convening for the convenient determination, what I inform you in answer and in compliance of what has been agreed to.

God and Liberty.

Chihuahua, August 9th, 1824
JOSÉ DE URGUIDO

To the Political Chief of New Mexico.   (*Rubric*)
      JOSÉ MARIA PONCE DE LEON. (*Rubric*)

PAGE 38

William Wolfskill. Barrows, H. D. Biographical Sketch of William Wolfskill, Wilmington, California Journal, Oct. 29, 1866. Vol. II, p. 116.

PAGE 39

Total 2013. Ruben de Celis. Bloom, Lansing. Old Santa Fe Mag. July 1913.

On the evening of the 26th — Pattie, Personal Narrative in Early Western Travels, Ed. Reuben G. Thwaite. Pub. by A. H. Clark Co., 1905, pp. 73, 74.

PAGE 41

Directly in front of me — Pike, Albert. Prose Sketches and Poems, p. 137.

On the evening of my arrival — Pike, Albert, Prose Sketches and Poems, 1833, p. 138.

PAGE 42

Fowler, Jacob, Journal of, Ed. Elliott Coues, pp. 137, 138.

PAGE 43

Dr. Willard — His notes were published at the end of Pattie's Personal Narrative.

Nidever. See addenda. MSS. Bancroft Library, Berkeley, California.

PAGE 44

The first route — Twitchell, Leading Facts, Vol. II, p. 116. August Storrs gave his route as "Fort Osage (established 1808, on Missouri River, long known as "Old Sibley") W.S.W. to the Arkansas, up the Arkansas N. of W. 240 miles, S. to the Cimarron; up the Cimarron W. 100 miles; and S.W. to Taos." In 1825, Congress passed a law calling for a survey of the trail as Storrs gave it. The chief surveyor, J. C. Brown, knowing of certain dangers of desert etc. made the line run to Taos through safer country than the traders were willing to take because of their desire for a more direct route. Brown's report was never published until long after its day of usefulness. Only a few mounds of earth were thrown up along the first part of the trail — this was the only practical outcome of all the hard work and heavy expense of Brown's three years of surveying.

PAGE 47

Thomas Forsythe wrote — October 24, 1831, in St. Louis. MSS. with State Historical Society of Wisconsin.

The inland trade — Missouri Intelligencer, Feb. 12, 1830.

Charles Bent. Chittenden, History of the American Fur Trade in the Far West. Vol. II, pp. 509, 510. Newspaper items:

"1829 — Spring caravan of about 70 persons and 35 wagons, — Charles Bent, captain; military escort under Major Riley; Samuel C. Lamma killed en route; return cargo valued at $30,000; reached Franklin early in November.

"1832 — Principal caravan under Charles Bent, date of departure not given, returned about November 1st with $100,000 specie and $90,000 other property. A party returning in the fall and winter of this year attacked by Indians on the Canadian, January 1 and lost all their property and one man.

"1833 — June 20. Spring caravan at Diamond Grove. 184 men, 93 wagons under Charles Bent; November 9, 100 of the above party returned with $100,000 specie and a large amount of other property. Gregg returned this fall."

1831 — Chittenden, Vol. III, p. 926. From a letter, we have, "In August last (1831) Mr. Charles Bent set out from St. Louis with a number of wagons loaded with goods for Santa Fe and drawn by oxen. His party consisted of from thirty to forty men, and if he succeeds with his ox wagons, the oxen will answer the triple purpose; 1st, drawing the wagons; 2nd, the Indians will not steal them as they would horses and mules; and 3rdly, in cases of necessity part of the oxen will answer for provisions."

PAGE 48

None of us were quite so brave — Sage, Rufus B., Rocky Mountain Adventures. 1841–1842. P. 59. *Grand Prairies* — Expression in use during the forties.

Trails. It must be remembered that many covered wagons went from Taos to Chihuahua following a trail much older than those which came from Missouri. The writer knows of but one description of the southern trail with the view-point from south to north, as early as 1838. This is in "The Life and Travels of Josiah Mooso," published by the *Telegram Print*, Winfield, Kansas, in 1888. It runs, "The old trail from Chihuahua to Santa Fe was at this time the great thoroughfare of the frontier and like most routes of its character, was a continuous line of skeletons, broken down vehicles and general wreck of the travel of the plains. Here we met the great 'freighting' wagon with its high bows and soiled ducking cover, drawn by eight or ten yoke of oxen, all under the care of a single teamster, who not only directs the movements of the team through its snail-like journey of the day but as night comes on, becomes the herder of the stock as it is liberated and allowed to feed by the side of the trail. Sometimes several trains are taken along in companies, then the stock is all herded together at night and the men are fed in a mess, while the wagons are placed in a circle in which the cattle can be enclosed.

"Again we meet the emigrant wagon with its occupants of men, women and children, with its coop of chickens suspended in the rear, numerous implements of husbandry attached to the sides of the wagon, and the usual complement of dogs keeping in close proximity to their nomadic habitations. The wagon is sometimes drawn by oxen, sometimes by one or two mules but not unfrequently by a yoke of cows, or a cow and a horse. Again a traveler has loaded all his effects upon a pony and walks happily by the side of his beast very much after the style of the Arab and his camel.

"The most novel outfit which the travelers met, however, was two young men with their effects on a cart, furnishing the propelling power themselves. They had traveled over a thousand miles and were in better condition than many of the mules and oxen that had traveled only half so far."

PAGE 49

Bent's Fort. Grinnell, George Bird, Bent's Fort and its Builders. Vol. XV, Kansas Historical Society, pp. 28–91. This is, by far, the best account of the old fort that has been written. Other authorities are Ruxton, George Frederick, In the Old West, Outing Co. 1915. Garrard, Lewis, Way-to-yah, H. W. Derby & Co. 1850. Farnham, Thomas J., Travels on the Great Western Prairies, 1841.

PAGE 53

Real name — Ward, Josiah, *The Denver Post*, Jan. 11, 1920.

PAGE 54

St. Vrain. Will Records, Vol. A, p. 54, Mora County.

South side of plaza. Bent and St. Vrain store was in the western part of the present Columbian Hotel.

PAGE 55

Calhoun, James S. Annie Heloise, Official Correspondence of James S. Calhoun, Washington, 1915, p. 42.

PAGE 56

Fur — Hill, J. J. Ewing Young in the Fur Trade in the Far Southwest, Pub. by Koke-Tiffany. Reprint, 1923, p. 4.

PAGE 58

Williams. Genealogy by Hon. Boutwell Dunlop, San Francisco, California.

As a specimen of the genuine trapper — Pike, Albert, Prose Sketches and Poems, 1833, pp. 37, 38. Conard, Louis H. " Uncle Dick " Wootton, 1890, W. E. Dibble & Co., pp. 201–202.

PAGE 60

Manuscript story — Hamilton, William Thomas. My Sixty Years on the Plains, 1905, p. 102. " For security, I placed William's manuscript in the safe and three days later (in 1873) the agency burned down." Agency was Crow Indian Reservation on Yellowstone River.

Peg-leg Smith. Bell, Major Horace, Reminiscences of a Ranger, 1853, p. 289. Heap, Gwinn Harris. Central Route to the Pacific, 1854.

PAGE 61

Baker. Hill, Alice P., Colorado Pioneers in Picture and Story, Brock-Haffner Press, Denver, Col., 1884, p. 37.

Cave man tactics — Ruxton, G. F. In the Old West, Doubleday, Nelson, 1915, p. 161.

PAGE 62

Of which Captain R. B. Marcy wrote — Marcy, R. B. Thirty Years of Army Life, pp. 358, 359.

PAGE 63

Where did you come from, Sir? — Finley, J. B. Pioneer Life in the West, 1853, p. 66.

PAGE 64

Munchies-Carcague — Neihardt, J. G. Splendid Wayfaring, 1920, pp. 128–132.

PAGE 66

Kephart Letter, Written to the American Missionary Magazine, Congregational Board, probably 1852.

PAGE 67

We are rejoiced — Gregg, Josiah, Commerce of the Prairies, 1844, Vol. II, pp. 40–41.

PAGE 69

Pike — Twitchell, Leading Facts, Vol. I, pp. 467–468. Major Z. M. Pike — The Sources of the Mississippi etc. 1810. John Binns, printer.

Tax on poultry — Twitchell, Leading Facts, Vol. II, p. 58.

PAGE 71

The story is — Prince, L. Bradford, Concise History of New Mexico, pp. 162–163.

PAGE 73

Wilson. Benjamin Davis Wilson was the second mayor of Los Angeles, California. MSS. Bancroft Library, Savage, Thomas, Berkeley, California.

PAGE 74

Carlos. Kendall, George W. Narrative of Texan Santa Fe Expedition, 1884, Vol. I, p. 131. *They are able to walk* — p. 298.

PAGE 76

We have come to fight — Sage, Rufus B. Rocky Mountain Life, p. 326.

PAGE 78

Tied to their horses — Gregg, Josiah, Commerce of the Prairies, 1844, Vol. II, p. 173.

PAGE 79

Whitman — Mowry, W. A. Marcus Whitman, Pub. Silver Burdette & Co. 1901, pp. 138, 332. Nixon, O. W. How Whitman Saved Oregon, Star Publishing Co., 1895, p. 339. Clarke, S. A. Pioneer Days in Oregon History. Vol. I, pp. 426–7. Account by Lovejoy.

PAGE 81

Truth-hunting Indians — McBeth, Kate, The Nez Perces, Since Lewis and Clarke, 1908, pp. 29–34.

PAGE 82

I came to you over a trail — Mowry, Marcus Whitman, p. 46. First published in the *Christian Advocate*, March, 1833.

PAGE 85

Emory — Emory, Col. W. H. Notes of a Military Reconnaisance, 1848, pp. 15, 18, 22, 33.

PAGE 86

Armijo — New Mexicans will always believe Armijo sold out to the Americans, through James Wiley Magoffin. People of old Mexico refer to them as " little brothers who were sold."

PAGE 87

At Pecos — Wallace, Susan B. The Land of the Pueblos, 1879, p. 33.

PAGE 90

Madame Tules — Gertrudes Barcelo, known as Madame Tules, Barcelona, Doña Tula, was the most famous gambling woman in the Southwest. She came from old Mexico, according to her adopted daughter, and drifted, perhaps in the eighteen twenties into Taos and was apparently not very successful. She then went to Santa Fe, made money and established a gambling house noted for its luxury and visited by the élite of the capital. She was said to have been, for a while, the power behind Armijo. Later she was friendly with the Americans and to her and a mulatto girl servant has always been given the credit of halting the first plans for the revolution to kill Americans in 1846.

A thrifty merchant's wife — The story was told to her son John Joseph, who was born in June 1847, when he was old enough to understand. He told the writer.

PAGE 92

I was only five years old — Told to L. Bradford Prince, Twitchell, Leading Facts, Vol. II, p. 235.

PAGE 95

Well, you see the purblos — Garrard, Lewis H. Wah-to-yah, 1850, pp. 131, 223, 231.

PAGE 96

479 men — Twitchell, Leading Facts, Vol. II, p. 240.

PAGE 97

The wind rose at dark — Fitzgerald — Garrard, Lewis H. Way-to-yah, 1850, pp. 149, 179.

PAGE 98

The trial — Garrard, Lewis H. Way-to-yah, pp. 206–231. Col. Price in his report to Adjutant General definitely named Tomas Ortiz and Diego Archuleta as heads of revolution.

PAGE 107

Padre Martinez — Sanches, Don Pedro, Life of Padre Martinez, 1903. Privately published. Incomplete. L. Pascual Martinez, a grand-nephew of Padre Martinez, Mrs. Albert Gusdorf, Benjamin Randall and other citizens of Taos gave information.

PAGE 110

Anderson, George. One of the writers for New Mexico History, Pacific States Pub. Co. 1907.

PAGE 112

Dr. David Waldo — Twitchell, Leading Facts, Vol. II, p. 118.

The Calf — From letters owned by the late Benjamin M. Read, Santa Fe, N. M.

PAGE 113

Letter by Padre Martinez, owned by L. Pascual Martinez, Taos, N. M.

Martinez children — Santiago Valdez, Vicente, Luz, Soledad and Julio Romero. His will mentioned every one.

Luis Pascual Martinez, the grandson of Pascual Martinez, the brother of Padre Martinez, carries on in the spirit of his forebears. At sixteen, Martinez left home to seek an education and enjoy religious freedom. After years of hard work he secured a High School diploma, took a business course, became a teacher in an Indian school and later was called to be secretary to the Congressman from New Mexico in Washington. He returned to Taos to become postmaster and is now in the U. S. Forest Service, a leading citizen of Taos to-day. He is a Mason and has the distinction of being the only Spanish-American who has ever been elected Master of the Bent Lodge No. 42.

PAGE 116

Leaning forward upon the pommel — McGehee, M. Rough Times in Rough Places, Century, March, 1891.

PAGE 117

In camp there was — Breckinridge, Thomas E. Cosmopolitan, August 1896.

PAGE 119

Richard Kern Diary — MSS. in Huntington Library, San Marino, California. By special permission.

PAGE 143

First lawyer — Bloom, Lansing, Old Santa Fe Magazine, July 1913, New Mexico under Mexican Administration, p. 271.

Fink's stages — Davis, W. H. H. El Gringo, Harper Bros. 1857, p. 14. Fink, stage proprietor; Billy, William McCoy; River Jordan, a small stream below Jefferson City.

PAGE 147

Well, gentlemen, I know Benedict — Twitchell, Old Santa Fe Mag. July 1913, p. 85.

José Maria Martin — Ibid. pp. 83, 84, 85.

PAGE 150

William L. McClure — Came to Taos in 1877. Merchant, Ranchman. Lived at Placita. Died 1929.

PAGE 152

Affair between people of Arroyo Seco and Indians — Taos archives. Court record 343.

PAGE 153

Trouble was brewing — Taos archives. Court record 446.

Guttman and Freadman vs. United States.

The following affidavit of testimony was taken in the U. S. Court of Claims in Washington. Copy belongs to the F. T. Cheetham library, Taos, N. M.

Literal translation of memorandum made by Cornelio Avila, July 12, 1864. Avila was a driver for the firm of Guttman and Freadman.

" July 1864 we were coming from the states with the trains of Guttman and Freadman and Company. We stopped at the arroyo of the cow [Cow Creek], Kansas, the 12th of July at about 10 or 11 o'clock in the morning. We unhitched the oxen and we turned them loose to graze and we started to cook dinner, when we saw a multitude of Indians that were coming. Then they sent a captive to see if the trains were of Americans or of Mexicans. We told them that they were trains of Mexicans and they told us that with the Mexicans they did not want anything. Then he went away and the Indians came all and asked for something to eat. When the Indians remained eating, the major domo sent us to gather the oxen, told us that it was not proper to have confidence in the Indians. When we were coming with the oxen, close to the wagons, the Indians took them away from us and drove them away. Then a part of the Indians went away with them and the other part remained doing damage to the wagons. They damaged four wagons only, they broke them, took out the grub, merchandise. They spread out the boxes of shoes. What they did not take away, they destroyed and spread on the ground. The oxen were one hundred and ten."

PAGE 154

Kephart, W. G. Letter written to American Congregational Board. Published in American Missionary Magazine, 1852.

PAGE 156
Peppery man — Chambers. W. G. Outlook Magazine, Oct. 1911.

PAGE 157
Volunteers. Muster roll for the Saguache campaign is owned by Benjamin G. Randall of Taos, N. M.

PAGE 158
One clear moonlight night — Conard, Howard Louis, " Uncle Dick " Wootton, W. E. Dibble & Co., 1890, pp. 206–214.

PAGE 159
Saschel Woods — Sherman, Edwin A. Fifty Years of Masonry in California, George Spalding & Co., 1897, Vol. I, pp. 48–49.

PAGE 160
Carson story — Told by Lina Scheurich, daughter of Teresina Bent Scheurich, to writer.

PAGE 163
Smith H. Simpson — Prominent citizen of Taos. Born in New York, May 8, 1832. Grandfather Valentine Simpson, a pilot for General Washington when he crossed the Delaware. At 13 years, apprenticed to a chemist. Left within three months to make his way. After much traveling and work of various sorts, especially that of clerk for Quartermaster in New Mexico and serving in Ute war in 1855, Simpson came to Taos to live in 1859. Made Captain of Spies and Scouts in 1862–3, in Navajo and Apache war. Wounded. Sent to Arizona. Mustered out 1866. Returned to Taos to engage in farming, stock-raising, land grant and money loaning business. Acted as confidential agent for Kit Carson, Indian Agent. Married Josefa Valdez. Children, Annie, Henry, Stefana, Margaret (Maggie), Raefalita, Samuel. Died in Taos, April 3, 1916.

PAGE 165
Zat Chivington — Hayes, A. A. New Colorado and the Santa Fe Trail, C. Kegan Paul & Co. London, 1881, p. 169.
You are stronger than we — Sabin, Edwin L. Kit Carson Days, 1915, pp. 346, 415.

PAGE 166
Letter from Abraham Lincoln — Family tradition from Christopher Carson, son of William, son of Kit Carson, now living in La Jara, Colorado.

PAGE 167
Pfeiffer's report — Sabin, Edwin L. Kit Carson Days, p. 436.

PAGE 168
I tell ye what — Rusling, James. Across America, 1874, p. 138.

PAGE 171
One night, a group of Taos men — Story by L. Pascual Martinez.

PAGE 174
Wootton was at work in the dark — Robinson, A. A. Santa Fe Employees' Magazine, Sept. 1912. " I remember being at Uncle Dick's house [since burned] in Raton Pass with William R. Morley, the night before the D. & R. G. and A. T. & S. F. war, so-called, broke out but I don't remember the

date. It was in the winter. We were advised about 11 P.M. by messenger from Trinidad that the D. & R. G. was moving a force of graders through the country back of Trinidad into Raton Pass.

On receipt of this news, Morley & myself went to Trinidad and from the town and its people we organized and had in the pass by 5 A.M. the next morning several grading outfits at work grading our line. One of these forces consisted of Uncle Dick nearly single-handed."

PAGE 175

John Dunn — Familiarly known as " Long John." Stage coach and automobile stage driver. Has had a colorful life as cowpoke, saloon owner and gambler in the early days and to-day ranks as a unique character in Taos and is noted for his wit and humor.

PAGE 180

John Bourke — Superstitions of the Rio Grande, Journal of American Folk Lore. About 1894.

Rev. Thomas Harwood — History of New Mexican Spanish and English Missions. 1850.

PAGE 183

Dr. T. Paul Martin — Came in 1889 from Shippensburg, Penn. after studying at College of Physicians & Surgeons, Baltimore, Has been prominent in all important matters pertaining to Taos ever since.

Alexander Anderson — Came to Taos in 1876. Carpenter, miner, mine owner and ranchman. Lived on a farm four miles west of Taos for many years. Bachelor. Died March 1, 1928.

PAGE 185

William Frazer — Scotchman. Came to the Hondo Cañon in 1877. Was a prominent factor in mining business for many years. Married and lived in Valdez, formerly San Antonio, New Mexico. Shot on July 16, 1914.

PAGE 188

Helphenstine and Hill — Miners. Little known of lives.

Gerson Gusdorf — Came from Germany as a boy. Salesman, merchant, now owner of the Don Fernando Hotel in Taos and one of the most prominent men in the town, especially interested in securing better roads.

PAGE 192

Bert G. Phillips — Artist. Arrived in 1898. First to stay in Taos as an artist. One of the very few who have always been interested in civic affairs.

PAGE 194

Frank Staplin — Lived in mining towns during booms, editor of various newspapers, including *New Mexican Record*. Now living in Santa Fe.

PAGE 196

Souvenir — Owned by Mrs. Nancy Witt, an old-timer and successful ranch owner.

PAGE 202

Fortner — Story, one of Jack Ferguson's.

PAGE 203

Harry Anderson — Came to Taos country 1881, prospector, miner, U. S. Forest Service lookout.

PAGE 204

Jack Ferguson — Real name Columbus Ferguson, prominent for years as a miner and mine owner, especially interested in the famous old Aztec and Mystic, high up on Baldy Mountain.

PAGE 212

Ernest L. Blumenschein — With Bert G. Phillips when both came into Taos in 1898. Came later to live.

PAGE 213

Lester Meyers — Photographer in 1898. Later business man in Carlsbad, N. M. where he now lives.

Albert Gifford — Lives now in Los Angeles, California.

PAGE 216

Albert Gusdorf — Came from Germany as a boy, to Taos as a young man, married Margaret (Maggie) Simpson, daughter of Captain Smith H. Simpson, a woman now prominent in civic and state affairs. Daughter, Mrs. Margaret Gusdorf Ryan.

PAGE 218

Carroll R. Dwire — Son of Rev. Isaac Dwire and wife who were, for many years, teachers at the Pueblo. Educated at Roswell Military Institute. Late Supervisor of Carson Forest, U. S. Forest Service.

PAGE 223

My Indian model — Joe Bernal, well known Taos Indian.

PAGE 228

Relay racers — This is a race of two sets of clans. These live on the north or south side of the plaza and so the race is often spoken of as one between the two pueblo buildings. It is *not* a race to decide which pueblo is to elect the new governor. That is decided by the council.

PAGE 232

Dr. Edgar L. Hewitt — one of the most noted scholars on the history of the Southwest of to-day.

PAGE 233

Bonfires — Bonfires play a part in religious processions in Spain.

Los Pastores — Cole, M. R. " Los Pastores," 1907, is by far the best book on the subject.

PAGE 234

The Devil — In Spain, the Devil used to appear dressed in black.

PAGE 236

Llano — a small town one mile south of Ranchos de Taos. Talpa lies about two miles to the east of Ranchos.

PAGE 238

Penitentes — Charles Lummis and George Wharton James wrote of this sect but the best authority is Alexander M. Darley's " Penitentes of the Southwest." Pub. by author in Pueblo, Colo. 1893.

PAGE 270

Every effort has been made to make this list complete of those who live here part of the year, at least. If there is any omission of a name it has not been intentional on the part of the writer.

III · BIBLIOGRAPHY

of most of the books consulted during the research
necessary for the writing of this book

1. Abel, Annie Heloise. Official Correspondence of James S. Calhoun. Washington. 1915.
2. Archives Nos. 3, 6, 23, 25, 159, 719, 883, 1168. Surveyor General's Office, Santa Fe, New Mexico.
3. Arch. Inst. Series V. 1890.
4. Anderson, George B. History of New Mexico, Its Resources and People. Pacific States Pub. Co. 1907.
5. Ayer, E. E. Reminiscences. MSS. in Bancroft Library, Berkeley, Cal.
6. Ayer, Mrs. E. E. Memorial *de* Fray *de* Benavides. 1916.
7. Bancroft, H. H. Arizona and New Mexico. 1889.
8. Bancroft, Mrs. M. G. MSS. notes in Bancroft Library in Berkeley, Cal.
9. Bandelier, Adolph F. Southwestern Contributions. 1890.
10. Bandelier, Fanny. Historical Documents Relating to New Mexico, Nueva Vizcaya and Approaches Thereto to 1773. Carnegie Inst. Washington. 1923.
11. Barrows, H. D. Biographical Sketch of William Wolfskill. Wilmington, Cal. Journal. 1866.
12. Bell, Major Horace. Reminiscences of a Ranger. 1853.
13. Bloom, Lansing. New Mexico under Mexican Administration. Old Santa Fe Mag. 1913.
14. Bolton, H. E. MSS. Tamáron in Bolton Collection. Berkeley, Cal. 1760.
15. Bonsal, Stephen. Edward Fitzgerald Beale. 1912.
16. Bourke, J. G. Popular Medicine Customs and Superstitions of the Rio Grande, Journal of American Folk Lore. 1894.
17. Breckinridge, Thomas E. Article in Cosmopolitan Mag. Aug. 1896.

18. Bureau of Eth. Reports. No. 14 gives Winship, George Parker, The Coronado Expedition. 1896.
19. Chambers, W. G. Article in Outlook Magazine, Oct. 1911.
20. Chittenden, H. M. American Fur Trade in the Far West. 1902.
21. Clarke, S. A. Pioneer Days of Oregon History. Vol. II.
22. Cole, M. R. Los Pastores, 1907.
23. Conard, Howard Louis, " Uncle Dick " Wootton, 1890.
24. Coues, Elliott, Journal of Jacob Fowler, 1898.
25. Cutler, Ben C. Condition of Indian Tribes, Gov. Report, 1867.
26. Darley, Alexander, The Penitentes, 1903.
27. Davis, W. H. H. El Gringo, 1857.
28. Documentas de Indias, Vol. XVI.
29. Dublan and Lazaro, Legislacion Mexicana. Tomo. I.
30. Emory, W. H. Notes of a Military Reconnaisance. 1848.
31. Finley, James B. Pioneer Life in the West. 1853.
32. Farnham, Thomas J. Travels of the Great Western Prairies, 1841.
33. Garrard, Lewis H. Way-to-yah or The Taos Trail. 1850.
34. Grinnell, George Bird. Bent's Old Fort and its Builders. Kan. Hist. Soc. Pub. Vol. XV. 1918.
35. Hackett, C. W. The Revolt of the Pueblo Indians. 1680. Texas Hist. Quarterly, June 1916.
36. Hamilton, William Thomas. My Sixty Years on the Plains, Trapping, Trading and Indian Fighting. 1905.
37. Harwood, Thos. History of N. M. Spanish and English Missions. 1850.
38. Heap, Gwinn Harris, Central Route to the Pacific. 1854.
39. Inman, Col. Henry. Old Santa Fe Trail. 1897.
40. James, Gen. Thomas. Three Years Among the Mexicans and Indians. Mo. Hist. Soc. Pub. 1916.
41. Kendall, George W. Narrative of the Texan-Santa Fe Expedition. 1844.
42. Kern, Richard H. Diary, MSS. in Huntington Library, San Marino, California. 1848–9.
43. Lowery, Woodbury. Spanish Settlements in the United States. 1513–1561, pub. 1901.
44. Macbeth, Kate. The Nez Perces, Since Lewis and Clark. 1908.

45. Marcy, R. B. Thirty Years of Army Life on the Border. 1866.
46. McGehee, M. Rough Times in Rough Places. Century Mag. Mar. 1891.
47. Missouri Republican. Article, April 20, 1826.
48. Mowry, W. A. Marcus Whitman. 1901.
49. New Mexico Reports. Vol. I. 1857.
50. Neihardt, J. G. Splendid Wayfaring, 1916.
51. Nidever, George. MSS. in Bancroft Library, Berkeley, Cal.
52. Niles Register. 1824.
53. Nixon, O. W. How Whitman Saved Oregon, 1895.
54. Oregon Hist. Quarterly. Vol. 24.
55. Pattie, James Ohio. Personal Narratives of Early Western History, 1905.
56. Peters, D. C. Life and Adventures of Kit Carson. 1858.
57. Pike, Albert. Prose Sketches and Poems. 1833.
58. Prince, L. Bradford. Concise History of New Mexico, 1912.
59. Rusling, James F. Across America. 1874.
60. Ruxton, George Frederick. In the Old West. Outing Co. 1915.
61. Sabin, E. L. Kit Carson Days, 1916.
62. Sage, Rufus B. Rocky Mountain Adventures. 1841–2.
63. Sanchez, Pedro. Memorias. Presbyter Don Antonio José Martinez. 1903. N. M. Printing Press.
64. Santa Fe Employees' Mag. Sept. 1912.
65. Sherman, Edward A. Fifty Years of Masonry in Cal. 1897.
66. Taos Archives. Court Records, 343, 446.
67. Twitchell, R. E. Leading Facts in New Mexico History. 1911–12. Military Occupation of New Mexico. 1909. Chief Justice Kirby Benedict. Old Santa Fe Mag. July 1913.
68. Wallace, Susan B. The Land of the Pueblos, 1879.
69. Wilson, Benj. D. MSS. by Thomas Savage. Bancroft Library, Berkeley, Cal.

INDEX

INDEX

INDEX

Index

96, 101, 105, 112, 125, 157, 163, 191,
292, 301, 303, 304, 311, 312, 322.
St. Vrain; Felicitas, 54; Felix, 54;
Vicinte, 54.
Stuck, Hans von, 268.
Sublette, Milton, 57.

Taledrid, 155.
Talpa, 179, 236, 330.
Tamaron, Bishop, 22, 281.
Taos Cañon, 15, 105, 252.
Taos Country, 15.
Taos Cresset, 195.
Taos, Don Fernando de, 15, 115, 118,
200.
Taos Fairs, 22.
Taos Indians, 10, 14, 18, 22, 114.
Taos Junction, N. M., 175.
Taos Pueblo, 9, 10, 11, 12, 42, 54, 76,
97, 105, 106, 282, 286, 301, 302.
Taos Society of Artists, 269.
Taos Valley News, 108.
Taplin, Kern's party, 140.
Tayberon, 1, 315.
Taylor, Hiram, 298.
Taylor, Walter L., 262.
Telegram Print, 322.
Tennessee, 223, Knox Co., 38.
Tewa, 3.
Texan-Santa Fe Exped., 74, 75, 97,
299.
Texas, 73, 78, 79, 84, 171; Texans,
38, 75, 76, 77, 78, 165, 171.
Thomas, Guy, 192.
Thor, Walter, 268.
Tibiana, Albert, 298.
Tiboux, 74.
Tigua, 7.
Tiguex, 7, 317.
Tipton, Wm. M., 319.
Tiwa, 4.
Tobacco Plant, 77.
Tobin, Tom, 158, 166, 249, 301.
Tomas, Workman's Party, 298.
Tomasito, 91, 98, 305.
Towih, 3.
Trails, Bent's Fort; 248, 322; Cimar-
ron Route, 45; Kiowa, 44; Navajo,
44; Santa Fe, 36, 44, 47, 102, 158;
Taos, 44, 45, 46, 47, 65, 101, 248;
Wolfskill, 56, Jackson, 56, Young,

56, Armijo, 56, Pattie, 56, Smith,
56.
Travis, Camp, 222.
Tres Piedras, 173, 174, 189, 317.
Trigo, Manuel de San Nepomuceno
y, 26.
Trinchera River, 306.
Trinidad, Colo., 174.
Trujillo, Lorenzo, 298.
Trujillo, Luciano, 213, 215.
Trujillo, Sostenos, 70, 320.
Tŭatá, or Place of the People, 316.
Tules, Madame, 90, 324.
Tupatu, 318.
Turco, El, 6, 7, 183, 317.
Turley, Simeon; Mill, 93, 141.
Twining, 190.
Twining, Albert C., 190.
Twitchell, Ralph E., 115.

Ufer, Walter, 264, 265, 266, 267.
United States, 33, 34, 47, 67, 78, 79,
81, 84, 85, 86, 88, 89, 109, 153, 169,
208, 243, 251, 265.
U. S. Army, 60, 90, 116, 306.
U. S. Dragoons, 78, 85, 97.
U. S. Hill, 156.
Uriarte, Nicolosa, 298.
Uribarri, Juan de, 21.
Urrisola, Manuel Partillo, 25, 284,
290, 319.
Utahs or Utes, 22, 60, 127, 196, 283,
288, 289, 308, 313, 314; Mohuache,
157.
Utah Territory, 313.
Ute Park, 175.

Valdez, 91, 241.
Valdez, Rafaelita, 110.
Valdez, Santiago, 113.
Valladolid, 2, 316, 317.
Valle, Alexandre, 165.
Valle, Gov. Francisco, Antonio Marin
del, 284, 319.
Valverde, 160, 164, 320.
Vermijo, Rio, 45.
Vigil, Gabilla, 207.
Vigil, Pedro, 41.
Villagrá, Gaspar de, 4, 8, 318.
Villapando, Pablo, 283, 286.
Villapando, Señorita, 23, 24, 319.